Linguistic Identity Matching

Bertrand Lisbach · Victoria Meyer

Linguistic Identity Matching

Springer

Bertrand Lisbach
Freiburg, Germany

Victoria Meyer
Zurich, Switzerland

ISBN 978-3-8348-1370-1
ISBN 978-3-8348-2095-2 (eBook)
DOI 10.1007/978-3-8348-2095-2

Library of Congress Control Number: 2013939631

Springer Vieweg

Springer is part of Springer Science+Business Media
www.springer.com

Foreword

by David Smith

My interest in identity matching comes from my years' fraud investigation and AML work. A few years ago, I would have expected that banks and other financial institutions would, by now, have reduced the AML process to a routine, low level back office function. How wrong I was!

At time of writing, the revolutions and uprisings in the Middle East have resulted in wide-scale sanctions where identity matching will be critical. The death of Osama bin Laden and the reported capture of a vast hoard of data will no doubt start a major anti terrorist financing effort.

Looking at this from a bank's point of view, this is a worrying time, given the scale of fines and sanctions imposed by regulators on both the firms and individuals. No decent bank wants to get caught out but this may not be as easy as it may appear. Before looking at how Linguistics should be a major step forward in Identity Matching it is worth considering the context in which it can be used in AML work in financial firms.

The Wolfsberg Group 2009 Statement on AML Screening, Monitoring and Searching usefully sets out 4 key areas involving matching:

- Screening (real time payment screening to prevent sanctions and other breaches)
- Monitoring (either live or delayed monitoring for unusual transactions)
- Client Screening (KYC not only at the opening of accounts but also at appropriate periods thereafter)
- Searches (typically in response to regulatory enquiries, updated sanctions lists, etc.)

The first major issue is scale – the volume of data in any large bank is vast, so the only realistic way of searching for names is using technology. Large banks that have grown, particularly by mergers, are frequently relying on legacy IT systems that were never designed with AML matching in mind. In addition, customer data may not be in the same format in different parts of the same bank and AML watch lists are not yet standardised between the various issuing authorities.

The scale and complexity all conspire to make automated matching very difficult. Because of the dangers of missing a relevant match (a "false negative"), often the systems are allowed to return large numbers of false positive hits, which then need to be manually sorted.

It is also worth considering the information contained on AML/sanctions lists. A full name with nationality, date of birth, address, etc would be very useful but is obviously not readily available for drug lords or terrorists, so matching even just a few names that are not presented in a set format presents a real challenge.

The information set out in this book is fascinating – the range of linguistic variations is quite amazing. How any matching worked before must be something of a mystery unless it is of the so-called exact name matching variety of a decade ago.

I am sure the book will be read with interest by AML professionals but I would be disappointed if it were not studied very carefully by regulators and authorities issuing AML/sanctions lists. If they are short of time I would recommend at least chapter one, some of chapters three to six, which get to grips with linguistics, and of course, chapter seven on errors. The how to match considerations are essential for AML professionals but would also be a good place for regulators to start before doing reviews of banks' AML procedures.

To me, a linguistic approach to matching is a more logical starting point anyway. Take, for example, a Mexican regional bank being ordered to search for names of one of the murderous drug gangs. If the search was being done manually, the staff, being local, would automatically be using their knowledge of the language, common variations, etc. whereas the same search at, say, a Jersey bank would not benefit from that local knowledge.

If linguistic matching can bridge that gap in knowledge then it could be key to ensuring that the danger of false negatives is eliminated whilst helping to reduce false positives.

David Smith is a forensic accountant with over 20 years' experience leading major fraud investigations. As the senior partner in KPMG Forensic Accounting, he worked extensively throughout Europe and the Middle-East. He currently works as a consultant dealing with investigations and corporate governance issues.

Contents

Introduction: Paradigm Shift in Identity Matching Theory

Identity matching in the world we live in

Searching identity data is something that many of us do every day. In a private context it is often carried out as an Internet search for local businesses or as a contact search on a social networking site. In a business context, identity searches form a fundamental part of many standard processes, from credit checks to customer data integration. Law enforcement and other government agencies also carry out huge numbers of identity checks every day in a bid to prevent and detect criminal activity. The combined effect of these search processes means that most of us will be the subject of a search far more often than we might think.

Anyone opening a bank account can expect their details to be automatically checked against databases of known criminals, terrorists and other sanctioned parties. These days, this control will often also include a search against international lists of politicians and their associates as part of the ongoing effort to combat corruption.

Within the realm of law-enforcement activities, many of us will be the subject of frequent identity checks. When we get on a plane, sign a mobile phone contract, rent an apartment or even purchase tickets to a football match, these checks will often take place behind the scenes. In a more mundane context, our identity details are searched through customer lists and other similar databases whenever we contact a customer service department or local government agency, and, whether we like it or not, direct marketing organisations are searching directories containing our contact details on a daily basis.

The basic function of all these identity searches is very similar, mostly focusing on name and date of birth information, sometimes together with address details, in order to identify whether two sets of personal details relate to the same individual. This can be a one off-search, such as when a customer contacts a call-centre, or part of a more formalised, automated mass search process. These bulk searches may take the form of regular screening of customer databases to remove duplicates and identify discrepancies. In other cases they may comprise the automated screening of new data records against an existing database, such as when a financial institution screens its customer records to determine whether any newly sanctioned parties are listed as clients.

With such a wide range of applications, identity matching techniques have assumed strategic importance for many global organisations. Today, identity searches are helping to manage corporate risks in areas as diverse as maintaining customer databases, avoiding unnecessary credit risks and enforcing regulatory requirements. Such processes require sophisticated technology in order to effectively manage risks and optimise data management procedures, with the result that an increasing number of software providers and consulting firms are focusing on this area.

The challenges involved

In a world of imperfect data and non-unique names, the concept of a match or mismatch is open to interpretation. Many tools determine the degree of congruence of each of the identity characteristics available and combine these to provide an overall score for the strength of the match. The higher the match score, the more likely it is that the records relate to the same individual, and the more effective it will be for the match to be subject to further, manual review. This is of crucial significance to many organisations as the resources required for manual review are often the most expensive part of their search processes. To these organisations, the importance of calculating a match score that accurately represents the likelihood of the two records relating to the same party cannot be underestimated.

In practice, getting this right has proved to be much more demanding than was originally thought. There are several reasons for this, many of which are discussed in detail in this book, but by far the most challenging aspect of identity search design lies in the complexity of the personal name.

The name is a complex feature because there are a myriad of linguistic, formatting and presentation variations that can cause the same name to be written in many different ways. These sources of variation can broadly be split between the linguistic (those deriving from different writing methods or phonetic sounds) and the non-linguistic (such as alterations to the order of name parts or simple typing errors).

Examples of non-linguistic variations include:

- **The use of initials**
  - *John Fitzgerald Kennedy*
  - *John F. Kennedy*
- **Changes to the order of name parts**
  - *John Fitzgerald Kennedy*
  - *Kennedy, John Fitzgerald*

- **The use of different fields in the data structure**
  - First Name: *John Fitzgerald*
  - First Name: *John*, Middle Name: *Fitzgerald*
- **Spelling and writing errors**
  - *Jon Fiztgerald Kenedy*
  - *John Fitz Gerald Kennedy*

While these sources of variation cannot be ignored if a matching program is to be effective, it is clearly not these, relatively simple, examples that make name matching such a challenging and complex science. The real challenge is in dealing with the linguistic sources of variation. Each culture, writing system and language adds its own influences to the ways in which names can be varied, so an accurate and reliable matching process requires innovative linguistic methods in order to address them.

Some of the challenges posed by linguistic name variants can be seen in the different ways in which the first president of Russia is referred to in the media. His name is converted from its original Cyrillic form (Борис Николаевич Ельцин) into *Boris Nikolayevich Yeltsin* in English-language media. The same name is likely to appear as *Boris Nikolaïevitch Eltsine* in articles written in French, as *Boris Nikolajewitsch Jelzin* in German articles or as *Bóris Nicoláievitch Iéltsin* in the Portuguese media; a standard spelling in the Latin alphabet does not exist.

The way that names converted from a non-Latin script are captured in a database can depend on many factors, including the country in which the individual's identity documents were issued and the language in which the details were input as well as the preference of the individual themselves. It is therefore important that a search tool is able to identify different valid transcription variants of the same name as potential matches. In order to match names such as *Yeltsin*, *Eltsine*, *Jelzin* and *Ieltsine* without capturing other, irrelevant names, the transcription standards which generate these variants have to be analysed and converted into machine-readable rules. Such rules should ensure that the lists of potential matches produced are the same, regardless of whether *Yeltsin*, *Jelzin*, or any other valid transcription variant, is used as the search term. This form of non-exact, or fuzzy, matching is a key element of computer linguistic science.

The term "fuzzy matching" has a very subjective definition and often strikes fear into the heart of corporate professionals, concerned that their expensive manual review resources may be wasted examining large amounts of irrelevant matches. For want of a better term, "fuzzy matching" is used in this book to include any form of non-exact matching, with the aim of highlighting the advantages and disadvantages of the many different ways in which this can be achieved.

In addition to transcription variants, linguistic variations also include names which are phonetically similar, diminutives of proper names and cultural variations. The most significant kinds of linguistic variation therefore include:

- **Transcription variations**
  – *Yeltsin, Eltsine, Jelzin, Ieltsin*
  – *Abdul Rahman, Abdurrachman*
- **Homophones**
  – *Meier, Mayr*
  – *Steven, Stephen*
- **Diminutive name forms**
  – *Bill* (for *William*)
  – *Jack* (for *John*)
- **Cultural variants of the same name**
  – *Steven, Stéphane, Stefan, Stefano, Estêvão, Esteban*

Each of these sources of variation are discussed in more depth in Part 1 of this book.

While non-linguistic variations in names can be adequately matched using traditional mathematical techniques, it is the more complex linguistic variations that are driving the conceptual changes in the way identity matching is carried out today. The importance of these linguistic variations has been brought to the forefront of matching debate in recent times, partly by the progressive effects of globalisation and international migration that have increased the variety of names that business processes have to deal with. The other major factor driving the debate stems from the international threat of terrorism and the rise in serious crime, which together have exponentially increased the costs associated with missing a potential identity match. At the same time, the global financial situation has left businesses reluctant to waste resources on reviewing extensive lists of fuzzy matches, leaving traditional matching methods unable to mitigate the risks involved at an acceptable cost.

In response to the need for increasingly sensitive matching systems, innovative computational linguistic techniques have been added to traditional mathematical matching methods to provide tools that are better suited to the challenges of today's global society. This has lead to dramatic increases in the quality of identity search results, both in terms of not overlooking relevant matches and in terms of picking up far fewer irrelevant matches so that manual review resources are more appropriately targeted.

For whom has this book been written?

This book has primarily been written for professionals responsible for assessing and implementing search methods within their organisations. It is also suitable for students and teachers of the diverse linguistic and computer science topics covered. It will particularly interest those involved in the study of linguistics, onomastics (the study of proper names) and computational linguistics.

Professionals will find coverage of many ideas, techniques and concepts that can be directly transferred to the working environment. This applies equally to software developers and administrative users in the operative environment as well as managers and risk specialists, who might like to focus more on the conceptual and strategic elements of identity matching. This book is not written with any particular industry focus, though many of the examples given are taken from the financial services industry, which is required to invest heavily in identity matching solutions in order to mitigate its inherent risks.

Professionals who might find this book useful include:

- those with strategic, managerial or implementation responsibilities within the compliance departments of financial services organisations
- those with responsibility for data quality management, including data de-duplication and master data management
- product managers and business analysts at software houses producing applications with an identity search component feature, including compliance or CRM suites, enterprise search platforms and Internet search solutions
- product managers and business analysts at intelligence data providers (including vendors of credit check data, watch lists, address data, news articles and other libraries)
- those working in investigative areas, such as forensic accountants, lawyers, private investigators and journalists as well as those working for law enforcement, government or social services authorities

Until now, the majority of the literature aimed at these groups has focused on identity matching as a purely technical issue and often failed to highlight the linguistic aspects that are vital for any effective solution. This book is intended to introduce the successful use of computational linguistics for identity matching to a wider audience and to encourage the attention that this relatively new science undoubtedly deserves.

The book runs through the relevant concepts chapter by chapter using practical examples to highlight their impact on the search process. Having completed this book, the reader should be able to:

- assess the reliability and accuracy of identity matching solutions currently available within their organisation
- develop precise requirements for future identity matching solutions to be developed, improved or purchased
- evaluate, benchmark and test identity matching solutions proposed for future use and critically assess the claims made by individual vendors with regards to the capabilities of their products

To conclude this introduction, a short note is warranted on a topic that is intentionally not covered in this book. No consideration has been given to the risks of abuse potentially connected with identity matching; all legal, ethical and social aspects have been omitted. This is not intended to detract from the relevance of discussion about the risks of personal data abuse, to which several other texts have been dedicated.

While high-powered and effective identity matching solutions have gained their legitimacy through their use in anti-terror operations and the fight against organised crime, it is undeniable that the power afforded by such systems has the potential to be misused. However, for the purposes of this text, we have focused on the linguistic, technological and economic features of efficient matching systems and the benefits that their legitimate use can afford.

Part I:
Introduction to Linguistic Identity Matching

Part I: Introduction to Linguistic Identity Matching

The importance of an individual's name as a determinant of identity is universally recognised across all major cultures of the world. For this reason, identity matching systems often focus on the similarity of names as a starting point for determining an identity match. As a result of increasing recognition that mathematical techniques alone are insufficient to address international naming variants, early attempts to solve the name matching challenge via mathematical means have been largely superseded by linguistic matching methods.

This shift in focus towards linguistic matching techniques has lead to a radical overhaul in the way search technology is designed. The ideas and terminology employed in the more modern search methods form the basis for Part I of this book.

Chapter 1 provides a brief introduction to the basic concepts involved in identity matching and its main component, global name matching. It uses terminology taken from information retrieval theory to define the objective of identity matching as obtaining maximum precision (the avoidance of irrelevant hits) and maximum recall (the inclusion of all potentially relevant hits) in the comparison of personal identity data. The chapter goes on to explain how linguistic search methods offer a solution to the early belief that improved recall could only be achieved at the expense of worsening precision.

Chapter 2 describes the many and varied fields of application for identity matching methods. Identity matching is a fundamental technique which supports many disparate processes in the financial services sector alone. These range from AML and counter-terrorist financing procedures through to customer relationship management and data quality control. Law enforcement and other investigative professionals also make extensive use of identity matching techniques in their efforts against fraud and corruption as well as organised crime and national security threats. Other applications for identity matching solutions can be seen in government departments and information service providers as well as in organisations that require high quality customer, employee or partner data for use in their selling, marketing and control functions.

Chapters 3 to 6 introduce the main linguistic sources of variation in names. A sound understanding of variation sources is required in order to define the requirements for a system that can deal with them appropriately. These chapters describe the concepts in detail and without assuming any prior knowledge of linguistics or onomastics on the part of the reader. The form and characteristics of personal names are discussed in the context of international naming conventions. The structure of a personal name varies widely between different linguistic and cultural backgrounds, as does the pronunciation and spelling. Transcription variants are highlighted as a key challenge in the identity matching process and, consequently, these chapters focus on Russian, Chinese and Arabic naming conventions as well as those adopted in Western societies.

Chapter 7 describes the non-linguistic spelling errors which can compound the linguistic variations discussed in earlier chapters. This chapter describes how analysing the various causes and types of spelling errors can help optimise the mathematical allowances made for them using conventional matching methods.

Part I's description of the various challenges faced by modern identity matching solutions provides the basic knowledge required to move on to Part II, in which the commonly used matching techniques are examined in detail and their relative advantages and disadvantages are compared.

Chapter 1: Basic Concepts

1.1 Identity Matching and Name Matching

The terms "identity matching" and "name matching" are sometimes mistakenly used interchangeably. In fact, name matching is not the only component in an identity matching process, though it is clearly the most challenging. Identity matching is a technique employed to determine whether or not two separate data records relate to the same person (where persons can be either legal or natural, and a legal person could be a company, foundation, trust or other organisation).

Matching two such "person records" typically involves calculating a metric to describe the similarity of the characteristics displayed by each. In the case of a natural person these characteristics include the name, date of birth, nationality and address as well as various reference codes such as passport and social security numbers. The characteristics of a legal person may include the name, legal status and place and date of incorporation, while its reference numbers may include tax codes and incorporation references. In both cases, in the absence of a unique identifying code, the highest weight is usually given to the person's name, as this is a key determinant of identity in most societies.

Name matching therefore forms the central part of the identity matching process. If two different data records show the same given names, *Barack* and *Hussein*, and the same family name, *Obama*, then the probability is high that both refer to the same person. For this reason, the congruence of name information is a key metric in determining a full identity match.

However, a name match on its own is by no means sufficient to presume an overall identity match. The incidence of common names such as *John Smith*, *Muhammad Hussein* or *Li Wei* means that other characteristics must also be considered in order to confirm a match. This is even more the case in countries such as China, where a large part of the population shares just a handful of family names, or Vietnam, where up to 40% of the population shares the surname *Nguyễn*.

At this point it should be noted that the term identity resolution is often used in conjunction with identity matching. Identity resolution (sometimes also referred to as entity resolution) is the application of identity matching and statistical techniques in the consolidation of person data across multiple data silos. Identity matching is the more general term for the matching of identity data in any context and is the term that is employed throughout this book.

1.2 Database Profiles and Search Profiles

For the purposes of this text, two types of data object are of particular interest: database profiles and search profiles. In broad terms, a database profile is a structured set of data characteristics relating to a particular person and stored in a database. It can also be referred to as a person record. A collection of person records is referred to in this book as a data population.

Identity matching techniques can be employed to match a set of database profiles against one another in order to identify any duplicates within them. The same techniques can be used across multiple sets of profiles in order to identify persons common to two or more different data populations. Such processes are referred to in this book as person data comparison.

Where person data comparison is carried out across multiple populations, its purpose may be to identify commonalities between the populations (for example, where one individual is a customer of more than one branch) or to identify additional information about persons recorded in one population from an external data source (for example, to identify whether any customers are recorded on a credit or sanctions watch list).

Identity matching techniques can also be employed to search a set of database profiles for a given person. The search profile is the collection of identity characteristics that are entered to a search engine in order to identify any matches within the database. This book refers to such targeted search activities as "person searches".

The terms introduced so far are summarised in the following table.

Term	**Definition**
Natural person	A human individual.
Legal person	An organisation such as a trust, association or corporation.
Identity characteristics	The separate features of a person's identity, such as name, date of birth, nationality, etc.
Database profile	The set of identity characteristics stored together in a data record relating to one person.
Data population	A collection of database profiles stored together in one databank.
Person data comparison	The comparison of one data population against another to identify any persons common to both populations. The term may also refer to the internal comparison of one data population against itself in order to detect any duplicates.
Search profile	A collection of identity characteristics that define the person to be looked for within a data population.
Person search	The search of a data population for the person defined by the search profile.

A practical example of an identity search can be seen in the standard process carried out when a bank account is opened. The bank clerk will create a search profile from the details contained in the applicant's identity documents. This search profile will then typically be compared against a number of data populations, including the bank's database of current and former clients, and watch lists of sanctioned persons and other higher-risk parties. Any database profiles with a sufficient degree of congruence with the search profile will then be added to the result list and returned to the clerk for manual review to determine whether they actually relate to the applicant. Where none of the database profiles have sufficient congruence with the search profile, this negative confirmation is returned to the clerk in place of the result list.

A data profile shown on the result list is referred to as a hit or match, and is often shown together with a match score, which represents the degree of congruence between the database profile and the search profile.

If it is determined that the individual has been sanctioned by a national or international body, the application for an account will most likely be rejected. Applications from persons determined to be Politically Exposed Persons, or other higher-risk parties, are likely to be subjected to further due diligence in order to determine whether the account opening is compatible with the institution's desired risk profile. Accurate results from the identity search process are therefore a key part of managing the organisation's risk.

1.3 True and False Positives, True and False Negatives

Theoretical discussions about identity matching often draw on terminology used in information retrieval science (the science of locating and retrieving information from large data repositories).

In assessing the results of a particular search, each database profile can be categorised in two ways. Firstly, whether or not it is actually relevant to the search profile, and secondly, whether or not it appears in the result list for that search. Those database profiles that appear on the result list are referred to as positive hits or matches. Those that do not, either because they are not relevant or because the search engine has failed to detect their relevance, are referred to as mismatches or negative matches.

Database profiles relevant to the search profile that appear on the result list are known as true positive hits. Those that do not appear on the result list are referred to as false negative hits. Similarly, irrelevant database profiles that appear on the result list are false positive hits, while those that are not returned in the search results are true negatives.

	Relevance to search profile	
	Relevant	**Not Relevant**
Appears on result list	True Positive	False Positive
Not on result list	False Negative	True Negative

The goal of every identity matching tool is to produce hit lists containing all relevant profiles and none of the non-relevant profiles. On the road to this seemingly simple goal, however, there are a number of challenges to be overcome. In addition to the technical and linguistic challenges, there are a number of conceptual issues to be considered, such as what determines a database profile's relevance or otherwise to the search profile. These will be considered further in Part III.

1.4 Hit Rate and Search Accuracy (Recall and Precision)

Information retrieval science also uses two scales to quantify the performance of the search process. Both of these measures are normally quoted as a percentage.

The hit rate, or recall, of a search measures the percentage of relevant database profiles that are returned in the result list (the number of true positive hits as a percentage of all relevant database profiles). A recall of 100% means that all relevant hits are identified so there are no false negative results.

The precision of a search measures the percentage of hits appearing on the result list that are relevant to the search profile (the number of true positive hits as a percentage of all profiles returned on the result list). A precision of 100% indicates that no false positive results have been produced.

In many search procedures, there is a trade-off to be considered between recall and precision, as a more precise search may have a higher risk of missing a relevant result. The optimum balance between recall and precision has to be determined in light of the relevant costs inherent in the specific business process in which the search procedure is used.

In the example of bank account opening procedures, the costs of inadequate recall can be significant, as the opening of an account for a sanctioned or otherwise undesirable party can incur large fines or even jeopardise continued banking licences. The costs of inadequate precision include the cost of the resources required to manually review the results of the automated search process. Ironically, very low levels of precision may also lead to some of the same costs as low levels of recall, as staff required to review high volumes of false positive results may inadvertently overlook a crucial true positive hit.

1.5 Linguistic Identity Matching

While almost all search procedures require some level of trade-off between recall and precision, it is worth considering this relationship in more detail. Clearly, a matching system which returns all database profiles for any search criteria provides a very low level of precision. As precision is improved, the risk increases that a relevant profile could be excluded from the results list. However, the extent to which recall may suffer as a result of a specified increase in precision is determined by the sophistication of the technology involved. This is where linguistic name matching can most greatly benefit the identity matching process.

Many traditional methods of name matching suffer a significant loss of precision if recall is improved. This is particularly the case with technology based on traditional measures of text comparison, such as Edit Distance methods (which are described in more detail in Chapter 8). Using such computational measures, the fall in recall as precision increases is a mathematical inevitability.

Linguistic name matching has, to a large extent, provided a solution to this problem. Linguistic matching is a relatively new field, based on knowledge drawn from linguistic sciences and from its sub-discipline, onomastic studies (the study of proper names). Mathematical and probabilistic algorithms no longer form the basis of matching technology, but have aquired a new, supporting role for the core fundament of linguistics.

Every linguistic matching rule has two functions; a matching function and an analytical function. The matching element applies the rules required to identify names that are valid linguistic alternatives. An example could be the rules required to match possible transcriptions of the Cyrillic name Ельцин, such as *Yeltsin*, *Jelzin*, *Eltsine* and *Ieltsin*. The matching element ensures an appropriate recall for the search process.

The analytical element ensures that each linguistic matching rule is only applied in appropriate circumstances. Using the above example, the analytic function would prevent the rules required to match *Yeltsin* with *Eltsine* being applied to produce a match between *Yan* and *Ane*, despite these examples being orthographically similar in the same manner: requiring the removal of the initial *y* and the addition of a final *e*. The analytical element, therefore, moderates the impact of increased recall on the precision rate.

In this way, the use of linguistic matching rules has revolutionised the identity matching arena and allowed organisations greater freedom to increase precision without running the additional risks associated with reduced recall. Linguistic matching techniques are described in greater detail in Chapter 10.

Chapter 2: The Application of Identity Matching Techniques

Although not a primary business process in itself, identity matching plays a crucial role behind the scenes in many modern organisations. As a discrete function that can be incorporated into a variety of different business processes, identity matching has a wide ranging scope that covers areas as diverse as risk management, customer support and data integration. Even within smaller organisations, there are often multiple processes that rely on identity matching techniques in some form. In larger organisations there may be dozens of systems incorporating the searching and matching of identity data, including customer service applications, human resource systems, data quality solutions, credit control functions and regulatory compliance systems.

This chapter describes how strong identity matching solutions can help manage risks in a wide variety of areas. These risk management advantages are maximised if identity matching methods are standardised so that comparable results are achieved wherever identity matching is applied within an organisation. In addition, the diversity of potential uses for identity matching techniques means that there are often significant cost and efficiency advantages to be gained from the standardisation of identity matching practices across an organisation, particularly in the areas of technology development, training, operations and licensing fees. The advantages of standardisation and a possible framework for achieving this are considered in Chapter 14.

This chapter looks more closely at the wide variety of application areas for identity matching techniques and the different ways in which getting the identity matching technology right can benefit an organisation.

2.1 Customer Relationship Management (CRM)

CRM is a broad discipline through which an organisation manages and develops its interaction with current, former and prospective clients. It incorporates communication methods and targeting strategies as well as marketing and promotion initiatives.

There are numerous ways in which linguistic search techniques can help to make the management of customer relationships more efficient. Effective search techniques are particularly important for ensuring efficient customer interaction in a call centre scenario. A call centre operative must be able to locate the relevant customer record using the caller's name where no reference number is available. Phonetic matching is useful in such cases as the operative will usually enter the name to the system as it sounds, which may not match its actual spelling. While generic phonetic matching is often too broad to be effective in such a situation, language-specific use of phonetic matching techniques can help ensure that relevant records are found without bringing up excessive numbers of false positive hits. This is explained in more detail in Chapter 6.

Another area where high quality identity matching techniques can benefit the CRM process is in ensuring that customer records across the organisation are fully integrated and do not contain duplicate records. A duplicate-free system allows an organisation to build more effective client profiles from which to design targeting, marketing and promotional initiatives. It also prevents customers from receiving duplicated or conflicting marketing information or promotional offers.

Being able to accurately identify all customer relationships with the same party is also crucial for credit risk management. Duplicate customer records may prevent an organisation from identifying potentially unprofitable client relationships, such as where the same person has obtained multiple credit facilities with different parts of the business.

2.1.1 Internal Know Your Customer (KYC) Checks

One way of ensuring that duplicate records are not created is for operatives opening a new client relationship to carry out a robust search of existing customer data prior to creating a new entry. These checks are usually run against a variety of databases containing details of current and former clients, including clients of other branches and locations.

In larger organisations, internal searches may be more complex than simply searching the customer register of each location. The details of prospective customers and specific marketing targets may be held in different systems and should also be included as part of the initial KYC search in order to ensure that all relevant information is appropriately linked. In certain circumstances, it may also be important to include employee registers and lists of suppliers and contractors in the initial KYC search so that any potential conflicts of interest can be identified and appropriate conditions applied to the new customer relationship.

In addition to covering all relevant data sources, it is important that KYC checks use flexible matching techniques to ensure that all related data profiles are identified. Differences that may prevent matching records from being identified include simple spelling errors (as described in Chapter 7) and phonetically similar variants (as described in Chapter 6), which may be introduced if the name of a prospective customer is entered to the system in a different but similar-sounding way.

The use of linguistic matching techniques becomes more important if the name of a customer has been transcribed from another script, as other parts of the organisation may have used different transcription variants to record their client relationships, particularly if records are maintained in different languages. Transcription variants are discussed in more detail in Chapter 4.

2.1.2 Customer Data Integration (CDI)

A further way of ensuring that customer data does not contain duplicate records is the regular matching of existing customer data in order to identify and consolidate any duplicate profiles. This process is known as Customer Data Integration (CDI).

Information began to be recognised as a strategic resource in the 1980's and since then numerous approaches have been developed to manage and make use of this resource in the most efficient manner possible. Over the same period, increased computerisation has rapidly expanded the volume of electronic data available, and the effects of globalisation have lead to multiple related databases being maintained around the world. Efficient data management practices are therefore increasingly required to deal with the challenges of disparate and often inconsistent data and, in particular, with the identification and linking of related records. CDI combines the technology and processes by which an organisation is able to centrally manage a complete record of all information held on each customer.

Duplicate records can be created if account opening staff do not recognise that records relating to the same party already exist, possibly as a result of poor search facilities. Duplicate records can also be present in a system through a customer having had records in different countries or different parts of the business with disparate data systems that were subsequently merged.

Duplicates can similarly be introduced following corporate take-overs or mergers, which require formerly separate organisations to merge their customer data. In such cases, mass de-duplication exercises may be required, and linguistic matching techniques can assist here by increasing the precision and recall of the automated procedure, thereby making the manual part of the process more efficient.

In organisations that use multiple different applications to manage related data, ensuring that all related records are correctly linked can prove a significant challenge. There are a number of reasons for this, including phonetic misspellings and differences in the way the information is collected and stored. For example, a call centre application may support the entry of name and address details in free-text fields in order to facilitate the swift documentation of the caller's message. In contrast, branch offices may use a system which requires the strict fielding of different parts of the identity information. In addition, details recorded in a face-to-face situation are more likely to be copied from official identification documents, making differences based on informal speech or phonetic similarities less likely. A CDI project may, therefore, have to integrate records such as those shown below.

Data from Call Centre Application

Kate Suzanne Jankowiz
Belrive Str. 20, 65920 Frankfurt am Main (Germany)

Data from Branch Application

Catherine	*Susan*	*Jennifer*	*Yankovits-Brunner*	
20	*Bellerivestrasse*	*Frankfurt/M*	*65920*	*DE*

It can be seen from the above example that the data matching challenges posed by CDI efforts extend beyond the linguistic variations to include fielding and word order. Double-barrelled names may cause additional problems, particularly as many individuals will typically use only one part of an officially double-barrelled name. Differences can also be seen in the way that address information is presented, though it should be noted that in terms of CDI, a mismatched address may not be sufficiently significant to discount a potential name match, as a customer's address details may change over time.

As a result of these additional considerations, it is particularly important that the linguistic tolerances built into the name matching process are appropriately precise, as greater flexibility will be needed in dealing with non-linguistic variations and the system overall should not produce excessive amounts of false positive hits.

2.2 Anti-Money Laundering and Counter Terrorist Financing

Some of the most interesting, complex and productive application areas for identity matching techniques can be seen in the fight against both money laundering and the financing of terrorists.

The definition of money laundering differs around the world but generally relates to the process of concealing funds derived from specified illegal activities (known as predicate offences). The standard pattern involves illegally obtained cash being placed into the financial system and then layered through multiple transactions before becoming integrated into the legitimate money cycle. Having formerly focused on organised crime, predicate offences in many countries now include more administrative crimes such as tax evasion and false accounting.

Terrorism financing is sometimes referred to as reverse money laundering as it often involves the diversion of legitimate assets for the funding of unlawful activity. Again the definition used in national legislation varies, with some states focusing on the financing of terrorist acts, though most have criminalised the financing of the terrorists themselves, in line with current international recommendations. In these jurisdictions, the scope of the law could extend, for example, to paying rent to the landlord of someone involved in planning a terrorist act.

Increased computerisation and enhanced regulation have meant that identity checks aimed at preventing money laundering and terrorist financing have now become a standard part of many daily activities. Nowhere is this more apparent than in the risk management processes of financial services organisations, which are required to gain a thorough understanding of the identity, relationships and activities of all their customers through a process known as Know Your Customer (KYC). Financial institutions with strong KYC processes are better placed to correctly manage the specific risks associated with each customer or, in cases where the associated risks are excessive, to reject the potential customer before the relationship becomes established.

In recent years, the KYC process has also become a standard feature in other industry sectors, as the reach of national security, anti-money laundering and anti-corruption legislation extends further and globalisation takes organisations into new and unfamiliar markets. This section looks at some of the main processes in which identity matching plays a key role in preventing money laundering and terrorist financing activities.

2.2.1 Due Diligence in the Financial Services Industry

It is arguably in the financial services industry that organisations face the greatest risks if their identity matching processes fail, as the penalties for providing parties involved in money laundering or terrorist financing with access to the financial system can be severe. In the worst case scenario, an organisation's ability to do business in one or more regions can be threatened, as regulators impose strict fines and consider withdrawing banking licences for breaches of sanctions or anti-corruption legislation. In addition, indirect penalties can include negative effects on the organisation's reputation and the cost of increased regulatory scrutiny going forward.

Financial services organisations use the Know Your Customer (KYC) process and its more robust counterpart, the Enhanced Due Diligence (EDD) process, to collect information about their customers and thereby mitigate the risk of accepting and maintaining a relationship with higher-risk parties.

KYC is the process by which financial institutions fulfil their obligation to assess, verify and store certain information about their clients' activities, relationships and sources of income. There is no set definition of the procedures involved and practices vary greatly around the world. That said, the KYC process does generally include confirmation and verification of:

- the client's identity
- the true beneficial owner of the assets (where this is not the direct client)
- the sources of wealth for the funds invested
- the economic activities and position of the client

In order to satisfy regulatory requirements, financial institutions may additionally be required to carry out Enhanced Due Diligence (EDD) on those segments of their client population which inherently pose a higher level of risk. These segments may include Politically Exposed Persons (PEPs) and any party potentially connected to acts of financial crime, corruption or extremist activity. In addition, EDD is often required on parties with connections to particularly sensitive industries or countries. A client's connection to such activities, industries or countries will often be identified by searching the intelligence sources described below.

There is also no set definition of the procedures that constitute EDD. It is generally considered to be a more robust extension of the KYC process and therefore requires a more in-depth understanding of the client's key relationships and associations with other parties, particularly where an individual has a role in a local or national government structure.

At the start of the KYC/EDD process, a prospective client's name will usually be checked against a variety of internal databases, as described in section 2.1.1, to identify any current or former client relationships. Following these internal checks, additional searches will be made against a variety of external compliance data sources in order to identify and assess any potential risks associated with the prospective client. In general, this process will involve an automated search followed by the manual review of the search results to identify true hits. Given the number of new client accounts opened every day, the manual review stage can be an expensive process, so it is important that the automated search is sufficiently precise to minimise this cost.

However, as the same name may appear in intelligence sources in several different ways, it is equally vital that the search used is flexible enough to identify matches even when the names are written differently. Without linguistic techniques, excessive fuzziness in the search configuration can leave an organisation with expensive resources tied up in the review and rejection of many irrelevant hits.

Chapter 10 looks at the ways in which linguistic search techniques have enabled organisations to find the optimum balance between the risk of missing a true match and the cost of reviewing irrelevant results. The rest of this section considers the various issues involved in searching particular types of compliance intelligence data.

Sanctions Data

Financial institutions may be heavily penalised for providing services to parties that are the subject of financial sanctions measures so a key step in the KYC process will usually be to check the prospective client's name against a variety of national and supranational sanctions lists, such as those issued by the United Nations, the European Union and OFAC in the United States. There will often be other national sanctions lists that must be included as part of this check depending on the locations in which the organisation operates.

Larger institutions will often purchase access to a consolidated intelligence database from a compliance data provider. These databases usually contain names from several different sources, including multiple sanctions lists. Often the institutions will download the consolidated list and use their own search technology to run the KYC check. Some organisations do not use their own search technology but rely on the on-line search capabilities offered by the data providers, though these may be relatively unsophisticated (often using methods described in Chapter 8 as First Generation search techniques).

Smaller institutions may limit the number of sanctions lists that they choose to search and go directly to the web sites of the individual issuing authorities, by-passing the data providers. Searches carried out this way are often very restrictive, as the relevant web sites mostly offer only very limited search facilities. They may simply involve running the "find" command on a PDF document, which inevitably limits results to exact matches. In addition, running separate checks on the websites of multiple sanctions-issuing bodies often produces duplicate hits, as many different authorities sanction the same individuals and entities. This duplication is usually removed by the compliance data vendors that provide consolidated lists.

In preparing lists of sanctioned parties, the issuing authorities may include variant names that the parties are known to have used in addition to their primary names. However, the number of valid variants of a name can be significant and, for this reason, most bodies do not attempt to include all possibilities. Data vendors often also do not include additional variants in order to avoid confusion as to exactly which names are officially sanctioned and must therefore be screened in order to fulfil regulatory requirements. As a result, a flexible search is vital to avoid missing a relevant hit, particularly given the nature of many sanctioned parties and the associated risk of their trying to obscure their true identity.

Other Watch Lists

Many financial services organisations will extend the search to watch lists issued by law enforcement agencies, financial regulators and professional watchdogs. These lists are also often obtained as part of a consolidated sanctions and watch list database from compliance data providers. As with sanctions lists, it is often also possible to search them directly on the website of each issuing body, though the same restrictions relating to search strategy and technology apply.

Data on Politically Exposed Persons (PEPs)

A further important data segment that is usually searched as part of a financial institution's KYC process relates to PEPs: those parties holding a position of political influence and their relatives and close associates. In recent years, this part of the KYC check has grown in importance as many nations have strengthened and more stringently enforced their anti-corruption legislation. Although such parties would not normally be denied financial services on the basis of their political associations, it is important that institutions providing services to such individuals are aware of the political connection so that any indication of involvement in bribery or corrupt activities can be swiftly followed up.

Access to PEP data is usually purchased from a compliance data provider, often consolidated with the sanctions and other watch list information. While the name variants appearing on sanctions and watch lists are usually provided by the issuing body, and therefore identical whichever data vendor is used, name variants for PEP entries are generally collected by each data provider from a review of official government websites and other publicly available information. Given the number of political positions that can be held worldwide, the frequency with which some regimes change and the difficulty of accessing this type of information for some parts of the world, this is a significant undertaking and the quality of the information collected can vary widely between providers. Simply identifying the primary name for each PEP worldwide requires considerable research, while coverage of additional name variants for each PEP is often unsystematic. For this reason, a flexible search is required to ensure that all PEPs are appropriately recognised.

However, global PEP registers may contain over half a million profiles, and it is important that the automated matching process does not throw up excessive numbers of false positive results, as considerable time can be spent investigating erroneous hits. PEP databases may include some level of additional identifying information such as nationality, domicile and date of birth, but such identifiers are not always available to facilitate the filtering of name matches. For this reason, it is important that the name matching process itself is sufficiently precise.

Media Archives

The KYC/EDD process is not limited to searches against structured databases, where the name information is clearly defined; media archives are often also included. There is often a considerable time lag between the first suspicion that a particular party is involved in some kind of financial misdeed and their formal entry onto an official sanctions or other public watch list. Similarly, a person may take up a political position some time before this is reflected in intelligence databases. As a result, the KYC process will normally also include a search against a variety of media archives to ensure that any publicly reported political activity or allegations of involvement in financial impropriety can be appropriately factored into the client acceptance decision.

Searches against such archives require a more complex technical approach than searches against structured databases, as an initial stage is required to identify the names within the documents, even where they are combined with non-name information. For example, a search for *Harry Taylor* should hit on the text "*Sarah Taylor* and her husband *Harry*". The standard functionality is still required within the name search itself so that this text would also be identified in searches for *Henry Taylor* or *Harry Tailor.*

The sheer volume of information available in most media archives can result in significant numbers of matches being identified, particularly when searching for common names or for names that are shared by media personalities. In addition, media articles are less likely than structured databases to provide additional identifiers, such as date of birth, thereby complicating the final determination of whether or not the information relates to the relevant party. These considerations make it imperative that any fuzziness in the media search configuration is appropriately targeted in order to prevent hit volumes from becoming unmanageable.

2.2.2 Transaction Screening and Monitoring

Anti-Money Laundering efforts came to prominence in the 1990's, partly as a result of the work of the FATF (Financial Action Task Force). A key consequence for the financial services industry has been the raising of minimum standards for the KYC process, as discussed above. A further consequence is the obligation to report suspicious transactions. One of the measures designed to facilitate this is the automated screening of electronic payment data against names from sanctions and other watch lists.

It is more difficult to search payment data precisely than it is to accurately search intelligence databases, as the format and narrative style of payment records often make it difficult to identify those parts of the text that contain names. While account numbers and references for specific countries and banks are usually recorded in a standardised way, narratives describing the beneficiary and purpose of the payment often allow free-text entries. It is not uncommon for such text to be distorted or truncated a number of times as it passes through the various electronic systems that comprise the global financial network, though work is underway to address this issue.

Given the volume of electronic transactions that are processed every minute, real-time screening, aimed at blocking transactions before they are executed, may be restricted to the riskiest names and the search is often configured more precisely than is appropriate in the KYC process. As a result, an additional off-line monitoring process, designed to identify suspicious transactions after they have been executed, is often employed. In general, post-event monitoring is able to include a wider register of names and terms and also to use a broader search configuration than its real-time counterpart (although it is still likely to be a narrower search than that used in the KYC process, given the volumes of transactions involved).

This off-line transaction monitoring may also involve the comparison of payment details against other payments, as a transaction may only become suspicious once it is identified as part of an unusual pattern. Identifying suspicious transaction patterns and transactions that do not fit the client's normal business profile is particularly important in combating the financing of terrorists. This is because terrorist financing involves funds from legitimate sources being channelled to extremist organisations, so the standard KYC and EDD processes often do not flag anything particularly unusual about the originating party. Fuzzy matching techniques can play a key role in identifying related transactions, as the free-text nature of beneficiary information allows significant flexibility in the way that names are written.

2.2.3 Due Diligence in Other Industry Sectors

In recent years, many countries have extended the reach of their legislation to penalise not only the money launderers and terrorist financiers themselves, but also their advisors and any third party involved in the laundering process who failed to carry out appropriate due diligence, regardless of their intentions. This being the case, many more organisations, particularly those in the legal and consulting sectors, are now carrying out increased due diligence procedures in order to verify their clients' identity and collect background information on their activities.

In addition, while earlier regulations focused on the movement of hard currency, more recent requirements have widened the scope of anti-money laundering legislation to include any economic asset, extending the risk of involvement in money laundering beyond the financial and consulting industries to areas such as property development and luxury goods.

2.3 Criminal Investigation and Crime Management

Over recent years, the trend for greater computerisation of criminal records and increasingly organised international cooperation has created many more opportunities for identity search techniques to assist in the fight against crime. White-collar crime investigation has particularly benefited from the use of such techniques, as the volume of electronic data available for analysis has increased dramatically.

Identity search tools are now used throughout the investigation and prosecution process, from the tracking of criminals across international borders, to the investigation of criminal networks and the analysis of large quantities of electronic evidence. This section highlights some of the areas that have benefited the most.

2.3.1 Law Enforcement and Border Control

Identity search techniques are a particularly useful tool for law enforcement agencies, who use them to search a variety of intelligence databases. Most national police authorities have access to databases of individuals who have been charged or convicted of crime, including the names of their known associates. Checks against such databases can be particularly helpful in investigating fresh allegations and, in these days of wider migration and large second and third generation immigrant communities, linguistic search techniques can significantly improve the quality of the results.

Identity matching techniques are also useful for authorities investigating organised crime, where identifying common contacts across different criminal cells can provide vital clues to unravelling a crime network. Over the last decade, international cooperation on such investigations has been significantly strengthened. As a result, the use of linguistic search techniques has become even more important to account for the different ways in which names can be written in different languages, particularly those transcribed from a non-Latin script.

Border control agencies also rely on identity search techniques to generate early warning of wanted criminals or terrorists en route to their borders. In many countries, the names of flight passengers will be checked against criminal and terrorist watch lists before the flight reaches its destination. Linguistic search techniques are also vital for these searches as wanted individuals may obtain travel documents using a variation of their own name in a bid to obscure their identity.

2.3.2 White-Collar Crime Investigation

Identity matching techniques often play a key role in the investigation of white-collar crime such as fraud, corruption or insider-trading. Such crimes may be dealt with by traditional law enforcement agencies but are increasingly being investigated by government departments and large consulting firms.

One of the most comprehensive examples of anti-fraud use of identity matching techniques can be seen in the UK National Fraud Initiative, which compares the personal details stored in many different public authority databases. These include the names of social security claimants, housing tenants, pension recipients, trading licence holders and many more parties receiving allowances or permits of some kind. The aim is to detect instances of inappropriately claimed grants and benefits by identifying claimants who are also recorded as working or receiving a pension, or are otherwise not entitled to the funds they are receiving. This data matching exercise has grown significantly since it was first introduced and recent advances have begun to include selected information from the private sector to further increase the reach of the program.

Following significant enhancements to global anti-corruption legislation, some of the largest private-sector white-collar crime investigations in recent years have focused on allegations of corruption. A useful technique in such investigations is to match an organisation's payment or supplier data against lists of local politicians, agents and facilitators in order to identify any payments which may have been made to influence a political decision or the allocation of a contract. Linguistic search techniques come into their own in such investigations, as they are able to focus on specific geographic areas, allowing the linguistic tolerances to be precisely targeted based on the relevant languages.

Other white collar crime investigations can also benefit from the use of linguistic search techniques. For example, investigators at a bank might match lists of the contacts of a known fraudster with the beneficiaries of payments made out of defrauded accounts. Contact matching is a technique used on many kinds of investigation, as proving a link between the parties able to carry out a particular action and those who benefited from it is often a key line of enquiry. This is particularly the case in insider trading investigations, where the contacts of traders making unusual profits may be matched against the contacts of those with access to inside information.

2.4 Information Search

2.4.1 Business Information Search

Today, vast amounts of data are available to business organisations, either free or at a cost. Free sources of information may include telephone and business directories, or on-line reference sources, such as library catalogues. A broader range of information is often available for a price and includes credit history records and marketing data, such as details of potential customers, as well as the compliance intelligence information discussed above.

Whatever the information source, it is only as useful as the tools used to search it. A credit history record warning of poor repayment potential is of no use if the search tool fails to identify the relevant record. Linguistic search methods can therefore be used to maximise the potential of investment in such information, particularly in cases where failure to identify relevant records can have serious financial consequences for an organisation, such as when searching credit history files or AML watch lists. In recent years, vendors of such information have become more aware of the dual need for high quality information and accurate search processes, and are starting to provide enhanced search facilities to increase the value of their product to their customers.

In addition to structured information sources, organisations may also purchase access to media and other document archives for marketing and research purposes. The issues related to searching such data sources are discussed in section 2.2.1 above.

2.4.2 Electronic Discovery

Electronic discovery is the process in civil litigation through which electronic data is provided for review by the opposing party. It relates primarily to data which originated in electronic form, such as e-mail, instant messaging and other document and databases files. It can also include paper documents that have been scanned into electronic images. The volumes involved have increased dramatically as the use of electronic files, email and electronic archiving systems has risen.

Searching electronic documents involves many of the same challenges as searching media archives (discussed in section 2.2.1 above) in that the name must first be located within the text before the appropriate fuzzy tolerances can be applied. An additional challenge is presented if the files to be searched are scanned images of hard copy documents, as they must first be processed with Optical Character Recognition (OCR) software to make them machine-readable. In such cases it may be appropriate to adjust the tolerances for character substitution as some characters may be more likely to be mistaken than others, depending on the quality of the software used. For example, an *S* may be read as an *8*, or a *D* as an *O*. Typographic tolerances are discussed in more detail in section 10.5.

2.5 Conclusion

This chapter has discussed some of the most common uses for identity matching techniques. In a large organisation there may be many more processes which rely at some level on identity search tools, whether as a database search for a specific identity or as part of a bulk data matching or de-duplication exercise. Such processes may be run either on structured databases or on unstructured data such as news articles and other document archives.

What these processes all have in common is the central role of the ability to match proper names from around the world. The use of different naming conventions around the world complicates the name matching process and this complexity is further increased by the proliferation of different transcription standards used in different languages to convert non-Latin scripts into standard Latin characters.

Proper names can be found in many data sources, including:

- customer, vendor and employee databases
- contact directories
- purchased information sources

- freely available directories on the Internet
- sanctions and watch lists for AML and CTF purposes
- law enforcement databases

Given the number of processes in which one or more such data sources play a key role, there are a great many ways in which linguistic identity matching can help improve the efficiency of an organisation's procedures.

Chapter 3: Introduction to Proper Names

A proper name can refer to any unique entity. In the context of identity matching, the proper names of individuals, organisations and other entities, such as ships, are the most relevant. Throughout this book, the term "proper name" is used in a restricted sense to refer to these classes of names.

This chapter looks in particular at the proper names of natural persons. It considers the basics of what makes up a person's name, together with the historical and cultural development of naming practices around the world. This lays the foundation for understanding the different features of proper names that are important for identity matching purposes and which will be considered in more detail in later chapters.

This book uses the term "naming system" to describe the structure of proper names and the function of the different parts within them, as well as the cultural norms and legal processes that might see a name changing over time. With language and culture playing such a huge role in the development of proper names, there are obviously very many different naming systems in use around the world. To highlight the differences in global naming systems, this chapter uses examples from four of the most widely used: the Western, Russian, Arabic and Chinese.

3.1 Important Characteristics of Proper Names

Before looking more closely at the different naming systems in use around the world, it is worth taking a moment to consider why proper names play such a key role in the identity matching process. There are three main reasons; their distinguishing function, their relative stability and their wide-spread use. Each of these is considered below.

3.1.1 The Distinguishing Function of Names

In many cultures, a name can be used to identify a person with relative certainty and thus provide a distinguishing feature. Of course, several people may have the same name, but this occurs far less frequently than people having the same nationality or date of birth. Each date during the last 50 years is a common birth date for hundreds of thousands of people. In most cultures, a person's name is significantly more distinguishing than this.

However, the relative distinction offered by particular name parts varies between different languages and regions. Thai families, for example, will usually have their own unique family name, while 40% of the Vietnamese population share the family name *Nguyễn*, making Vietnamese names far less distinctive. In the English speaking world, even the most common names are still relatively distinctive. *Smith* is one of the most common surnames in these communities, but only around 1% of the population has this surname, demonstrating that there are still plenty of other, more distinctive names in use.

Even if specific given or family names are not particularly unique, used in combination, they are much more distinctive. *James*, *Ralph* and *Smith* are all common name parts in themselves, but the name *James Ralph Smith* is far more distinguishing as a full name.

3.1.2 The Relative Stability of Names

A further useful feature of proper names is their relative stability. Most people and legal entities will go through their whole lives without changing their name completely. In some cultures, names may change at specific points in a person's life, often on marriage. In some cases new name parts are added to the original; in others, the original name part may be dropped. Outside of such cultural norms, names tend to change only infrequently during a person's lifetime, and in some countries the legal changing of a natural person's name is permitted only in very restricted circumstances. That said, this stability is more a feature of official, registered name information than of names that might be used informally, such as nicknames and shortened name forms. The names of non-natural persons such as organisations and other entities, such as ships, may also change more frequently.

While names may not always be completely stable over time, they are often more so than other identity characteristics such as address information, which can change frequently. Even national identification numbers are not always reliably constant. For example, the migrant workers forced to move on at the start of the first Gulf war already had national identification numbers from their home countries, as well as residence permit numbers issued by Kuwait, and many of them travelled through several other permit-issuing jurisdictions in the period that followed. Names, albeit subject to spelling variations, remained relatively constant while "national" identification numbers came and went. This was a particular challenge for the international agencies attempting to monitor the fortunes of the displaced migrants.

3.1.3 The Widespread Use of Names

The final characteristic of proper names which makes them such a valuable part of the identity matching process is their omnipresence throughout our global society. While social security numbers or tax registration codes may provide a more unique identifier, they are not always used in every country, or even within all classes of society. Even the date of birth is an erratically used identifier. In some cultures it is common for an individual to use only the year of their birth, and women may use their husband's birth year if they have no record of their own.

Even in cases where full identity details are known, they may not have been captured in the database or archive to be searched. This is particularly true when searching media archives or other free-text information sources, as these often contain little identifying information other than the person's name.

In such cases, the name may be the only identifying feature available for matching. It is therefore appropriate that the matching process is optimised to make full use of this complex characteristic.

3.2 The Historical Development of Naming Conventions

The way that names have developed over time has varied enormously across different geographical and political regions. While it is a common misconception in the West that international names follow much the same pattern as those used in Western society, in reality a naming structure is often valid only within its own language area and the specific culture and administrative system in which it has developed. Typically, it is the same phenomena (including urbanisation, administration and colonisation as well as political revolutions) that have shaped the development of names in different regions, but the resulting naming systems may be entirely different.

In the Western world, naming structures have been relatively stable for many years, but in other parts of the world the development of naming conventions and cultural norms is still ongoing. A full description of the history of naming practices around the world would be a topic for a separate book in itself. This chapter aims to highlight just some of the trends that have shaped global naming conventions and to demonstrate the reasons why the differences in naming structures pose additional challenges during the identity matching process.

3.3 Western Names: the Germanic Example

Although the naming conventions in use across the Western world are largely similar, historical and linguistic influences have lead to a number of smaller variations. This section focuses primarily on the naming conventions prevalent in the Germanic language areas of Northern and Central Europe to demonstrate the way in which naming practices have changed over time.

3.3.1 Given Names and Auxiliary Names

The term "given name" is used in this book to depict a name given to a child entirely at the discretion of its parents or other family. Long ago, the Germanic peoples mostly only used one given name for each person. While the size of each settlement was still relatively small it was usually clear which individual was referred to with the use of a given name without any additional identifiers. Where individuals shared the same name, a second, auxiliary name part was added. Two men named *Karl* may have come to be referred to as *Karl der Lange* (*Tall Karl*) and *Karl der Kurze* (*Short Karl*). Additional given names came into use as the arrival of Christianity in the region made biblical names popular. However, the inventory of commonly used given names decreased steadily over the years as children were customarily named after their ancestors. At the same time, settlements and villages grew larger, making the use of auxiliary names more widespread.

Auxiliary names tended to be derived from particular characteristics of the individual. Occupational titles were commonly used, and the effects of this can often be seen in common Germanic family names today. *Müller* (miller), *Schmidt* (smith), *Schneider* (tailor), *Fischer* (fisherman), *Weber* (weaver), *Schulz* (magistrate), *Wagner* (wagon maker), *Becker* (baker), *Hoffman* (farm steward), *Schäfer* (shepherd), *Koch* (cook), *Bauer* (farmer) and *Richter* (judge) are all examples of common family names derived from the occupational auxiliary names of old.

Other auxiliary names described personal characteristics. These include names derived from physical traits, such as *Klein* (small), *Groß* (big), *Kurz* (short) and *Lang* (tall), and hair colours, such as *Weiß* (white), *Schwarz* (black) or *Rot* (red). Traits of character were also used as auxiliary names including *Kühn* (hardy), *Gut* (good) and *Fromm* (pious) and names were also derived from particular life circumstances, such as *Neumann* (new man) for the newly settled.

Some auxiliary given names described the region, the town or the country in which the person originated. Examples include *Deutscher* (German), *Schweizer* (Swiss), *Hess* (Hessian), *Bayer* (Bavarian), *Schwab* (Swabian), *Böhm* (Bohemian) and *Mannheimer* (from Mannheim). A further group of auxiliary names referred to the person's residence or the name of the farm that the person lived on, such as *Busch* (bush), *Wiese* (meadow) or *Zumstein* (at the stone). Auxiliary names derived from the place of origin or residence often became the basis for titles for the aristocracy, but many other types of auxiliary names can be seen as common family names today.

3.3.2 Patronyms

An important form of auxiliary name is the patronym (a name derived from the father's name) and, to a lesser extent, the matronym (derived from the mother's name). These names were also originally used to distinguish between two individuals of the same name, so that *Karl Johnson* was distinguished as being the son of *John*.

Occasionally, a patronymic name may simply be the name of the father, but more usually they are amended with a suffix or prefix to indicate descent. Patronyms of Germanic origin tended to be suffixed with *-son, -sen, -s, -z, -man* or *–mann*; for example, *Johnson, Robertson, Hansen, Pedersen, Peters, Friedrichs* or *Petermann*. In Scottish and Irish names, they may be prefixed with *Mac-, O'-* or *Fitz*, as in *MacDonald, O'Connor* or *Fitzgerald*. Other patronyms, such as *Alexander, Martin* and *Frank* have been formed without an affix, which explains why so many male given names are also used as family names today.

With or without affix, names derived from the names of forefathers are mostly used in the modern Western context as family names, handed down through generations. One notable exception can be seen in Icelandic names, where patronyms (and occasionally matronyms) are in standard use in place of family names and continue to represent the name of the immediate father. As an example, the son of *Stefan Eriksson* might be *Karl Stefansson*, while his daughter might be *Anna Stefansdottir.* A recognition of such standards is clearly important when using identity matching to identify family groups.

3.3.3 Family Names

Family names developed largely as a result of urbanisation and the desire of administrators to be able to unambiguously relate to their citizens. As populations grew, a single given name, with or without a descriptive auxiliary name, was no longer sufficient.

The examples given above have demonstrated how many of today's Western family names are derived from the patronyms and auxiliary names used many years ago. The key difference between these auxiliary names and the family names that they became is that family names are passed down through generations of the same family, so that as *Karl der Lange* became *Karl Lange*, his son would also have the family name *Lange*, however tall he was.

While the use of these descriptive auxiliary names as family names has lead to a relatively small number of family names becoming very common, the original regional pronunciations lead to a multitude of variations in their spelling. The name *Meyer*, originally used as an auxiliary name meaning a steward of the manor, was transcribed in many different ways, often based on the way the word was pronounced in each region, resulting in variations including *Meier, Maier, Mayer, Majer, Meyer, Maijer, Meijer, Mair, Meir, Mayr* and *Meyr.* Pronunciation has converged over the years so that in modern usage these names sound very similar and can cause confusion. Additional variations were caused by the transcription of names with multiple parts as either one or several words, such as *Vanderburg* or *Van der Burg.* These are particularly important features to take into account when matching identity data that has at some point been transcribed from the spoken word, for example in a customer call centre.

3.4 Other Features of Western Naming Systems

The Germanic example provides a good introduction to naming concepts in use in the Western world. The process of descriptive auxiliary names becoming family names took place across most of Europe and is also seen in many other parts of the world. The name *Smith*, for example, is seen not only in its Germanic forms *Schmidt*, *Schmitt*, and *Schmid*, but in many other societies too, such as the French

Lefèvre and the Italian *Ferrari* as well as the transcribed Russian *Kuznetsov* (Кузнецов) and Arabic *Haddad* (حداد), all of which are common names in their respective regions.

Compared to the naming systems in use in many other parts of the world, conventions in Western societies can be considered relatively mature in that the pace of development in naming practices has virtually ground to a halt. The basic Western standard combines one or two given names with a family name that is passed down through generations and many electronic databases are designed to store names in this format, with three fields for "first name", "middle name" and "last name". However, it is not uncommon for a person to have more than two given names, and additional names are often entered to the "middle name" field.

Compound given names are common in some cultures and are often incorrectly entered into databases as separate given names. A good example of this can be seen in the Spanish tradition, where middle names are generally not used. For example, a compound given name such as *Juan Pablo* may be entered into a database with *Pablo* as the "middle" name, making erroneous matches with individuals whose full given name is either *Juan* or *Pablo* more likely.

This problem is less frequent in the English speaking world but does still exist, as in the compound name *John Paul*, which may or may not be written with a hyphen. In other languages, it is common to concatenate compound names, as in the German *Hanspeter*, which electronic registers may also display as *Hans-Peter* or *Hans Peter*, or erroneously as first name *Hans*, middle name *Peter*.

Different traditions also exist in the composition and use of family names. Much of Europe and North America adopts a single family name shared by all members of the same family, with a woman often taking her husband's name on marriage and this name being passed on to their children. This differs from the practices in use across Spanish and Portuguese speaking areas, where children often take one (or more) family names from each parent to create a compound family name.

In the Spanish variant, the first family name of the father is traditionally placed before the first family name of the mother to form the child's family name. For example, *Juan Antonio Lopez-Sanchez* has inherited the name *Lopez* from his paternal grandfather and the name *Sanchez* from his maternal grandfather. Partly to avoid confusion between given and family names, the two parts of the family name may be joined with the conjunction *y* (or sometimes *e*), as in *Juan Antonio Lopez y Sanchez*. Women do not usually change their name on marriage so parents will normally have different compound family names to those of each other and their children.

As in the Spanish convention, Portuguese tradition places emphasis on the name inherited from the paternal grandfather as the "main" family name. However, in Portuguese-speaking regions, it is more common for this name to be placed after the one taken from the maternal grandfather so that the two parts are the opposite way round to those in a Spanish compound name.

Tradition in Portuguese-speaking areas also provides for a child to inherit up to two family names from one or both of their parents, which may result in a three or four-part family name. This can also be seen in cases where a woman opts to adopt her husband's family name(s) on marriage in addition to her own.

In both the Spanish and Portuguese traditions, it is possible for each part of a compound family name to consist of more than one "word". The former Portuguese Prime Minister *José Socrates Carvalho Pinto de Sousa* takes the name *Carvalho* from his mother and the name *Pinto de Sousa* from his father. This, combined with the possibility of up to two family names being inherited from each parent, can make the complete family name complex to match, often resulting in large numbers of partial matches. Partial matches are significant because individuals with very long family names may choose to be known under just part of their official name, but they can also include large numbers of irrelevant hits if common name parts are involved.

Outside the Spanish and Portuguese conventions, compound names are often formed on marriage. While it is common in the English-speaking world for a woman to replace her family name with that of her husband on marriage, the couple may alternatively take a hyphenated name, and in Continental Europe the maiden name is just as likely to be maintained in some way as it is to be dropped altogether. For example, if Frau *Schmidt* marries Herr *Meyer*, her name may be shown in official documents as Frau *Meyer-Schmidt*, Frau *Meyer Schmidt* or Frau *Meyer (-Schmidt)*. In some countries, the man may also be shown in official registers as Herr *Meyer-Schmidt*. Despite an officially double-barrelled name, both the man and the woman will often use only the man's family name, again raising the issue of partial matches.

In the US, it is not uncommon for the mother's maiden name to be passed down to the children as a matronymic middle name even if the mother herself has ceased to use the name. This is seen less often in the UK, demonstrating that differences in naming conventions exist even within language communities. Another small but important difference in terms of identity matching can be seen in the American use of middle names as the main identifier, so that someone commonly known as *Jack Morton* may officially be called *William Jack Morton* and refer to himself in writing as *W. Jack Morton*. Again, this convention is relatively less common in the UK. This is significant for identity matching purposes as a match between *Jack Morton* and *William Jack Morton* is more likely to be a true match if William is an American.

The above examples are just a few of the many ways in which differences exist within Western naming conventions, all of which must be understood and incorporated into any good identity matching system to ensure that each part of the name is treated appropriately. The differences between Western naming conventions and those used in other parts of the world are even more substantial, as the rest of this chapter will demonstrate.

3.5 The Russian Example

The Russian naming system is significant not only because of its use throughout the Russian Federation, but also because of the influence it has had on naming conventions in other regions of the world. As a result of the vast expansion of the Russian empire, and later the Soviet Union, the Russian naming system was introduced to many other cultural areas, including some outside the Slavic region. Since the dissolution of the Soviet Union, many former Soviet republics have taken steps to return to their traditional naming systems. This process is still ongoing, particularly in Central Asia, where it is not uncommon for there to be more than one established way to represent a person's name. This is a particular challenge that has to be addressed when matching names from this region.

A Russian proper name typically exists of three main parts: a given name, a patronym and a family name. A typical example is Борис Николаевич Ельцин or its English transcription *Boris Nikolayevich Yeltsin*.

Given names often have many diminutive forms, which may be used when addressing a good acquaintance. These diminutives do not always display an obvious connection to their related full name. For example, diminutive forms of *Vladimir* include *Vova*, *Volodya* or *Vovochka* and diminutive forms of *Aleksandr* include *Sasha*, *Sanya*, *Shurik* and *Alik*.

In more formal situations, a Russian might be addressed with their full given name together with their patronym, though as a result of Western influences it is becoming customary to use only the given name. The Russian patronym is built from the given name of the father together with a suffix dependent on gender. Boris

Yeltsin's father was called *Nikolai*, giving him the patronym *Nikolayevich*. His sister would have had the patronym *Nikolayevna*. In very informal situations, a person could be addressed using the patronym only. In these cases, a diminutive form of the patronym may be used, such as *Mikhalych* for *Mikhailovich* the son of *Mikhail*.

The concept of the family name was introduced to Russia in the 18th Century and today is a fixed and hereditary part of the Russian naming system. Historically, the endings of family names are also different for men and women, as is seen in the transcription of the name of Yeltsin's widow, *Naina Iosifovna Yeltsina*. Following Western influence, it is becoming more common for an individual to be referred to using only their given and family names in Russian language media. In addition, it is not uncommon for Western media to erroneously assume that a wife's family name must be the same as her husband's and refer to Naina, for example, as *Naina Yeltsin* rather than *Naina Yeltsina*.

Only the given and family names in the Russian naming system have direct equivalents in the Western convention. If a database has only fields for these two names, the patronym may be recorded in either, though both are technically incorrect. In a standard three-field name register, the patronym is often entered as the "middle name". This is also not ideal, as patronyms have specific features that are different from given and family names and ideally these should be incorporated into the matching process. For example, it is sometimes necessary to review matches that are based on the middle name and family name, so that the singer *James Paul McCartney* could be identified by searching for *Paul McCartney*. This is not the case with the patronym and family name so it would be useful to be able to distinguish between patronyms and true "middle" names.

3.6 The Arabic Example

A good understanding of the Arabic naming system is extremely important for those involved in international identity matching efforts. It is one of the more complex naming systems and has had enormous influence on the development of proper names throughout the Islamic world. For the purposes of simplicity, this section uses the term Arabic to describe the Islamic Arabic tradition. Other sections of Arabic society follow different conventions to the traditional Islamic system described here. For example, Christian Arabs often follow a system closer to that used in the West.

The Arabic naming system is deeply rooted in the Islamic cultures established across the Middle East and Northern Africa. However, some variations do exist within these regions as a result of earlier colonial influences and the more recent effects of globalisation and the Internet. Consequently, and despite the strong hold of the traditional Arabic system, it could well be that naming conventions in these areas will continue to evolve for some time to come.

One traditional form of Arabic name consists of up to five different elements: the Ism, the Kunya, the Nasab, the Laqab and the Nisba.

Ism

This is roughly equivalent to the Western given name. Children and young people are mostly addressed using their Ism. In most cases, adults are not addressed this way, even by family members.

Kunya

Adults may be addressed using their Kunya. This refers to the person as the father (transcribed as *Abu* or *Abou*) or mother (transcribed as *Umm, Um, Oum, Oumm*) of the first born son. In this way, *Abu Mahmud* is the father of *Mahmud*. This is normally used from the moment the son is born. Occasionally, if older adults do not have a son, an arbitrary boys name may be placed in the Kunya name form.

Nasab

This element has some similarities with European patronymic names. It may contain many sub-elements, referring to the father, grandfather and so on. The name is often introduced with the Arabic word for son (transcribed as *Bin*, *Ben* or *Ibn*) or daughter (transcribed as *Bint*, *Bent* or *Ibnat*), so that *Mahmud Bin Faisal Bin Muhammad* is the son of *Faisal* and grandson of *Muhammad*.

Laqab

Many Arabs have a Laqab, which represents some positive characteristic, and this is often the name by which the person is addressed. A common example of a Laqab takes the form "Servant of God". A frequent transcription of عبد ال (servant of) is *Abd al-* and this is often followed by one of the many names of Allah used in the Koran. *Abd al-Rahman, Abd al-Aziz* and *Abdullah* are examples of such constructions, the female versions of which would be *Amat al-Rahman,*

Amat al-Aziz and *Amatullah*. The *Abd al-* construction is a common name form and can also be used in the Ism. However, it should be noted that not all names that use this structure are from the Islamic-Arabic culture. Christian names may also use this form, as can be seen in the name *Abdul Isa*, which can be roughly translated as Servant of Jesus.

Nisba

The Nisba is the closest name part to the Western family name. It is usually a description of the place of origin of the family, though it can sometimes be a description of the occupation. The Nisba can consist of more than one element, signifying an individual's belonging to a particular family and to a particular clan.

In Arabic names that contain all five basic name parts, they are usually represented in the order Kunya, Ism, Nasab, Laqab, Nisba; for example, *Abu Murad Faisal Ibn Muhammad Ibn Salim Abd al-Rahman al-Husseini*. The difficulties of trying to force such a name into the standard three name fields of Westernised databases are clear.

Arabic names may also contain honorific titles. The main ones are شيخ (*Sheikh*, often transcribed as *Sheik*, *Shaykh*, *Shaikh*, *Cheikh* or *Scheich*), حاج (*Hajj*, also transcribed as *Haj*, *Hadj*, *Hadsch*, or *Hag)* and حاجي (*Hajji*, also transcribed as *Haji*, *Hadji* or *Hagi* and may be found in other variants such as *Al-Haji*). *Sheikh* is used to identify an elder person or scholar, or sometimes the holder of a governmental position. This title may rarely appear in its female version *Sheikha*. *Haj* or *Haji* designates a Muslim who has completed the pilgrimage to Mecca and may also be used in some communities to denote an elder.

In most cases, only some of an individual's name parts or titles are used publicly but there are no standards for the selection of these. The Ism and Kunya can loosely be translated to the Western given and family name construction, but this is often not the name form used.

A review of media articles covering the Arabic world highlights the variety of different name part combinations used to refer to different individuals. The former Iraqi dictator is known in the Western world as *Saddam Hussein*. More accurately, his name was *Saddam Hussein Al-Tikriti*, as *Hussein* is the Nasab, being the Ism of Saddam's father, though the *Ibn* or *Bin* that often introduces the Nasab is not used in this case.

A similar situation is seen in Western media reporting of the former Egyptian president *Gamal Abdel Nasser*. *Gamal* and *Abdel* are often mistakenly taken to be the first and middle name with *Nasser* as the family name. In fact, *Abdel Nasser* is the name of the individual's father and a form of the *Abd al-* construction discussed above. To separate the *Abd al-*, no matter how it is transcribed, from the rest of the name element is not valid. In addition, to take and match this common prefix as a name part in its own right would significantly increase the risk of false positive matches.

As discussed above, Arabic names have been, and still are, subject to foreign influences. However, the Arabic naming system has itself had enormous influence over naming systems in many other parts of the world. Arabic is considered to be a holy language, and many Arabic names have become popular in societies with a strong Islamic culture, particularly in parts of Africa, Iran, Afghanistan, India, Malaysia and Indonesia. In these countries, Arabic names are often used in local variants. For example, *Mohd*, a version of *Muhammad*, is a common name in Malaysia and Indonesia but is used less often in the Arab world. Arabic names are also increasingly commonly used outside Arabic-speaking countries as a result of migration.

The pervasive nature of Arabic names, the complexities of their format and issues caused by their transcription combine to make the matching of Arabic names one of the most challenging elements of international identity matching projects.

3.7 The Chinese Example

Many Chinese proper names consist of two or three main parts: a family name and a personal name; or a family name, a generation name and a personal name. Often, these name parts consist of one Chinese character and are monosyllabic. The former Chinese leader 毛澤東 (*Mao Zedong*, sometimes transcribed as *Mao Tse-tung*) is a good example of a Chinese name with three monosyllabic parts.

The first part of the former leader's name, 毛 or *Mao*, is his hereditary family name, demonstrating how inappropriate the Western term "last name" is when discussing family names of this origin. There are only a few hundred distinct family names in use in China, which means that many families in China's vast population share the same name. The most common is 王, which can be transcribed as *Wang* or *Wong* and is the family name of over 90 million Chinese people.

The family name is often followed by a generation name, which is shared by all siblings of a generation. The generation name of *Mao Zedong* is 澤 or *Ze*, and his brothers were named *Mao Zetan* and *Mao Zemin*. The generation name is never used without the personal name.

The personal name, in this example 東 or *Dong*, can be used alone or together with the generation name. Its function resembles that of the Western given name, but its position at the end of the full Chinese name means that it is often misused as a family name in Western style records. Ironically, confusion may also arise as a result of the tendency of some Chinese people to swap the order of their names when communicating with Westerners, precisely in the hope of avoiding such misunderstanding.

Notwithstanding confusion caused by the order of Chinese name parts, the family name and personal name can be represented quite easily in the Western naming model. The generation name, on the other hand, causes difficulties since it is neither a given nor middle name in the Western sense. In addition, it is not always recognisable from the transcribed form whether a whole "word" is the personal name or a combination of the generation and personal name. This is partly because these two name parts are not always written separately when transcribed, depending on local traditions. For example, 亞南 may be written as *Yanan* in mainland China, *Ya-Nan* in Taiwan or *Ya Nan* in Hong-Kong.

This, combined with the fact that some Chinese given names do have more than one syllable can cause confusion between the name parts. For example, from the romanised version, it is not clear whether *Huang* is a personal name or a combination of the generation name *Hu* and the personal name *Ang*. The apparent similarity of these romanised name elements belies the fact that they are transcribed from entirely different Chinese characters.

The Chinese administrative and writing conventions have had a significant influence on naming conventions in other Asian countries, notably Japan, Korea and Vietnam. Often, Japanese and Korean names are written in Chinese characters rather than the native script. Following the French colonisation of Vietnam, names in this country are mostly written in the Latin script, though still follow the Chinese three part system with the family name represented at the front.

3.8 Conclusion

This chapter has provided an introduction to the wide variety of naming conventions used around the world. It has summarised some of the key features of naming systems in use in Western, Russian, Chinese and Islamic-Arabic societies in order to demonstrate how widely international naming conventions may differ. In practice, many variants of these naming systems exist even within their own language areas; the examples given, therefore, are by no means comprehensive.

Looking further afield, other language areas use different naming systems entirely. These include the numerous and complex naming structures that have developed across sub-Saharan Africa and some parts of Asia, including the multi-language communities of the Indian sub-continent. In many of these regions, naming conventions vary widely and are continuously developing as a result of changes in political regime and modern international influences. The result is a huge variety of naming traditions in use around the world.

It is not necessary to fully understand the historical development of international naming systems to appreciate the challenges that must be addressed by effective identity matching systems. However, what is required is an understanding of the basic structure of names from each system and the function of each name part as well as the variations that may be seen in practice.

This chapter has highlighted the following features of international naming structures that provide particular challenges for the identity matching process:

Structural differences

Most databases used for identity matching purposes have been designed with the Western name format in mind. The storage of non-Western names in such a structure can lead to inconsistencies as different fields may be used to record the same type of name elements. It can also lead to information loss as the significance of each name part may be masked by the way it has been recorded in the Western structure.

Multiple name systems

Many countries have several proper name systems in active use, some of which may be hybrid forms of other national naming conventions. As a result, the same person's name may be represented in several different ways, even within their home country.

Changes to naming systems

A country may have changed its naming system relatively abruptly as a result of war or political upheaval. This can lead to complications in the identity matching process if the data being compared has been collected at different points in time.

Life events

Some cultures traditionally change the way a person is referred to based on particular life stages or events. This is another reason why the same person may be represented in a database with a different name.

Most of these features are complicated to address and require specific tolerances to be built into the matching process. However, the enforced recording of all names in the Western format ought to be less complex to solve. Ideally, databases used for identity matching purposes should not be based on Western naming conventions but on a generic model that is flexible enough to accommodate many different styles and formats of name without losing any of the information contained. The aim should be not to store name elements with different characteristics without somehow recording any attributes that may be useful in the identity matching process. Some of the larger international regulatory bodies are now starting to re-design their databases with this in mind, but this is the exception rather than the rule.

In practice, many of the databases used for identity matching purposes simply form existing components of standardised systems and are typically based on Western naming conventions. As identity matching is usually not the core of the application as a whole, it is likely to be some time before software developers consider an overhaul of this narrowly defined standard for storing name information.

In addition, the database structure is not the only reason why international names may not be stored in the most appropriate format. Identity data are often collected without full knowledge of the true function of each name element, particularly where those charged with inputting the data are unfamiliar with international naming conventions. It is, therefore, usually necessary to design flexible matching rules that allow for the loss of structural information in names of non-Western origin.

The structural issues posed by different naming conventions are compounded by the intricacies of the associated linguistic and typographical issues. These additional challenges are discussed in the following chapters.

Chapter 4: Transcription

The previous chapter considered the variations that can be introduced when proper names are converted from one person name system to another and explained that this frequently occurs when non-Western names are stored in a database designed around Western naming conventions. This chapter considers a related but significantly more problematic source of variation in proper names: the variations that are caused by transferring proper names from one writing system to another.

There may be many valid romanised versions of the same non-Latin names, and the differences between them can be considerable. This is a particularly important consideration in the design of any identity matching system used for compliance, law enforcement or national security purposes, as watch lists published for use in such systems often focus on romanised versions of names, despite including a significant number of names originating from countries where the Latin script is not used.

The variations caused by the use of different transcription standards can be so significant that they result in names that do not obviously appear related to the untrained eye. Consider the name Хрущёв, which can equally be written as *Khrushchev* or *Chruschtschow*; the name القذافي, which may appear as *Gaddafi*, *Khadafy* or *Quathafi*; or the name 黃, valid transcriptions of which include *Huang* and *Wong*. From these examples, it is clear that specialised linguistic techniques are required in order to identify and match valid variations of the same name without also generating huge numbers of false positive matches. This is both a technically and a linguistically complex task. Consequently, many popular identity matching applications are, as yet, unable to reliably match different transcription variants, and some of the organisations using these tools are unaware of the limitations.

The consequences of failure in this area can be severe. Consider the fate of a bank that has opened an account for a known money-launderer whose name is published on an internationally recognised watch list. Regulators impose fines, strengthen their on-going compliance requirements and possibly even withdraw operating licences, while nervous clients move their funds to other institutions.

A post-mortem reveals that the account opening clerk had carried out all the necessary due-diligence checks but the system had failed to notice that the client had opened the account using a different transcription of his name to the one published on the official watch list. Colossal damages, and no one to blame but the technology.

This chapter introduces the challenges involved in the matching of transcription variants. The number of scripts in use world-wide and the multiple transcription standards that may be applied to each make this an extremely complex area. For the purposes of simplicity, this chapter provides examples using romanised names from the Russian, Arabic and Chinese writing systems, but it should be borne in mind that an effective matching solution should cover many more scripts and transcription standards than those considered here.

4.1 Transcription, Transliteration and Translation

The process of converting a name from one writing system to another is referred to as transcription or transliteration. Though these terms are often used interchangeably, they have subtle but important differences in their meaning.

4.1.1 Transliteration

Transliteration is the process of converting characters from text presented in one script (the source script) into the corresponding characters in another script (the target script).

In many cases, a particular alphabet or script is shared by several different languages. For example, many Western languages such as English, Spanish, French and German use the Latin alphabet, while many Slavic languages such as Russian, Bulgarian and Ukrainian are written in the Cyrillic script. Which Latin character is equivalent to which Cyrillic character depends on the conversion standard being followed. Transliteration standards aim to provide a direct one-for-one conversion for each character so that text can be transliterated and then unambiguously reverse-transliterated back to the original. Such standards are popular for use in automated transliteration processes but are of limited use in the identity matching sphere as they are rarely the conversion standards used in practice by those wishing to transcribe their names. For example, the standard for transliterating Cyrillic characters into the Latin script set out by ISO 9 converts the Russian name

Ельцин into *El'cin*, but this name is much more likely to be written as *Yeltsin* in the English-speaking world.

Transliteration would have little relevance for the identity matching topic if it were not for the fact that many software developers confuse the ability to transliterate a name with the ability to deal with transcription variants. Matching Ельцин with *El'cin* (and vice versa) is easily achieved but far less useful in an identity matching context than being able to match Ельцин with *Yeltsin*, *Jelzin* and *Eltsine* and recognising that these transcriptions, and the other commonly used transcription variants of this name, should all match to each other.

4.1.2 Transcription

While transliteration focuses on the process of converting characters from one script to another, transcription involves the conversion of text from one language to another (that uses a different script) in such a way that native speakers of each language would pronounce the text in a similar manner. For example, an English speaker would transcribe the name Ельцин to *Yeltsin*, while a German speaker would transcribe it to *Jelzin* in order to achieve a similar pronunciation. To consider transcription as the process of converting a name from one script to another is only half the story; the source language and target language are equally as important considerations as the source and target scripts when transcribing a name.

A frequent English transcription of the Arabic name عبد الرحمن is *Abdurrahman*, while a more common French transcription would be *Abdourrahmane*. In each case, a native speaker would pronounce the transcribed name approximately the same way as an Arabic speaker would pronounce the original. However, if an English speaker pronounced the French version, or vice versa, different sound patterns would result. For each source language, there may be several ways of transcribing text into each different target language. As section 4.4 explains, *Abdurrahman* is by no means the only variant of this name that is commonly used in English texts.

Though the process of transcription frequently results in many different variants for the same name, it may also have the opposite effect. Different names from the source language may end up with identical transcriptions in the target language. Where this happens, the differentiation is lost and the original spelling can no longer be deduced with certainty from the transcribed version. For example, سليم and سالم are two frequent parts of Arabic names. Although they are spelled differently, they sound similar to Western ears and are both often transcribed as *Salim*, whereas they can be distinctly transliterated as *Slym* and *Salm*.

While academics and computer linguists often favour transliteration over transcription for the increased certainty it offers, in practice, names are more often transcribed using the most comfortable spelling in the target language. This applies as much to authorities issuing official identification documents as it does to journalists and others writing in the media. There are several reasons for this. Firstly, the scientific transliteration standards are not widely known by those with no linguistic training. Secondly, even if the standards are known, they may not produce a practical spelling for use in the target language. For example, a scientific transliteration of Хрущёв is *Chruščëv*, which is not particularly useful for communicating the correct pronunciation. This example also demonstrates the third reason why scientific transliterations are not widely used. They often require the use of diacritics, such as the caron, or inverted circumflex, above the *s* and *c* in *Chruščëv*. These markings interrupt the readability of the name for those unfamiliar with their usage and are not easily accessible on Western computer keyboards.

For all these reasons, the scientific transliteration of names is not common, so it is the transcription variants which are of the greatest relevance to the identity matching process.

4.1.3 Translations

Before closing this introduction, it is worth mentioning translated versions of names. Translation is the conversion of a word (or name) from one language into another without losing its meaning. In practice, names are rarely translated. For example, an English translation of علاء is grandness, but an Arab of this name would not call himself *Grandness* when entering the UK or US. He would most likely use the transcription *Ala*. Similarly, *Mr Black* would not be known as *Monsieur Noir* in France or call himself *Herr Schwarz* in Germany. However, translations are not totally irrelevant for the name matching process and are discussed in more detail in Chapter 5.

4.2 Latin and Non-Latin Scripts

Different communities around the world use many different writing systems to graphically communicate the languages they speak. The basic elements of these writing systems can be referred to as characters, with the main characters of the Latin script being the 26 letters of the Latin alphabet. Some extensions to the basic Latin script add diacritic marks to indicate an alteration of the sound communicated. This can be seen in the French *é* or the German *ö*, both of which sound different to their unaccented counterparts.

The Cyrillic and Arabic writing systems are also examples of alphabetic scripts. In simplified terms, each character in an alphabet represents a phoneme: a consonant or vowel sound. The Arabic alphabet, like many Semitic scripts, does not contain characters corresponding to short vowel sounds and these are usually omitted in written language.

Other writing systems, such the Kana used in Japan, use characters that typically represent syllables rather than individual phonemes. Logographic scripts, such as the Chinese, use pictorial characters that represent syllables with a specific meaning, as opposed to simply indicating sound patterns. For example, the character 王 (*Wang*) means "king" and represents one of the most common family names in the world.

The Latin alphabet dominates the continents associated with the Western culture, such as the Americas, Australasia and most of Europe as well as most states of Sub-Saharan Africa. Globally, around half of all people write their names using writing systems other than the Latin script. The following map shows the prevalence of different scripts around the world.

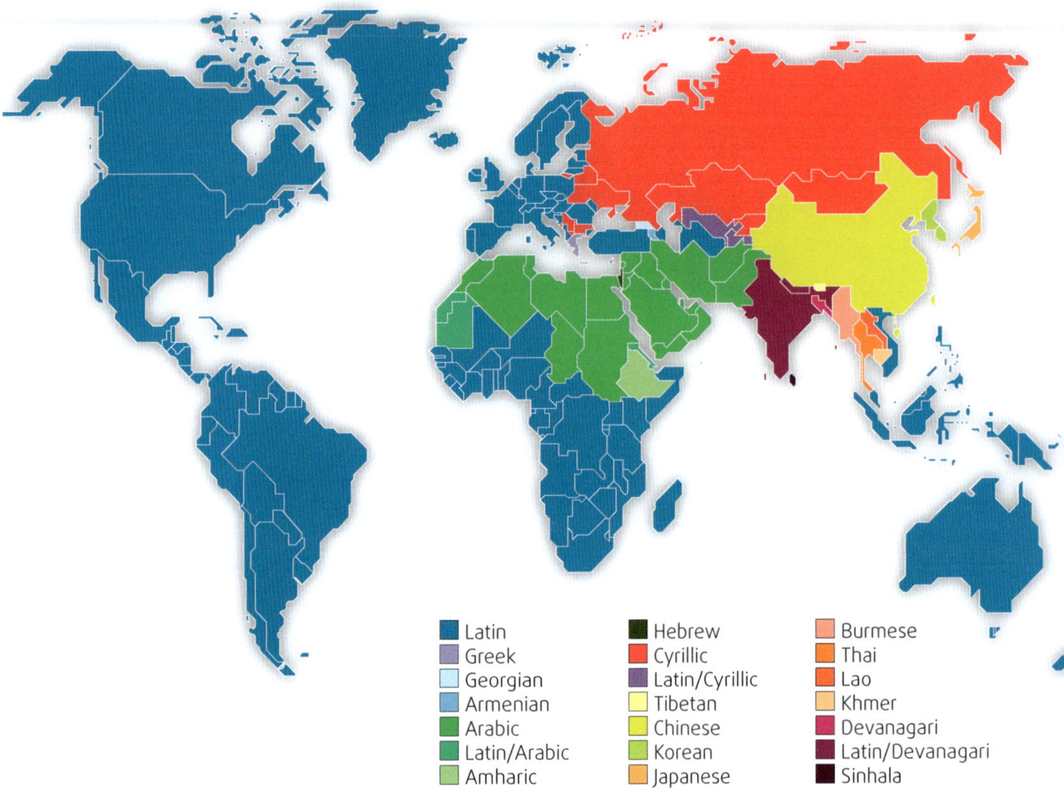

Figure 4.1: The prevalence of some of the most prominent writing systems worldwide. The map shows only the dominant script within each country and does not distinguish between different scripts of the same group (for example, Russian-Cyrillic versus Bulgarian-Cyrillic)

Non-Latin alphabets dominate Asia and Northern Africa. In parts of Eastern Europe and Northern Asia the Cyrillic alphabet is widely used. The Chinese, Japanese and Korean scripts dominate Eastern Asia, while the situation in South East Asia is more complex. The Latin alphabet has been adopted in Malaysia, Indonesia, Vietnam and the Philippines but not in Myanmar, Thailand, Laos or Cambodia, where specific native scripts are more common. Despite the special status of the English language on the South Asian subcontinent, non-Latin scripts still dominate. In Pakistan, Iran, the Arabic states of the Middle East and Northern Africa, the Arabic script (or derivations thereof) are most widely used.

From an historical point of view, the description provided here is not much more than a snapshot. Wars, migration, cultural revolutions and the dissemination of different religions have lead to different scripts being adopted and abandoned over time. Such situations often result in manifold transcription processes that mutate the composition of proper names over the longer term.

The recent history of Azerbaijan provides a good example of this process. The land was part of Persia until 1813 when it was abandoned to Russia as a consequence of one of the Russo-Persian wars. Over the next century, the inhabitants of Turk origin continued to use the Perso-Arabic script. A Latin-based script was later introduced against the backdrop of the various reforms that followed the 1917 Russian Revolution and the resulting alphabet was known as the Uniform Turkic Alphabet. Azerbaijani names were then romanised from their original Arabic versions.

A decade later, Stalin began his wholesale campaign of Russification. This resulted in the replacement of the Latin script with the Russian-Cyrillic script across the Soviet Union. Azerbaijani names that had been romanised from Arabic just a few years earlier were then transcribed into Cyrillic. Adjustments to the cultural naming system were made in line with this process and the adoption of the Russian patronym became obligatory. Subsequently, following the dissolution of the Soviet Union, a Latin-based script, closer to the one used in modern-day Turkey, was introduced and names were converted from the Cyrillic into this new Latin script.

The emphasis given to the Latin script by regulators, law enforcement and other watch-list-issuing bodies means that the conversion of names into the Latin script from other alphabets can be considered the most important form of transcription from an identity matching point of view. Though some watch lists provide supplementary name variants in the original script, few do so in a systematic way. In addition, most software tools used in the matching of these lists are designed with core matching functionality focused on the Latin script. Few have the ability to carry out reliable fuzzy matching using names in non-Latin scripts.

For these reasons, the rest of this chapter focuses on the romanisation of names from prominent non-Latin script languages, though many of the same principles apply to the transcription of names to and from other writing systems.

4.3 Romanisation of Cyrillic Names

4.3.1 History and Spread of the Cyrillic Alphabet

The Cyrillic alphabet became established in the Bulgarian Empire in the 10th Century and is based on an early form of the Greek alphabet. As a result, it has many similarities with the Latin alphabet, which was also based on the Greek script. Wherever the Greek alphabet was unable to provide a character to represent the required phonemes, additional characters were borrowed from the earlier Glagolitic script. This early script was created by the brothers Cyril and Methodius, who brought Christianity to the Slavic people in the 9th Century. Cyril's followers further advanced his work to create the Cyrillic script.

The map below charts the usage of the Cyrillic script around the world.

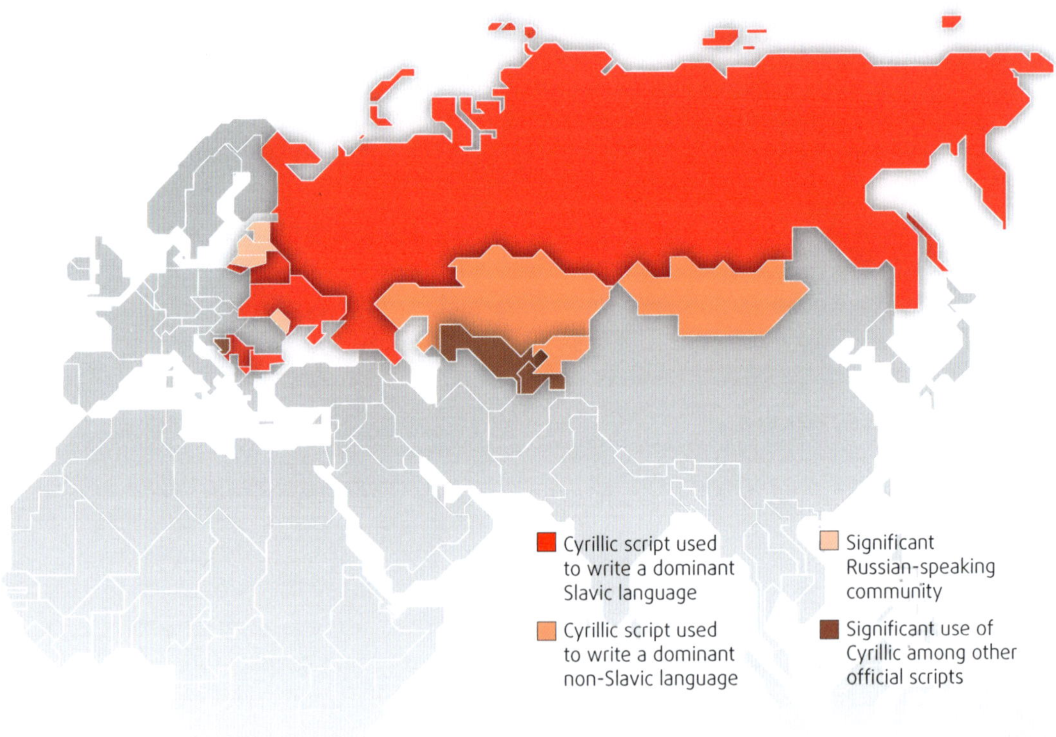

Figure 4.2: Spread of the Cyrillic Alphabet

Today the Cyrillic script is used mainly for writing Slavic languages, such as Russian, Ukrainian, Belarusian, Serbian, Macedonian and Bulgarian. As a result of Soviet influence, a number of Altaic languages such as Kazakh, Kyrgyz, and Mongolian as well as Persian languages like Tajik and even the Chinese language Dungan also use the Cyrillic script. Owing to the historical influences of Russian culture, some communities use the Cyrillic script to write a number of other languages. These include the Central Asian language Uyghur, which is often written in the Arabic script but may also be written in Cyrillic (for example, by the Uyghur community in Kazakhstan).

Most of the languages mentioned above use specific extensions to the core Cyrillic alphabet to account for particular phonetic phenomena. For this reason, the Cyrillic alphabet should more properly be referred to as the Russian-Cyrillic, the Ukrainian-Cyrillic, the Kazakh-Cyrillic and so on. The differences become quite complex at some points, with different languages assigning different sounds to the same character. For the sake of simplicity, this section focuses on the use of the Cyrillic alphabet in the Russian language area.

4.3.2 Sources of Variation in Names Romanised from Cyrillic

As the Cyrillic alphabet is relatively similar to the Latin script, names transcribed from Cyrillic tend to be written the same way within each target language area. In the English press, *Gorbachev*, *Yeltsin* and *Medvedev* are nearly always written in these forms. However, variations emerge when the names are transcribed into different target languages. This is due to the fact that different languages assign different sounds to different Latin characters and sequences of letters. While a German would pronounce *Jelzin* (the most common German transcription of this name) in a very similar way to the way an English person would pronounce *Yeltsin* or a Russian would pronounce Ельцин, native English or French speakers would pronounce *Jelzin* in a significantly different way.

The following table demonstrates the common English, German and French transcriptions of the names of Presidents of Russia or the Soviet Union since Khrushchev. Approximately a quarter of all Cyrillic characters are transcribed differently in these three languages. From the 24 name parts in the table below, only 4 (*Nikita*, *Leonid*, *Konstantin* and *Boris*) are represented the same way in all three languages (ignoring diacritics). The name *Khrushchev* is one of the most extreme examples. From the 6 characters in the original Cyrillic name, the only letter which is consistently romanised across all three target languages is the Cyrillic р, which transcribes to an *r* in English, German and French.

Russian Cyrillic Original	English Transcription	German Transcription	French Transcription
Никита Сергеевич Хрущёв	Nikita Sergeyevich Khrushchev	Nikita Sergejewitsch Chruschtschow	Nikita Sergeïevitch Khrouchtchev
Леонид Ильич Брежнев	Leonid Ilyich Brezhnev	Leonid Iljitsch Breschnew	Léonid Ilitch Brejnev
Юрий Владимирович Андропов	Yuri Vladimirovich Andropov	Juri Wladimirowitsch Andropow	Iouri Vladimirovitch Andropov
Константин Устинович Черненко	Konstantin Ustinovich Chernenko	Konstantin Ustinowitsch Tschernenko	Konstantin Oustinovitch Tchernenko
Михаил Сергеевич Горбачёв	Mikhail Sergeyevich Gorbachev	Michail Sergejewitsch Gorbatschow	Mikhaïl Sergueïevitch Gorbatchev
Борис Николаевич Ельцин	Boris Nikolayevich Yeltsin	Boris Nikolajewitsch Jelzin	Boris Nikolaïevitch Eltsine
Владимир Владимирович Путин	Vladimir Vladimirovich Putin	Wladimir Wladimirowitsch Putin	Vladimir Vladimirovitch Poutine
Дми́трий Анато́льевич Медве́дев	Dmitry Anatolyevich Medvedev	Dmitri Anatoljewitsch Medwedew	Dmitri Anatolievitch Medvedev

Table 4.1: Common English, German and French transcriptions of the names of Soviet and Russian presidents.

As discussed above, some of these variations can be explained by the fact that different letters represent different sounds in the three languages. For example, the Cyrillic character в represents a sound in Russian that is transcribed in English as *v* and in German as *w* (as in *Gorbachev* and *Gorbatschow* – which would be pronounced similarly by native English and German speakers respectively). In some cases, characters are added to the transcribed version in order to provide for correct pronunciation. This can be seen in the *Y* in the English transcription *Yeltsin* and the *J* in the German transcription *Jelzin*, both of which serve to soften the initial *E*.

The French transcriptions contain some characters which are themselves silent but provide indications as to how other characters in the name should be pronounced.

This can be seen in the trailing *e* in the names *Poutine* and *Eltsine*, which prevents the *in* from being pronounced as a nasal vowel, similar to the way an English speaker would pronounce *an*. Nasal vowels do not exist in English or German, so the English and German variants do not require the use of this trailing *e*.

As an exception, the trailing *e* is missing from the French transcription *Konstantin*. This is because *Konstantin* is a name used relatively often in French speaking countries and, as a result, it is pronounced with a nasal vowel at the end, in contrast to the original Russian pronunciation. In the Francophone press, the transcription variants *Konstantine* and *Constantine* can also be found. Although they are used less commonly than *Konstantin*, these variants are likely to encourage a more accurate pronunciation in the Francophone world.

While pronunciation has the most significant influence on transcription standards, some of the variations shown above can be attributed to the visual similarity of some Cyrillic characters to letters of the Latin alphabet. For example, the Cyrillic character ё (as in Горбачёв) is often transcribed as an *e* in the English *Gorbachev* and the French *Gorbatchev*, but the common German transcription *Gorbatschow* using *o* is closer to the original Russian pronunciation.

4.4 Romanisation of Arabic Names

4.4.1 History and Spread of the Arabic Script

The Arabic script has its roots in the Phoenician alphabet, which was also the basis for the Greek and hence the Cyrillic and Latin alphabets. However, beyond its roots as an alphabetic writing system, the Arabic script is visually very different from the Latin and Cyrillic scripts. It is written from right to left and always in cursive script, with no minuscules or majuscules and most characters taking on a different form depending on their position in each word or name.

As the language of the Koran, classical Arabic forms the foundation for Modern Standard Arabic. This is the literary language that is taught at universities and allows Arabs from around the world to communicate with each other. In practice, many variations and dialects of Arabic are used in different countries. The media often uses Modern Standard Arabic, though Egyptian Arabic is also commonly used as a result of the significant role of Egyptian television and radio stations throughout the Arabic world.

The following map charts the usage of the Arabic script around the world.

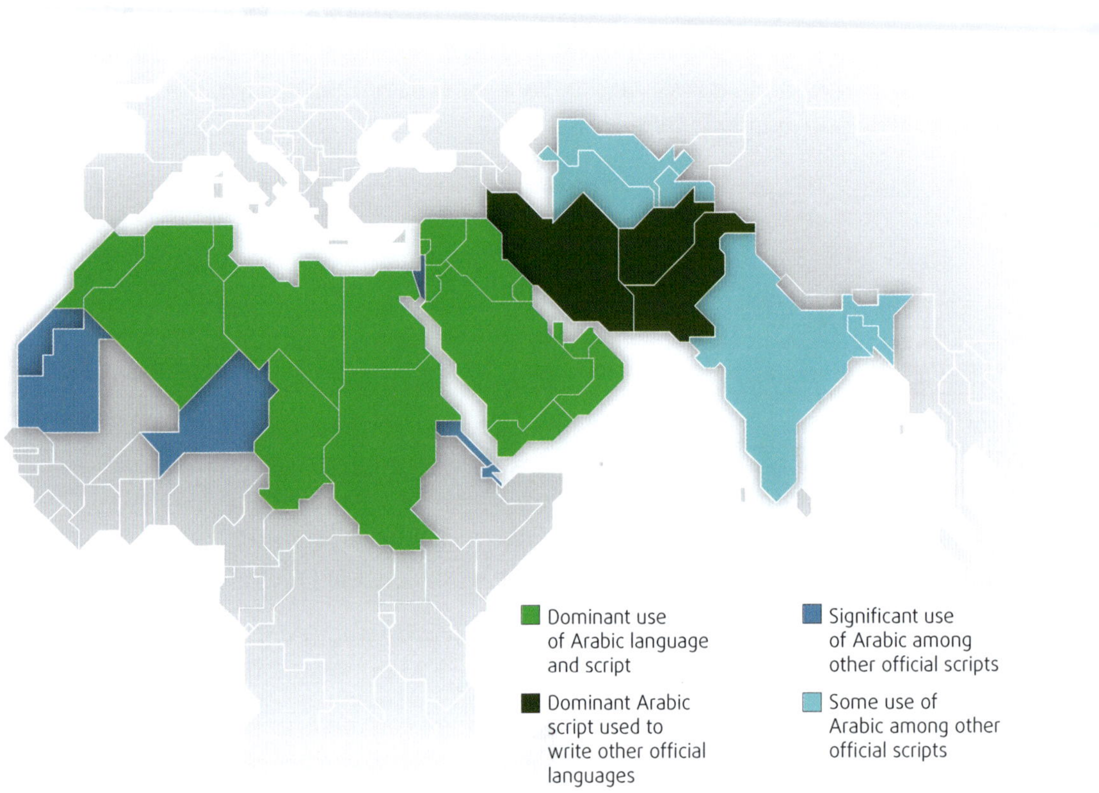

Figure 4.3: Spread of the Arabic Script

Around 500 million people use the Arabic writing system, though only around half of these have Arabic as their native language. With some modifications, the Arabic script is also used to write West African languages, such as Hausa and Fula, though these are often written in the Latin script as a result of colonial influences. The Arabic script (or variations thereof) may be used to write some Turkic languages, such as Kazakh and Uyghur, as well as various Indo-Iranian languages, such as Persian, Kurdish, Pashto and Urdu. It is also used in some parts of Malaysia and in some Chinese provinces, particularly in areas with a strong Islamic culture.

For the sake of simplicity, this section focuses on names originating in the Arabic language, but it should be noted that transcription issues arising from the romanisation of names from other Arabic-script languages provides an even more diverse range of challenges for the identity matching process.

4.4.2 Sources of Variation in Names Romanised from Arabic

As with the transcription of Cyrillic names, many of the variations in transcriptions from Arabic are caused by differences in the pronunciation of different target languages. However, these variations are compounded by differences in the composition of the Arabic alphabet, which includes more consonants than its Latin counterpart. Some of these sounds have no direct equivalent in any Western language. These include the glottal stop (ء) and the pharyngealised glottal fricative (ع). Often such characters are not reflected in the transcribed version. Where they are included, this is often not done in a consistent manner. In some cases, an apostrophe may be used, as in *Mu'tasim*, which is one way of transcribing معتصم.

Other characters have a written equivalent in some Western languages but not in others, such as خ, which represents a sound like the *ch* in the German name *Bach* or the *J* in the Spanish name *Jorge*. There is no precise equivalent for this sound in the English or French languages. These languages tend to use *kh* to transcribe this sound, as can be seen in the transcriptions of the name خالد, which can be transcribed as *Khalid*, *Jalid* or *Chalid* depending on the target language.

A further source of variation is the vast number of different dialects in which Arabic is spoken. The differences are not usually expressed in the written form, which commonly reflects Modern Standard Arabic rather than the dialect. However, the varying phonetics of the Arabic dialects often result in different transcription variants of the same Arabic names. For example, in the Egyptian dialect, the character ج is pronounced like the *G* in the English name *Gavin*. Arabs from other countries may pronounce it like the *J* in *John*. As a result, the Arabic name جمال is sometimes transcribed as *Gamal* and sometimes as *Jamal*, or even as *Djamal* or *Dschamal*.

There are some Arabic characters which can be transcribed in the same way into the Latin alphabet. For example, the letter *d* may be used to represent both ض and د, which are clearly distinguishable to Arabic speakers but only subtly different in the way they sound to Western ears. For the first of these two characters, an *h* may be added to provide differentiation to the transcribed version of د. However, this in itself can lead to confusion as the Arabic character ذ may also be transcribed as *dh*, and an *h* may also represent the characters ح or ه, so that *dh* may represent the characters ض or ذ, or the combinations دح or ده. This phenomenon means that several distinct Arabic names may share the same romanisation.

The few characters used for vowel sounds in the Arabic alphabet can also be the subject of transcription confusion. For example, و can create a vowel sound, as in the name يوسف (*Yusuf*) or create a consonant sound, as in the middle of the name جواد (*Jawad*). The vowel sound is transcribed in English as *u*, *oo*, *ou* or sometimes *o*, whereas the consonant sound is usually transcribed with a *w*. In French, both the consonant and vowel sounds are more often transcribed as *ou*. This means that an identity matching system must ensure that the *ou* in Arabic names recorded in French text matches both to the *w* and to the *u*, *oo*, *ou* and *o* combinations in Arabic names found in English text.

Another relevant feature of the Arabic writing system is the optional addition of diacritics indicating the doubling of a particular consonant. The name *Mohamed* can be written with this diacritic as محمّد or without as محمد. This results in a number of different transcription variants with or without the double *m* such as *Mohammed* and *Mohamed*.

The name *Mohamed* is a good example of a particular challenge posed by the Arabic writing system: the fact that short vowels are not written. *Mohamed* consists of only four characters in the original Arabic: م (*m*), ح (*h*), م (*m*) and د (*d*). This feature may cause confusion in names that differ only in their vowels, which are spelt the same way but pronounced differently. For example, the name عبيد can be pronounced in two very different ways, commonly transcribed in English as *Abid* and *Obaid*.

A final important characteristic of the Arabic name construction is the use of compound names that including the particle *al*. This was discussed in the context of the *Abd al-* construction in section 3.6 but can also be seen in names such as شمس الدين (*Shams al-Din*) meaning the Sun of Religion and نور الشمس (*Nur al-Shams*) meaning Light of the Sun. The different parts of these compound names can be combined to give different transcription variations. For example, the name عبد الرحمن, meaning Servant of God, consists of three connected name elements; *Abd* (عبد), *al* (ال) and *Rahman* (رحمن). When romanised, these three parts can be written separately (as in *Abd al Rahman*), together (as in *Abdalrahman*) or as a hybrid of the two (as in *Abdal Rahman* or *Abd Alrahman*).

There are also a number of different ways in which the particle *al* can be transcribed. Owing to a particular feature of Arabic phonetics, the *l* in *al* is not always pronounced as such but in some cases may serve as the phonetic doubling of the following consonant (in this case an *r*). Some transcriptions ignore this fact, as in *Abdulrahman*, while others partially take it into consideration by dropping the *l*, as in *Abdurahman*, and others fully include the effect by dropping the *l* and doubling the *r*, as in *Abdurrahman*. In addition, the vowel used in the *al* particle can vary, as demonstrated in the variants *Abdarrahman, Abderrahman, Abdirrahman, Abdorrahman* and *Abdurrahman*.

These different linguistic phenomena associated with the particle *al* combine to provide transcription variations as diverse as *Abd al Rahman, Abdul Rahman* and *Abderrahman*. Additionally allowing for transcription variations in other parts of this name provides around a hundred commonly used transcription variations for the full name. Chapter 9 considers the range of possible transcription variants for this name in more detail in its discussion of generative algorithms.

Some examples of common variants of this name are shown in the table below together with English, French and German variants for a number of other common Arabic names.

Arabic Original	Transcription Variants
عبد الرحمن	Abd al-Rahman, 'Abdurrahman, Abdurakhman, Abdourrahmane, Abdur Rahman, Abdel Rahman
محمد	Muhammad, Mohamed, Muhammed, Mhamed, Mouhammad, Mukhamed
يوسف	Yusuf, Yousuf, Yousef, Youssef, Yossef, Youssif
جمعة	Jumaa, Joumah, Djum'a, Dschum'aa, Djomaah, Joum'aa
سليمان	Suleyman, Soliman, Souleymane, Suleiman, Soulaiman
عز الدين	Izzadin, Ezedine, Ezzedin, Izz al-Din, Ez aldeen, Izzuddine
عبيد	Ubaid, 'Ubeid, 'Obayd, Oubeyd, Abid, Abeed, 'Abeed
حسين	Hussein, Houssayn, Hosain, Hoseyn, Hussen, Housain
معمر	Mouammar, Muamar, Mu'ammar, Moamer, Mo'ammar, Maummar, Momar
القذافي	Qaddafi, Kadhafi, Gadhafi, Al Quathafi, Khadafy, Kazzafi, Gheddafi, El Quathafi
معتصم	Motassem, Mutasim, Moatasem, Moatassime, Mu'tasim

Table 4.2: Examples of diversity in transcription variants of common Arabic names.

4.5 Romanisation of Names from the Chinese Script

4.5.1 History and Spread of the Chinese Script

The Chinese writing system is one of the oldest still in use today. Its characters are logograms and each represents a syllable with a specific meaning rather than the equivalent of a Latin letter. Many Chinese name parts consist of just one of these syllables. For example, the Chinese character 王 is a common family name that can be transcribed as *Wang* and conveys the meaning "King". While an alphabet generally consists of between 20 and 50 characters, the Chinese script consists of many thousands of characters, each representing one of these meaningful syllables. However, only a few thousand are in regular usage.

The following map charts the usage of the Chinese script.

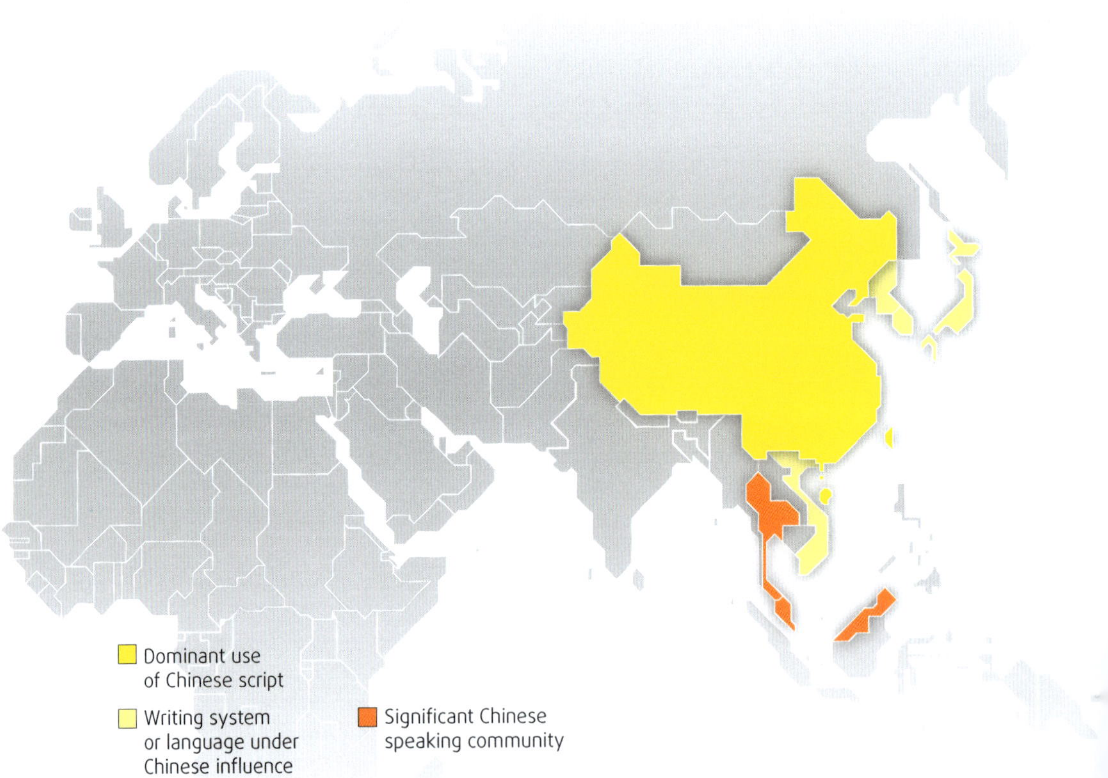

Figure 4.4: Spread of the Chinese Script

The term Chinese is confusing when applied to language. There are many languages spoken in China which use the Chinese script. Mandarin is the language most widely spoken within China and is the mother-tongue of almost a billion people. Several other relatively significant languages are spoken alongside Mandarin. The most important are Wu, spoken by around 80 million Chinese, and Cantonese and Min, which are each the mother-tongue of around 70 million Chinese.

The Chinese script is also used to write some non-Chinese languages. Originally, Japanese, Korean and Vietnamese were all written using Chinese logograms. Japanese and, to a lesser extent, Korean are still partly written using these characters. However, over the course of time, the pronunciation, appearance and meaning of these characters has deviated from those of the original Chinese version.

Since the 1950's, the People's Republic of China has instigated several reforms of the Chinese writing system, one result of which has been the introduction of simplified versions of commonly used characters. The reforms have been adopted by Singapore but not yet by Taiwan and Hong Kong, which means that there are currently two different writing systems in place. Though this has little impact in terms of transcription variants, it does mean that any identity matching system should be able to match names in both the traditional and simplified Chinese characters.

4.5.2 Sources of Variation in Names Romanised from the Chinese Script

Transcription variations in Chinese names can be significant as a result of the differences in the numerous transcription standards in use. Over the last few centuries, several attempts have been made to standardise the romanisation of the Chinese script, initially by Western missionaries, scientists and colonial officials, and more recently by the Chinese authorities. From the numerous systems developed over the years, around ten are still in use today. These systems vary greatly, primarily because they were each designed around different Chinese languages and dialects, which use the same script but have different phonetics. Other variations were introduced as a result of the different Western languages preferred by the scholars who developed the systems.

In an attempt to reduce the ambiguities of transcription, Chinese names may be communicated using Chinese Commercial Code, which represents Chinese characters using four-digit numbers rather than Latin characters. However, due to the development of different versions of the code, even this does not eliminate ambiguity entirely and romanised variants are more widely used.

The most well-known romanisation systems for Mandarin Chinese are the Hanyu Pinyin, Tongyong Pinyin, Wade Giles and Mandarin Yale. The Hanyu Pinyin standard is by far the most commonly used since its adoption as the official transcription standard in many of the relevant countries, though standards used for the romanisation of proper names may still vary.

Hanyu Pinyin is the official romanisation system of the People's Republic of China. Singapore and Taiwan have also adopted this system, though it is likely to be some time before Hanyu Pinyin effectively replaces the usage of Tongyong Pinyin and Wade Giles in Taiwan. This is particularly the case for Taiwanese names, which are often transcribed using the Wade Giles system. It is also likely that Hanyu Pinyin will take longer to become established in Hong Kong and among the large number of Overseas Chinese. There are 20 million Overseas Chinese in Indonesia, Malaysia and Thailand alone, and over 40 million worldwide. The names of people in these communities will most likely remain romanised in systems other than Hanyu Pinyin for some time to come.

A variety of different systems exist for transcribing other Chinese languages. For example, the Cantonese Yale system is widely used for transcribing Cantonese, though Jyutping and the Standard Cantonese Pinyin are commonly used in Hong Kong and the Sidney Lau system also remains in use. Further systems exist for transcribing other Chinese languages and for transcribing Chinese characters used outside the Chinese language area.

The following table provides examples of transcriptions for characters representing some of the most common Chinese family names and demonstrates the wide variations that exist in their transcription.

Chinese	Hanyu Pinyin	Jyutping	Other variants used in PR China, Taiwan and Singapore	Other variants used in Japan, Korea and Vietnam
李	Li	Lei	La, Lee, Lii	Lee, Ly, Rhee, Ri, Yi
王	Wang	Wong	Heng, Ong, Vong, Wong, Yu, Yuh	O, Vương, Wang

Continued ...

Chinese	Hanyu Pinyin	Jyutping	Other variants used in PR China, Taiwan and Singapore	Other variants used in Japan, Korea and Vietnam
張	Zhang	Zoeng	Chang, Cheong, Cheung, Chong, Jhang, Jang, Janq, Jeung, Teo, Teoh, Tiew, Tio, Tiu, Zêng	Cho, Jang, Trương
劉	Liu	Lau	Lao, Leo, Liou, Lou, Low, Lyou	Luru, Ryu, Yu
陳	Chen	Can	Cen, Chan, Chern, Chun, Jan, Jen, Jenn, Jhen, Tan, Ting, Zhen, Zan	Chin, Hin, Trần
楊	Yang	Joeng	Eaw, Ieong, Iu, Yêng, Yeo, Yeoh, Yeong, Yeung, Yong	Dương, Yang, Yo
黃	Huang	Wong	Hwang, Wang, Vong, Ng, Eng, Wee, Oei, Ooi, Bong, Uy, Ung	Hoang, Huynh, Hwang, Ko
趙	Zhao	Ziu	Chao, Chiu, Chio, Jiu, Tio, Teo, Teoh, Chew	Cho, Jo, Triệu
周	Zhou	Zau	Chao, Chau, Chew, Chiew, Chow, Chou, Jau, Jhou, Jou, Joe, Zeo	Châu, Chu, Ju, Shu
吳	Wu	Ng	Eng, Go, Goh, Gouw, Ngo, Ung, Woo	Go, Kure, Ngô, Oh

Table 4.3: Selected transcription variants of the most frequent family names.

The first column in the table above shows the Chinese characters that represent some of the most common family names. The next three columns show common transcription variants if these characters are used in a Chinese context. The final column shows transcription variants of the same characters if used in Japan, Korea or Vietnam. In contrast to the transcription variants of Russian or Arabic names, it is often very difficult for Westerners to recognise any connection between transcription variants of the same Chinese character. Depending on the context of the identity matching process, it may not be necessary to match all transcription variants of each character with each other, but even where this is the case, the differences that must be accounted for are significant.

Though a single Chinese character may have many different possible romanisation variants, it is also possible for many different characters to have the same romanised version. The Chinese writing system consists of many thousands of characters, but the Hanyu Pinyin transcription system is restricted to around 400 distinct romanisations (excluding tone markers, diacritics and other marks). One reason for this is the tonal nature of the Chinese languages. Different characters may be pronounced in a similar way but using a different tone, just as Western speakers might alter their tone to differentiate between a statement and a question. This variation in tone has no direct equivalent in the Latin script so the different Chinese characters that differ only in their tone may be transcribed the same way. Tones may be indicated with the use of diacritic marks or superscript numerals but these are often omitted, so many Chinese characters have the same Hanyu Pinyin romanisation. If transcriptions resulting from other romanisation systems are also considered, the situation becomes even more ambiguous, with potentially hundreds of characters sharing the same transcription.

This ambiguity should be considered in the context of the huge population of people with Chinese names, many of whom share just a few distinct family names. The fact that different names may lose their distinction on transcription contributes to a significant problem with precision when matching names of Chinese origin.

This lack of precision is often unintentionally compounded by attempts to minimise false negative results caused by the significant differences in transcription variants. Sophisticated linguistic techniques are necessary to match the diverse transcription variants without generating excessive numbers of false positive results. Unsophisticated attempts to broaden matching rules so that Chinese transcription variants are matched often lead to very poor precision.

Balancing precision and recall in the matching of Chinese names is a complex science. However, there are a few characteristics of typical Chinese names and their transcription that can be incorporated into the matching system to improve its precision. For example, the order of the generation and personal name is usually fixed, so there is no need to allow for them to be reversed. In addition, the relatively low number of family names in use means that it is possible to create a reference table that will help identify Chinese family names for the majority of the population.

There is also a low probability that different transcription standards will be used to transcribe different parts of the same name. This may happen, for example, as

Taiwan moves away from the Wade Giles system towards the Hanyu Pinyin, but in general, the mixing of transcription standards within a name is not common.

These are simple ideas that must be sensitively combined with more complex linguistic and onomastic features to create a matching system with both acceptable recall and precision when matching names of Chinese origin.

4.6 Conclusion: Transcription as the Achilles Heel of Name Matching

This chapter has demonstrated how names originating in non-Latin scripts can often be transcribed in several (or even many) different ways. Examples have been provided using names transcribed from the Cyrillic, Arabic and Chinese scripts; the vast number of scripts and potential source and target languages in use around the world only compounds the number of potential variations that should be accounted for.

Despite a multitude of efforts to encourage standardisation, many different romanisation standards continue to be used, both by official authorities and in the media. In this sense, a particular transcription variant cannot be said to be correct or incorrect; it is simply more or less common in a particular language area or region. Given this, any system which incorporates the matching of non-identical names should give the highest priority to the matching of transcription variants. Providing for the matching of all possible transcription variants cannot be done with mathematical algorithms without jeopardising precision. It can only be achieved using techniques based on specific linguistic research.

The most important linguistic concepts which must be considered when designing methods to match transcription variants include:

Source language

Individual writing systems (whether character or syllable based) are often shared by different languages that differ widely in their phonetics. As a result, names identical in their original script may be transcribed very differently if they originate from different source languages. In some cases, this can result in variants that are not visibly connected to the Western eye, such as 張, which can be transcribed as *Zhang* when used in Mandarin or as *Tiu* if used in Min Nan, or 吳, which can be written as *Wu* if used in Mandarin or *Ng* if taken from a Cantonese context. This last Chinese character is also a common Korean name, which is often romanised to *O* or *Oh*.

Target language

The language into which a non-Latin script name is transcribed can have a similarly wide-ranging effect on the resulting transcription variants. This is because different languages assign different sound qualities to different Latin characters when used in particular combinations. As a result, *Yeltsin*, *Jelzin* and *Eltsine* all represent the Russian name Ельцин, depending on the target language. Though this text has focused on the English, French and German transcription variants, other systems such as the Spanish, Portuguese and Italian standards should also be considered in the design of a robust identity matching system.

Romanisation standards

Even within the same source and target languages, different transcription variants often exist. For example, the name عبد الرحمن may appear in very many ways in English texts, such as *Abdurrahman*, *Abdel Rahman* and *Abd ar-Rahman*. There are many reasons for this, including the different weights afforded by each transcription standard to the sound pattern and to the original spelling.

Clearly, such issues are complex to research and even more complex to represent in an automated matching system. As a result, many of the popular matching systems in use today are weak with regard to matching transcription variants, even if they are relatively sophisticated in dealing with other sources of variation in names. Similarly, assessing the ability of an identity matching system to effectively match transcription variants requires specialised knowledge. This means that the users of a matching system may not be aware of its failings in this area. The topic is often also poorly understood by the software sales representatives with whom users discuss their requirements. Many times, the ability of a tool to match transcription variants is confused with the ability to romanise particular scripts, so that a tool which is able to convert and match Ельцин to the ISO standard *El'cin* is mistakenly thought to be a tool which can match the more common variants, including *Jelzin*, *Yeltsin* and *Eltsine*, with each other.

Some data vendors have attempted to counter the frequent lack of sophistication in matching systems by adding common transcription variants to the data profiles they provide for each individual. However, it is unlikely that such enrichment could ever be truly comprehensive, and as it increases the volume of data that has to be matched, it cannot really be seen as a practical way forward.

This chapter has described the matching of transcription variants as the Achilles heel of modern identity matching processes. Chapter 10 introduces a solution that provides for the matching of transcription variants using linguistic identity matching techniques. The rest of Part 1 looks at other important sources of variation within proper names.

Chapter 5: Derivative Forms of Names

5.1 Aliases and Derivative Names

It is not uncommon for a person to be known by a name other than their primary, official name. Some of these other names may be alternate forms or derivatives of the officially registered name. Others may be completely different, with no connection at all to the official name. Such alias names may be used for many different reasons. Criminals may seek alternate identities to escape detection, entertainers may choose to perform under a stage name and writers may allow themselves the freedom afforded by a pseudonym. In these cases, there is no predictable connection between an individual's official name and the alternate name they have chosen for themselves. *Eric Arthur Blair*, for example, is more widely known as the writer *George Orwell*, and many readers are unaware that the classics created by *George Eliot* are, in fact, the work of *Mary Anne Evans*.

Freedom fighters and revolutionaries may adopt a nom de guerre to conceal their identities, to provide separation between personal and political lives, or as a mark of respect to cultural traditions. The adoption of such names is particularly common among communist leaders such as *Lenin*, who was born *Vladimir Ilyich Ulyanov* and *Saloth Sar*, more widely known as *Pol Pot*. Other leaders who have adopted alternative names include *Mikhail Yuhanna*, better known as *Tariq Aziz*, former Deputy Prime Minister of Iraq, and *Joseph-Désiré Mobutu*, former President of the Democratic Republic of the Congo, who awarded himself the more prestigious name of *Mobutu Sese Seko Nkuku Ngbendu wa Za Banga*, though this was often shortened to *Mobutu* or *Mobutu Sese Seko*.

People may also use alternate names for religious reasons. This may be on appointment to a particular position, as on the appointment of *Pope Benedict XVI*, who was born *Joseph Aloisius Ratzinger*, or on conversion to a new religion, as was the case when *Cassius Marcellus Clay* converted to Islam and became known as *Mohammed Ali*. Similarly, *Stephen Demetre Georgiou* converted to Islam and changed his name to *Yusuf Islam*, though he is still perhaps more widely recognised under his former stage name of *Cat Stevens*.

Name changes on cultural or religious grounds are often seen when a person moves to a new country with a strong national culture. For example, immigrants to Israel may adopt Hebrew names. *David Grün* was born in Poland but became *David Ben-Gurion* (בן גוריון) before becoming the first Prime Minister of Israel, and *Golda Meyerson* became *Golda Meir* (מאיר) during her political life in Israel after moving there from the United States.

In the Western world, one of the most common cultural reasons for a person to change their name is on marriage. While in some parts of Europe it is common for a woman to add her husband's name to her own to create a double-barrelled name, many women will drop their maiden name and take their husband's family name instead. Less frequently, the man may take the woman's family name.

Adopted names cannot be matched using rules-based algorithms or dictionary-style reference tables. The fact that the official and alternate names refer to the same person must be recorded as part of the individual's profile in the target database. Some people, such as more prolific fraudsters, may have many different aliases that need to be recorded to ensure that data relating to the individual can be efficiently located in a search.

The concept of alternative names is not restricted to natural persons. Companies, associations and other groups may also change their names, legally or otherwise, during the course of their existence. For example, the consulting firm *Accenture* was formerly known as *Andersen Consulting*. While such commercial name changes are well documented, others may be more difficult to track. Criminal and terrorist organisations, in particular, often change their names as allegiances shift. For example, the Algerian movement *The Salafist Group for Preaching and Combat* largely became *Al Qaeda in the Islamic Maghreb* after it aligned itself with the wider Al Qaeda organisation.

The amount of research that goes into the collation and verification of alias and former names is one reason why organisations often prefer to purchase intelligence information from commercial data vendors rather than to compile compliance databases internally. A comprehensive database of names and their aliases is essential, as no matching process can be expected to match names that are both linguistically and orthographically unrelated.

The rest of this chapter focuses on other ways in which an individual may be known under an alternate name; ways which may be more predictable, perhaps as a result of linguistic features or cultural convention, and which modern matching technology should be able to tackle relatively effectively using onomastic reference tables.

These types of derivative names can be classified into hypocorisms, such as the diminutive name forms used by *Bill Clinton* (*William*) and *Tony Blair* (*Anthony*), and names that may have been translated from another language. Though less commonly used than hypocorisms, translations can still be seen in the names of people migrating between different language areas, such as the religious scholar born into a Russian family as *Ivan Feofilovich Baron von Meyendorff,* who was known as *Jean Meyendorff* while working in France, and as *John Meyendorff* during his time in the United States.

5.2 Hypocorisms

Common given names often have established derivative names in a particular language. These are often hypocorisms, or diminutive versions, of the original name. Some examples of hypocorisms from the English, Spanish and Russian language areas, where the use of derivative name forms is particularly common, are shown in the table below.

English Name	Derivative form (examples)
Elisabeth	Bess, Bessie, Bet, Beth, Betsy, Bette, Betty, Elise, Eliza, Ella, Elle, Elsa, Elsie, Libby, Lilibet, Lily, Lisa, Lisbeth, Lissie, Liz, Liza, Lizbeth, Lizzie
James	Jamie, Jim, Jimmy
Katherine	Kat, Kate, Katie, Kathy, Katy, Kit, Kitty
William	Bill, Billy, Will, Willie, Willy
Richard	Dick, Dicky, Rich, Richie, Rick, Ricky
Robert	Bert, Bertie, Bob, Bobbie, Bobby, Rob, Robbie, Robby
Victoria	Tori, Tory, Vic, Vicki, Vicky, Vikki, Vickie

Continued ...

Spanish Name	Derivative form (examples)
Alfonso	Chete, Fon, Fonsi, Fonso, Loncho, Poncho, Poto, Sito
Antonio	Anto, Antoñete, Antoñito, Toni, Toño, Tucho
Concepción	Conce, Concha, Conchi, Conchis, Conchita
Francisco	Chencho, Chisco, Cisco, Curro, Fran, Pacho, Paco, Pancho, Papico, Patxi, Quico
Isabel	Bela, Chabe, Chabel, Chabela, Chabeli, Chava, Chavela, Isa
María del Carmen	Maika, Mamen, Maricarmen, Mayca, Menchu, Maricar
María José	Coté, Majo, Mariajo, Marijó, Marijose

Russian Name	Derivative form (examples)
Mikhail	Miha, Misha, Mishanya, Mishenka, Mishka, Mishutka
Sergei	Seriy, Seryoga, Seryozhenka, Seryozha, Seryozhka
Svetlana	Sveta, Svetik, Svetka, Svetochka, Svetyushka
Vladimir	Volodenka, Volodka, Volodya, Vova, Vovan, Vovka, Vovochka

Table 5.1: Examples of hypocorisms (diminutive forms) of common English, Spanish and Russian given names.

These examples display a number of characteristics of derivative names that are relevant to the name matching process. The first is that derivative names can be built on any part of the original name. For example, the names *Elle* and *Elisa* are derived from the first part of the name *Elisabeth*, while the names *Liz* and *Lisa* are based on the middle of this name, and *Beth* and *Betty* are derived from the final part.

It can also be seen from the table above that derivative forms are not necessarily "short" forms. The use of suffixes is a common way to form derivative names, with the result that many are longer than their original form, as can be seen in the name *Seryozhenka*, a derivative of *Sergei*.

Derivative name forms, even when well established within a particular language community, may not bear an obvious connection to the original name to those from other language areas. For example, native English speakers may not recognise the name *Sito* as a derivative form of *Alfonso*, or *Sasha* as a derivative of *Aleksandr*, just as native speakers of other languages may not recognise *Jack* as a derivative of *John*, or *Harry* as a derivative of *Henry*. The examples above also demonstrate that the same name may have different hypocorisms in different languages. *Bella* and *Izzy* may be recognisable to an English speaker as derivatives of the name *Isabel*, but a Spanish woman of this name is more likely to be referred to as *Chavela* or *Chabeli*, like the Spanish journalist *Chabeli Iglesias*.

Derivative forms of compound names may seem particularly unusual to readers from countries where multi-part names are less common. For example, the compound name *Maria del Carmen* can be shortened to *Mamen* or *Maricar*, which non-Spanish speakers may not recognise as being diminutives of the longer name. Compound names pose a particular challenge in the name matching process as the component parts must be recognised and matched as such. Neither *Mamen* nor *Maricar* should match to *Maria* or to *Carmen*, only to the compound *Maria del Carmen*.

In some cases it is possible to detect common creation patterns for derivative names within a given language area, such as the use of the suffixes *–ie* or *–y* in Anglophone countries. However, despite these detectable patterns, their application is not sufficiently standardised to enable derivative names to be effectively matched using a rules-based approach. The most appropriate way of matching such names is to use dictionaries collected through onomastic research in each relevant language area. Such dictionaries link common names to their recognised hypocorisms and other derivative forms. They must be built and used carefully in order to avoid over-matching. Some names may have identical derivatives (such as the name *Jo* from either *Joanne* or *Josephine*). It is important that the dictionary is used in such a way that allows *Jo* to be matched with both *Joanne* and *Josephine* without matching *Joanne* and *Josephine* to each other.

Though derivative names are often only used for unofficial purposes, this is not always the case, as a traditional hypocorism may be used as the official registered name. For example, a woman known as *Josie* may hold a passport in the name *Josie* or *Josephine*. However, in general, the more official the situation, the more likely it is that the original form of the name will be used, meaning official identification documents are less likely to contain a hypocorism. Journalists, on the other hand, more usually write articles using the name by which an individual is popularly known, thereby contributing to the legitimacy of the derivative name. The politicians *Bill Clinton*, *Tony Blair* and *Nick Clegg* are almost never referred to as *William*, *Anthony* or *Nicholas*, much as the president of FIFA, *Sepp Blatter*, is rarely referred to as *Joseph* and *Che Guevara* is not widely known as *Ernesto*. In most cases, a particular individual is only referred to using one of the standard derivatives of their official name; for example, *Bill Clinton* is not referred to as *Will*. In some cases, hypocorisms may be derived from the family rather than the given name, for example *Gazza* from *Gascoine* or *Smithy* from *Smith*, but the use of these names is far less common and almost never achieves the semi-official status that derivatives of given names may have.

Given the widespread use of derivative names, sometimes to the extent that the official name is no longer recognised as the individual's real name, the ability to match these names effectively is an important requirement for any identity matching system.

5.3 Translated Names

Translation may be defined as the conversion of a term from one language into another language without altering its meaning. Proper names are not often translated in this sense as the meaning of a name is usually irrelevant to the identity of the person. However, some names do have accepted alternatives in different languages and these may be used when a person moves between language regions.

In the past, before the stability of person names gained the importance it has today, immigrants often adapted both their given and family names to sound more familiar to natives of their adopted countries. For example, *Hans Müller* moving from Germany to the US may have adopted the name *John Miller*. Accommodating translation variants is standard practice for genealogists investigating family histories, and the practice of adapting names on immigration continues with sufficient frequency to also be of interest to identity matching professionals. For example, the commodities trader *Marc Rich* was born in Belgium as *Marcell Reich*. His family changed their name to *Rich* after emigrating to the United States.

The likelihood of immigrants changing their name varies from country to country. In some jurisdictions, changes to an individual's name are only permitted in very restricted circumstances; in others, they are positively encouraged. As discussed in section 5.1 above, many immigrants to Israel choose to Hebraise their names. This can be done in a number of ways, one of which is the direct translation of the original name into Hebrew.

The closeness of the two languages and cultures involved may also play a role in determining whether a person may be known using a translated version of their name. For example, the Russian name Сергей Николаевич Рубинов (*Sergey Nikolayevich Rubinov*) may be written as Сяргей Мікалаевіч Рубінаў (*Syarhey Mikalayevich Rubinau*) in Belarus. This example compounds some differences in transcription with the fact that the original Cyrillic versions are different in themselves, having been translated from the Russian to the Belarusian version.

Though it would be technically possible to create a reference table containing translations of common family names, this would be an enormous task and the effort involved disproportionate to the number of individuals actually adopting a translation of their family name. The use of such a reference table in the matching process would also likely lead to excessive numbers of false positive matches. For this reason, if translations are to be accommodated in the matching process, they are usually only considered for given names.

The translation of a given name is often the immigrant's choice as they seek to make their name easier for the inhabitants of their new country to understand, though the translation may also be assigned by the natives themselves. The following table shows a selection of possible translations from the European region.

English	German	French	Italian	Spanish	Croatian	Swedish
John	Hans/ Johannes	Jean	Giovanni	Juan	Ivan	Johannes/ Jens
Joanne / Jane	Johanna	Jeanne	Giovanna/ Gianna	Juana	Ivana/ Jana	Johanna
Joseph	Josef	Joseph	Giuseppe	José	Josip	Josef
Judith	Judith	Judith	Giuditta	Judit	Judita	Judit
Julia	Julia	Julie	Giulia/ Giuliana	Julia	Julijana	Julia
Elisabeth	Elisabeth	Elisabeth	Elisabetta	Isabel	Elizabetta	Elisabet
Peter	Peter	Pierre	Pietro/Piero	Pedro	Petar	Peter/Per
Steven/ Stephen	Stefan	Stéphane/ Etienne	Stefano	Esteban	Stjepan	Stefan

Table 5.2: Selection of possible translations for European given names

As with the hypocorisms discussed earlier, it is possible to detect some recurring patterns. For example, the English *J* is regularly replaced with the phonetically similar *Gi* in the Italian translation. However, translation variants are the result of a historical process that does not follow systematic rules, so rules-based matching methods are not appropriate for matching translated names. If it is deemed appropriate to include such matches in a particular identity matching process, dictionaries compiled using linguistic and onomastic research must be applied.

5.4 Derivative and Translated Forms of Names of Legal Persons

The phenomena of derivative and translated names apply also to the names of legal persons, though sometimes in a slightly modified form.

The names of legal persons frequently contain generic terms, indicating either the nature of their business or legal form. Such terms are often easily translated, particularly if the name parts look alike, as in *Bank, Banque, Banca* or *Society, Société, Sociadad.* The translation of legal form such as *Limited* to *Limitada* may also occur, as may the translation of place names. For example, the German re-insurance institution *Münchener Rückversicherungs-Gesellschaft Aktiengesellschaft*, or *Münchener Rück*, is better known in English as *Munich Re.*

A common source of variation in the names of legal persons is the use of abbreviations and acronyms. *IBM* stands for *International Business Machines, Interpol* is short for *International Criminal Police Organisation* and *Oxfam* was originally an abbreviation of the name of the *Oxford Committee for Famine Relief.* These examples show the very different ways in which abbreviated legal person names can be formed. Given the lack of standardisation in the way they are created, abbreviated names for organisations should be stored within the profile in the identity database, as any rules which could be defined for matching them are unlikely to be effective and may lead to over-matching.

However, abbreviations for indicators of legal form are relatively standardised, such as *PLC* for *Public Limited Company* and *GmbH* for *Gesellschaft mit beschränkter Haftung.* In these cases, dictionary tables which reference common legal forms and their standard abbreviations can be used in the matching process.

A final point of note in relation to variations in the names of legal persons is the usage of numbers, dates, punctuation marks and other symbols. For example, an organisation called the *People's Liberation and Welfare Army, 5th July* may use the symbols + or & instead of the world *and*, and may write 5th as *fifth* or 5. Dealing with such variations should be a standard component of any identity matching system used to match the names of legal persons.

Chapter 6: Phonetically Similar Names

It has long been recognised that phonetically-motivated misspelling is a frequent cause of variation in names. Some of the earliest attempts at name matching were based on an understanding that names are often misspelt in a way that sounds similar, so that *Taylor* may be misspelt as *Tailer*, or *Wight* as *White*. Such errors may result if the person writing the name is doing so from hearing it spoken rather than from seeing it written out. It may also be that the writer has seen the name written out but remembers only the sound pattern rather than the exact spelling. In case of doubt, a person may be more likely to recall the spelling that is most familiar to them.

This chapter looks at variations in names that occur as a result of the relationship between pronunciation and spelling. Pronunciation is a complex topic and one that is highly language specific, so any consideration of the effect of pronunciation on spelling must be made in the context of the relevant language. However, even within individual languages, the various peculiarities and ambiguities in pronunciation mean that great care has to be taken in trying to identify names that are pronounced in the same way.

Unfortunately, the widespread use of largely unsophisticated phonetic matching methods has lead to a general reluctance to consider phonetically similar matches. However, as Chapter 10 explains, modern phonetic matching techniques can be used to great effect and it is important to understand the nature and origin of phonetic misspellings so that these more modern methods can be correctly applied.

6.1 Homophones

Homophones are words or names that sound the same. These are relatively common as, in many languages, several different sequences of letters may call for similar pronunciation. For example, *Meier*, *Meyer*, *Maier*, *Mayer*, *Mejer*, *Majer*, *Mair* and *Mayr* may all be pronounced in a similar way. This applies equally to family names and to given names, such as *Stuart* and *Stewart*, or *Kathryn* and *Catherine*.

One feature which sets homophones aside from other linguistic variations, such as those caused by transcription standards, is that homophones are essentially misspellings. Phonetic misspellings are errors that individuals could avoid, whereas variations in transcription could only be avoided if entire communities agreed on one transcription standard to be used universally. If a person called *Meier* is referred to as *Meyer*, this is incorrect. However, referring to a person called Ельцин as *Jelzin* is no more correct or incorrect than referring to them as *Yeltsin*. Looked at another way, it could be said that there is a higher likelihood that the names *Jelzin* and *Yeltsin* refer to the same person than there is that the names *Meier* and *Meyer* refer to the same person, though this depends on a number of factors, including the context in which the data was collected.

In this respect, phonetically similar names are not the most important linguistic variants that should be covered by modern identity matching systems. However, as one of the most common causes of spelling variations, they must be dealt with appropriately and in a manner sensitive to international language variations.

6.1.1 Pronunciation and Spelling

Broadly speaking, there is a slightly clearer connection between spelling and pronunciation in languages such as German, Italian, Spanish or Polish than is apparent in English or French. In English, for example, an *ee* sound can be expressed by many different character combinations, including *i, e, y, ie, ei, ee, ea* and *ey*. Similarly, an *oo* sound can be represented as *u, ugh, ew* or *oo*. This flexibility in writing vowel sounds provides the basis for many homophonic names such as *Hugh/Huw, Lee/Leigh, Dianne/Dyan, Aimee/Amy, Tailer/Taylor* or *Wheeler/Wealer*. Consonant sounds may also pose challenges, as in the English "silent" *p*, which allows *Thompson* and *Thomson* to be pronounced in a similar manner.

Similar examples can also be seen in French names. For example, French names ending with an *o* sound may end with the letters *au, aux, ault, aulx, eau, eaux, o, oc, ocs, os, ot* or *ots*. The names *Renault, Reno, Reneaux* and *Renaud*, therefore, all sound similar. The nasal vowels in French also have numerous spellings so that names like *Dupond* and *Dupont* are pronounced the same way. However, these names would all be pronounced in a much more distinctive way if spoken using the conventions of the English language.

When a child learns to read, they learn to associate different sequences of characters with different sounds; the conventions of their native language determine which sounds are associated with which character sequences. In general, therefore, the way a name is spelt dictates the way in which it is pronounced by speakers of each language and dialect.

The extent to which this generalisation holds depends on a number of factors. For example, internationally familiar names such as *David* or *Tony* are less likely to be pronounced using non-English conventions, as their English pronunciation is more well known. Less familiar names, such as *Siobhan* (*Shi-vawn*), are more likely to be phonetically misspelt. Possible misspellings include *Siobhain, Siobhann, Siobhon, Siovhan, Shivaune, Shivaun, Sioban, Shivonne, Shivaughn, Shivaughne, Shavaughan, Shavaugn, Shevaun* and *Chevonne*. All of these are based either on the name's original pronunciation or on the way that someone unfamiliar with the name might assume it to be pronounced.

The education level of the speaker therefore also plays a role, as the more highly educated or well-travelled are more likely to be aware of the correct pronunciation of foreign names. Those with a narrower perspective may simply apply the phonetic conventions of their own language. For example, a native English speaker unfamiliar with the German language (and classical music) might mispronounce the family name of the composer *Richard Wagner* as an English *Wag-ner*, rather than the more German sounding *Varg-ner*. Similarly, though some English speakers seeing the name *Bach* in a German context might recognise its correct German pronunciation (with the *ch* pronounced similarly to the Scottish loch), others might pronounce the name as *Batch* or *Back*, potentially leading to confusion in its spelling.

6.1.2 International Variations in Pronunciation

Native speakers of different languages may pronounce the same name in different ways. For example, while the German names *Roth* and *Rot* can be considered homophones, if the names were known to derive from an Anglo-Saxon context it could be assumed that the names would be pronounced differently, as the combination *th* is generally a softer sound than a *t* in an English context. Similarly, the German names *Scholze* and *Scholtze* would be pronounced the same way by a German but might sound different if spoken by a native English speaker. Identifying names which sound alike should ideally, therefore, be carried out in the context of their language origin. In this last example, not only might a German speaker confuse these two names, but an English speaker, on hearing the name *Scholze* correctly spoken, might introduce an erroneous *t* in an attempt to reproduce the hard sound of the German *z*.

Conversely, if a name is habitually used in a language context other than its language origin, alternative pronunciations may develop. In English speaking countries, for example, commonly used names of French origin may be pronounced differently, so that *Dubois* may be pronounced in the French way as *Du-bwa* but may also be spoken using English phonetic conventions as *Du-boyz*. It is therefore important to ensure that matching techniques are able to accommodate alternative pronunciations, as different variations may be introduced depending on the way the name is pronounced.

6.2 Linguistic Matching and Phonetics

The prevalence of phonetic misspellings makes them an important class of variation to be dealt with in an identity matching system. However, as will be discussed in Part II, early attempts at phonetic matching were not always effective and often resulted in over-matching. This inevitably lead to a reluctance to include phonetic matches in identity matching systems and that reluctance is still evident today, despite the improved methods now available.

Perhaps because of the long-standing focus on the matching of similar sounding names, linguistic matching techniques are often confused with phonetic matching methods. This is a common misconception which ignores the fact that a true linguistic matching system will account for differences resulting from transcription variations and alternative cultural naming conventions as well as matching names which are phonetically similar.

In addition, not all phonetic matching methods can be seen as true linguistic techniques. The first attempts to systematically match homophones were made several decades ago (as discussed in Chapter 8) and a number of these very rudimentary phonetic techniques are still in common usage despite their obvious shortcomings. Many of them focus on just one (often the Anglo-Saxon) phonetic convention and cover only a small number of the relevant characteristics so cannot be said to adequately deal with phonetic variations, even within the context of their target language. Given the global context in which most identity matching systems now operate, such methods are rarely appropriate.

The difficulty in matching similar sounding names is in accounting for all the specific peculiarities of given languages and all the possible combinations thereof. Proper names usually consist of several different syllables, each containing many different character combinations, each of which may be pronounced in a number of ways. This often leads to many different possible homophone variants for one original name. As a result, the most effective way to deal with the matching of phonetically similar names is through targeted linguistic rule sets, as dictionary-type tables of homophones are unlikely to be comprehensive and generic algorithms cannot hope to deal with the complexities of multiple languages. Such rules are defined through detailed analysis of the connection between spelling patterns and sound patterns in each major language and are discussed further in Chapter 10.

Chapter 7: Typos

7.1 Variations, Spelling Mistakes and Typos

The term "variation" is relatively neutral and does not necessarily imply that a mistake has been made. Chapter 4 looked at transcription variants, which are technically neither correct nor incorrect. Similarly, the derivative forms of names discussed in Chapter 5 are not technically incorrect variations; they are simply more or less likely to be used to refer to a given person. In contrast, the phonetically-driven variations considered in Chapter 6 are errors in the spelling of a person's name, though as linguistically motivated errors they form some of the most frequent misspellings of person names.

The following table shows how both linguistically and non-linguistically driven spelling variations can be considered to be either correct or incorrect.

	Correct variants	Incorrect variants
Linguistic	Includes transcription variants such as *Jelzin* or *Yeltsin*.	Includes homophones such as *Stewart* instead of *Stuart*.
Non-linguistic	Includes the omission of the legal form or other generic parts of a company's name, for example *British Gas* instead of *British Gas Services Limited*.	Includes typographic errors such as *Stusart* instead of *Stuart*.

Table 7.1: Differentiation of variation types

This chapter considers spelling errors that are not linguistically motivated. Such errors are commonly known as typos as they frequently result from hitting the wrong key on a computer keyboard, but they may also stem from other sources, such as the ambiguities that may be introduced through low-quality scanned or faxed copies, or through difficulties encountered in reading handwriting.

An understanding of the source of such non-linguistic spelling errors can help determine the most appropriate methods for dealing with them.

7.2 Motor Function and the Role of the Keyboard

In the days before the introduction of the typewriter and computerisation, non-linguistically based spelling errors followed a less predictable distribution pattern. These days, a reasonable indication of the likelihood of various types of spelling error can be obtained from an understanding of human motor function and the design of the computer keyboard.

That said, when designing an identity matching system, it is also important to consider the origin of the data being matched. Motor function and keyboard design will always affect the distribution of spelling errors in any data that has been manually input to a computer system. However, if the data has been typed up from older, handwritten records then handwriting style will also play a role, just as phonetics will be an important driver if data is being input as a result of a telephone call or other spoken record.

Leaving aside these other influences for the moment, some of the most common types of non-phonetic spelling errors in names are:

- Insertion: an additional character is inserted, as when an adjacent key on the keyboard is struck along with the correct key so that *Stuart* becomes *Stusart*.
- Replacement: a character is replaced with an incorrect one, as when an adjacent key on the keyboard is struck instead of the correct one so that *Stuart* becomes *Stusrt*.
- Omission: a character is omitted altogether, as when a key is not struck strongly enough so that *Stuart* becomes *Sturt*.
- Transposition: the positions of two characters are swapped, as when the motor activities of the right and left hands are not correctly synchronised so that *Stuart* becomes *Staurt*.

The longer a name is, the higher the probability that it will contain one or more of these typos. Typically, typos occur less frequently at the beginning of a name than they do in the middle or at the end. These features can be used to prioritise matches containing typos. For example, it may be more appropriate to match longer names containing two different characters than to match shorter names that differ by only one character. Similarly, a different initial character may be a better indicator that two names should not be matched than a differing character at the end of the name.

Keyboard design influences the probability of each particular combination of character insertions, replacements and transpositions, as the proximity of one character to the intended character determines the likelihood that it will be struck in error. Where the adjacent keys to the intended character are not letters but digits or punctuation marks, the error may be more easily spotted and corrected by the writer. However, if such errors are not corrected they may have more severe consequences for name matching processes, which may not be prepared for the introduction of non-alphabetic characters and may even treat such characters as a boundary between two separate name parts.

Other physical properties of the keyboard also play a part, including the size of the keys and how hard a key has to be struck in order for the character to be registered. If the identity data to be analysed comes from a particular source, it may be possible to identify particular features which make one kind of spelling error more likely than another. For example if the originating keyboard has a "sticky" key, the character it relates to may be more likely to be omitted.

7.2.1 Regional Influences

Regional differences also influence the likelihood of particular combinations of characters being involved in a typo, as different regions favour keyboards with different layouts, altering the groups of characters which are adjacent to each other. The QWERTY keyboard (named after the first six letters on its first alphabetic row) is widely used in the Anglophone world, but the most commonly used keyboard in France uses the AZERTY layout, while the first six characters on the German keyboard are QWERTZ. These differences must be taken into consideration when designing a precise system for matching and weighting particular typos. Adjacent-key typos are a common type of spelling mistake, but the particular character combinations that they involve will depend on the layout of the keyboard.

If a person uses a keyboard unfamiliar to them, the likelihood of their making an error with non-adjacent keys increases. For example, an English person using a German keyboard may habitually transpose the letters *Y* and *Z* as the positions of these characters are swapped on English and German keyboards. Further differences exist between the English and French keyboards, increasing the likelihood of typos involving keys that are not adjacent if a French person uses an

English keyboard. In particular, the position of the *M* on the French keyboard is occupied by punctuation in other keyboard layouts. A typo involving this key could cause an identity matching system to assume a word border in place of the *M*.

The availability of diacritics on different keyboards may also play a part in the kind of errors that are made. Those unfamiliar with their use often replace the accented character with the same basic character without the diacritic. A correct, un-accented transcription of the name *Müller*, for example, would be *Mueller*. Those unfamiliar with the effects of the diacritics might incorrectly write the name as *Muller* so an identity matching system should be able to match both variants.

7.3 Optical Character Recognition

In recent years, the scanning of hard copy documents for electronic storage has become an increasingly common activity. This may be done as part of a standard electronic archiving programme and is also often carried out to facilitate document retrieval during large-scale litigation or research projects. If the images created by the scanner are to be searched for names, they must first be treated with optical character recognition (OCR) software to identify the text they contain and convert this text into machine-readable characters.

Over the last decade, the quality of OCR tools has improved dramatically but, for a number of reasons, the results are still often imperfect. Marks on the original hard-copy documents may cause errors in character recognition and the use of more artistic fonts may lead the software to mistake the characters being read. For example, the letters *O* and *B* may be mistaken for the numbers *0* and *8* respectively, the lower-case *l* may be mistaken for the number *1* or a capital *I*, and the pair of letters *ri* may, in some fonts, look similar to the lower case *n*. OCR tools often use sophisticated language dictionaries in order to help them determine the most probable combination of characters present, but these are of less use when the software is trying to read names, as many names do not appear in such dictionaries.

Developments in OCR tools have improved their ability to recognise characters and allowed the operator to suggest corrections in cases of uncertainty. However this manual intervention is often omitted, particularly in large-scale conversion processes, and the potential for recognition errors remains.

7.4 Typos in the Identity Matching Process

While linguistically motivated variations are more common than simple spelling errors, the correct treatment of typos is still an important requirement for any identity matching system. It is particularly important when searching informal documents such as email correspondence or chat messages, or data derived from non-optimised OCR processes.

Many identity matching systems have included typo-handling features for years as these are relatively less complex and easier to build than linguistic matching features. The more sophisticated techniques prioritise various character combinations based on the likelihood of their being a typo. For example, *Stusart* is more likely be a reference to *Stuart* than *Stumart*, based on the proximity of the characters on a QWERTY keyboard, just as *Stuant* is more likely to refer to *Stuart* than *Stuast*, based on an OCR process applied to a standard font.

Where the identity data has a particular creation history, it is worth considering the kinds of misspellings that may have been introduced at that time. For example, during the 1990's, there was a particular drive to computerise many of the banking and other financial services records from the 1930's and 40's. Time and cultural adaptations significantly altered styles of handwriting during the intervening fifty years, so that those entering the identity data to the computer may have misrecognised particular characters. For example, the letters *f* and *s* could easily be confused in such a situation. Similarly, without an understanding of the context of the documents, other errors could be made in transcribing names. For example, in historic documents, the name *M. Dupont* is just as likely to refer to a French man named *Monsieur Dupont* as it is to refer to an individual with the first initial *M*. In such a situation, *Albert Dupont* may well be a good match to *M. Dupont*. Where possible, it is always useful to factor such peculiarities of the data collection process into identity matching routines.

Such specific cases aside, in modern identity matching processes it is often appropriate to consider typos based on motor function, keyboard design and OCR errors as the most likely to occur. Basic algorithms for handling typographic errors have been around for years and are discussed in more detail in Part II. These algorithms can be made more effective if they are adapted to incorporate an analysis of the statistical causes of non-linguistic errors, prioritising those character combinations that are most likely to be involved in typos or OCR errors.

There may also be some benefit to incorporating the frequency distribution of common names into the matching methods. For example, *David* and *Davis* could be considered less likely to refer to the same person, despite *d* being next to *s* on many keyboards, because both are common names. Conversely, *Johndon* could be considered a relatively better match to *Johnson* because *Johnson* is common and *Johndon* far less so.

There are many ways in which the algorithms designed to match names containing non-linguistic errors can be modified and implemented to provide improved precision and recall. As a result, many matching systems perform far better in this area than they do with handling the more complex linguistic variants. However, there is still much to choose between the best performing and worst performing implementations so it is always worth checking that all appropriate optimisation techniques have been applied. These modifications are discussed further in Chapter 10.

Part II:
Name Matching Methods

Part II: Name Matching Methods

Part I introduced the basic characteristics and qualities of proper names as applied to legal and natural persons. It described the various different sources of spelling variations that are most often the reason for the same name being represented in different ways. In doing so, it introduced some of the requirements necessary for a comprehensive name matching system.

Part II looks at the methods for matching person names that have been developed over the years and compares them with the requirements identified in Part I. Chapters 8 and 9 look at first and second generation name matching methods and highlight their relative advantages and disadvantages. Chapter 8 also examines some of the reasons why first generation methods are still so widely used in today's business processes despite their obvious weaknesses.

Chapter 10 introduces third-generation matching solutions. It is these more modern solutions that herald a new dawn and the age of truly linguistic name matching. They have emerged from the new paradigm for name matching and are based on a deeper understanding of the different sources of variation in names that were described in Part I.

Chapter 11 summarises the results of a simple benchmark study, in which methods of the first, second and third generation are compared using publicly available data. As expected, the results of the study show obvious improvements in both precision and recall using third generation techniques. Given the reduced risks associated with improved recall and the lower costs associated with greater precision, it is likely that these third generation methods will, over time, become standard in professional name matching systems.

Chapter 8: Name Matching Methods of the First Generation

8.1 Introduction

Computer algorithms have been used for automatic name matching for over half a century. For the most part, earlier efforts used methods that were not originally developed for matching names but were borrowed from other disciplines. Those that did focus specifically on comparing proper names did so in a largely superficial way. As a result, none of the first generation of methods used for matching names (G1 Methods) effectively cover the requirements of global name matching, though some do still have a limited role to play when used in conjunction with other, more sophisticated techniques.

G1 Methods are more widely used in today's business processes than might be expected given their limitations. However, this situation is not uncommon for a market in transition, particularly one operating in such a complex technical and linguistic area. Economic factors also play a significant role in the continued popularity of G1 Methods. On the supply side, such simplistic methods have inherently low design and development costs, as expertise in linguistics and onomastics is not required in order to bring software based on G1 Methods to market. On the demand side, buyers are often attracted by the relatively low purchase and maintenance costs, while the significantly greater costs associated with the risks of under-matching and the efforts to follow up on over-matching are often less immediately apparent.

Four of the most important G1 Methods are:

- Levenshtein Distance
- N-Gram methods
- Soundex
- Thesaurus-based methods

The first two are techniques for the comparison of two character strings, such as words or names. Sometimes referred to as simple pattern matching methods, their aim is to quantify the differences in the character sequences. Both are often used in name matching solutions, though neither was originally developed for this purpose.

Soundex, however, was developed as a name matching technique and can be considered the grandfather of several modern name matching methods. It was initially patented at the beginning of the twentieth century and has since been modified in a number of different ways, though the basic features have remained the same. The algorithm is used to generate a simplified representation of the name, known as a similarity key, which can then be compared to the keys generated from other names. This is an early version of the technique known as phonetic encoding, as similar sounding letters are simplified to the same encoded character.

The final set of G1 Methods discussed here are techniques based on thesauri similar to those that have long been used for text processing and translation. The difference is that, rather than containing synonyms or translations, the thesauri used in these techniques contain spelling variations and derivative forms of proper names.

This chapter looks at the different classes of G1 Methods in more detail and considers their practical application for modern name matching processes. It highlights the relative strengths and notable weaknesses of each technique in dealing with the various classes of name variation that were introduced in Part I. In conclusion, this chapter considers the various factors that have combined to keep G1 Methods in use in many of today's name matching processes, despite the improvements available in more modern techniques.

8.2 Pattern Matching with Levenshtein Distance

8.2.1 Similarity and Edit Operations

One of the most popular measures of "fuzziness" in name matching, Edit Distance, is defined as the minimum number of basic operations required to convert one name into another. In this context, basic operations include:

- the insertion of a character (e.g. Yeltsin ⇨ Yexltsin)
- the omission of a character (e.g. Yeltsin ⇨ Yeltsn)
- the replacement of one character with another (e.g. Yeltsin ⇨ Yqltsin)

Defined in this way, the Edit Distance is known as the Levenshtein Distance, after the Russian mathematician Vladimir Levenshtein. Levenshtein Distance has become so widely used that the coding necessary to calculate it is a standard feature in many database systems. It is a popular feature in commercial software as the concept is easy to understand and the algorithm easy to implement. Its popularity has lead to Levenshtein Distance becoming almost synonymous with the term Edit Distance, though other Edit Distance metrics do exist.

In practical application, the question arises of how close the Levenshtein Distance has to be in order for two names to be considered a match. A tolerance for a Levenshtein Distance of one would match *Yejltsin* with *Yeltsin* but would have to be increased in order to match *Yejltsir*, which has a Levenshtein Distance of two. Clearly, the higher the distance tolerated, the greater the number of false positive matches generated. This being the case, any improvements in recall must be directly paid for in reduced precision.

In an attempt to partially mitigate this factor, Levenshtein Distance is often used in conjunction with the string (name) length in name matching processes. Acceptable tolerances will depend on the purpose of the process but will often be similar to the following:

Number of characters in name	Tolerated Levenshtein Distance
< 5	0
5–8	1
9–12	2
> 12	3

Table 8.1: Possible Levenshtein Distance tolerances based on name length

In this way, systems are able to take account of the fact that the relative significance of a deviation in spelling decreases with increases in the length of the name. For example, *Lee* and *Lex* are far less likely to be misspellings of each other than *Leederheimer* and *Lexderheimer*, despite the same deviation (the replacement of an *e* with an *x*) being present in both pairs.

The reasons for the reduced significance of single character deviations in longer names are clear. On the one hand, the opportunity for typing errors to be introduced is greater in longer names. On the other hand, it can be seen that the relative proportion of concurring characters is greater in longer names that deviate by only one character; only 67% of the characters in the names *Lee* and *Lex* concur, while 92% of the characters are the same in the names *Leederheimer* and *Lexderheimer*.

8.2.2 The Application of Levenshtein Distance for Name Matching

The key weakness of Levenshtein Distance when used for name matching is that it disregards the nature of the characters being inserted, omitted or replaced. As discussed in Part I, variations in names stem from a number of different sources. Based on these sources, some character variations are more likely to indicate an alternative version of the same name than others. This knowledge can be used to increase the precision of name matching techniques, but as a pure string comparison algorithm, Levenshtein Distance treats all character variations equally.

Predictably then, Levenshtein Distance does not appreciate the differences that may arise through the use of different transcription standards. This can be demonstrated by examining the most common English, German and French transcriptions of Ельцин.

English	German	French	Levenshtein Distance
Yeltsin	Jelzin		3
Yeltsin		Eltsine	2
	Jelzin	Eltsine	4

Table 8.2: Levenshtein Distance of English, German and French transcription variants of the Cyrillic name Ельцин.

It can be seen that matching all of these common transcription variants would require a tolerance of Levenshtein Distance 4. This is effectively unworkable in a practical name matching application, as this tolerance level would, for example, match *Yeltsin* with *Meli*, *Jelzin* with *Dell* and *Eltsine* with *Coutine*. Such poor precision would clearly be unacceptable.

Phonetic relationships are also ignored. From a linguistic perspective, the replacement of a *y* with an *i* or a *c* with a *k*, as in *Vicky* and *Vikki*, may be far less significant than the replacement of *y* and *c* with more linguistically distant letters such as *t* and *e*. Levenshtein Distance does not distinguish between *Vikki* and *Viekt* as matches for *Vicky*. As discussed in Chapter 9, some second generation techniques, such as Editex, have attempted to introduce some phonetic discrimination to edit distance metrics.

The position of the deviating character within the word is also ignored for the purposes of calculating Levenshtein Distance. The position of the difference can have a stark effect on the phonetic similarity of the names; for example, *Eric* and *Erick* are linguistically closer than *Eric* and *Keric*, though both pairs of names differ only by the insertion of a *k*.

Levenshtein Distance also ignores the significance of the position of the deviating characters on a keyboard, so that the replacement of a *b* with a *v*, two characters which are adjacent on most Western keyboards, is treated the same way as the replacement of characters represented by keys that are further apart. As discussed in the next chapter, this weakness was partially addressed in some second generation pattern matching techniques such as Keyboard or Typewriter Distance.

The final most significant weakness of the original Levenshtein Distance metric (as used in identity matching) is its treatment of character transpositions. As discussed in Chapter 7, transpositions are common typing errors due to the motor abilities required to coordinate the left and right hands. One pair of transposed characters in a name would require tolerance of a Levenshtein Distance of two in order to match the name with its original spelling. In many cases this would have an unacceptable effect on precision. To compensate for this, the second generation Damerau-Levenshtein metric, discussed in the next chapter, considers transpositions to be one single edit operation.

As a result of its lack of bias between different classes of character deviations, Levenshtein Distance would be most appropriate for use where variations in spelling is caused entirely by random errors. As Part I demonstrated, spelling variations are rarely completely unpredictable. Most name variations are the result of different transcription standards or phonetic alternatives, or represent derivative forms of names. Even those which can be truly referred to as non-linguistic spelling errors are most often the result of keyboard typing mistakes or OCR errors. As discussed in Chapter 7, variations from these sources are far more likely to involve some particular combinations of characters than others. Ignoring this in any name matching system will significantly reduce its precision.

8.3 Pattern Matching with N-Gram Methods

8.3.1 Comparison of Substrings

N-gram methods are based on the idea of splitting a string of characters into smaller chains, or substrings, with a pre-defined length. Often, the chains are set to a length of three characters and known as 3-grams or trigrams. For example, the name *Thompson* can be split into 6 trigrams: *tho, hom, omp, mps, pso* and *son*. In other cases, names may be split into chains of two characters (bigrams) or four characters (tetragrams).

A common application area for n-gram methods is language detection in longer text, as each language has a particular statistical distribution of n-grams. When n-grams are used in a name matching context, the objective is to determine the number of concurring n-grams in a given pair of names. If a sufficient proportion of n-grams are the same, the names are considered a match.

In the example of the phonetically similar names *Thomson* and *Thompson*, it can be seen that of the eight distinct trigrams formed by the two names, three are present in both names. This indicates a relatively high congruence.

<table>
<tr><th colspan="7">Trigrams</th></tr>
<tr><td>Thomson</td><td rowspan="2">tho</td><td rowspan="2">hom</td><td>oms</td><td>mso</td><td></td><td rowspan="2">son</td></tr>
<tr><td>Thompson</td><td>omp</td><td>mps</td><td>pso</td></tr>
</table>

Table 8.3: Trigrams in the names Thomson and Thompson

The number of concurring n-grams between the two names would be higher using bigrams and lower if tetragrams were used. Only one tetragram (*thom*) is shared by the two names.

However, other homophones may vary significantly in their n-gram comparisons. The name *Tomsen* shares only one trigram with Thomson.

<table>
<tr><th colspan="6">Trigrams</th></tr>
<tr><td>Thomson</td><td>tho</td><td>hom</td><td rowspan="2">oms</td><td>mso</td><td>son</td></tr>
<tr><td>Tomsen</td><td>tom</td><td></td><td>mse</td><td>sen</td></tr>
</table>

Table 8.4: Trigrams in the names Thomson and Tomsen

And has no trigrams at all in common with *Thompson*.

Trigrams						
Thompson	tho	hom	omp	mps	pso	son
Tomsen	tom		oms		mse	sen

Table 8.5: Trigrams in the names Thompson and Tomsen

8.3.2 The Application of N-Gram Methods for Name Matching

N-gram methods have similar drawbacks to Levenshtein distance when used for name matching, in that they do not take into account the nature of the discrepant characters. Linguistically motivated variations are treated the same way as random differences. *Yeltsin* and *Jelzin* have no trigrams in common and would therefore not be considered a match using trigram methods alone. The congruence would still be low if bigrams were considered, as the two variations have only *el* and *in* in common.

The key difference between n-grams and Levenshtein Distance is that the positioning of the discrepancy has a greater effect on concurring n-grams than it does on the distance metric. The Levenshtein Distance between *Thomson* and *Thompson* is identical to the distance between *Thomson* and *Thomsons*. However, the former pair of names contains three concurring trigrams, whereas the latter pair contains five. This is because deviations at the beginning or end of a name have a lower impact than those in central positions. Generally speaking this random downgrading of variations in the initial and final characters is not desirable for name matching purposes. If any character position should be taken into account, it would be preferable if deviations at the beginning of the name should be considered more, rather than less, significant. As discussed in Chapter 9, some of the second generation methods for string comparison have incorporated this idea.

As with Levenshtein Distance, n-gram methods have no significant role to play in modern name matching techniques. They may be applied in the handling of truly random spelling errors but, as previously discussed, in most contexts these form only a small minority of the variations encountered when dealing with proper names.

8.4 Phonetic Encoding with Soundex

8.4.1 Phonetic Similarity Keys

Soundex is a phonetic algorithm that was patented in the early 1900's and came into widespread use in the 1960's. Unlike the G1 Methods discussed so far in this chapter, it was specifically designed for use in name matching processes.

In its day, Soundex provided a new approach to the matching of names. The idea was that, rather than comparing the character strings directly, each name should first be converted into a similarity key representing its phonetic characteristics. By today's standards, the algorithm used is so simple as to be effectively useless, but there is no doubt that the concept of the similarity key lives on in many more modern techniques. In the context of global name matching, the Soundex algorithm also has the disadvantage that it focuses entirely on Anglo-Saxon phonology and is therefore even less effective for matching names originating in other cultures.

The basic Soundex algorithm consists of the following steps:

- Leaving the first character untouched, replace the remaining consonants as follows:
  - B, F, P, V = 1
  - C, G, J, K, Q, S, X, Z = 2
  - D, T = 3
  - L = 4
  - M, N = 5
  - R = 6

- Remove any duplicate digits.
- Leaving the first character untouched, remove all remaining characters (A,E,I,O,U,W,Y,H).
- Match based on the first character and the first 3 digits of the resulting code (adding 0's if the code has less than 3 digits).

Applying this formula to the name *Kennedy* gives the similarity key K530. The names *Kenedy*, *Kanadie*, *Kant*, *Knuth* and *Komet* all share this similarity key and would therefore be considered matches using the Soundex method of comparison. This tendency to over-match is one of the key criticisms of the original Soundex algorithm.

8.4.2 The Application of Soundex for Name Matching

Overall, Soundex is now considered an inappropriate technique for use in most name matching processes. For a number of reasons, it suffers from both poor precision and poor recall.

As discussed in Part I, names vary in the way they are written based on a number of factors, only one of which is phonetics. Transcription variants are equally, if not more, important in the matching process as phonetically similar names. Soundex does not systematically account for such variations. For example, the most common transcription variants of Ельцин would not match using Soundex (the similarity keys for *Yeltsin*, *Jelzin*, *Eltsine* and *Iéltsin* being Y432, J425, E432 and I432 respectively).

In addition, to the extent that name variations are phonetically driven, they are not dependent solely on Anglo-Saxon phonetics. The Soundex algorithm does not consider the phonetics of any other languages and so does not match many phonetically similar names. The French homophone names *Bodins* and *Baudaint*, for example, could not be matched using Soundex as their codes are B352 and B353 respectively. Even in the case of Anglo-Saxon homophones, Soundex is often not a reliable method of matching names. One reason for this is the requirement that for names to match they must start with the same character. The name *Kandle* (K534) would not match *Candle* (C534) because the first character is fixed.

Soundex also ignores the phonetic context of each character, so that the phonetically equivalent *Thomson* (T525) and *Thompson* (T512) would not match and nor would homophones such as *Leigh* (L200) and *Lee* (L000). The pronunciation of each character in a name is affected by both the preceding and following characters, and this is not taken into account in the original Soundex algorithm.

NYCIIS Soundex is a popular variant which appeared in the 1970's and included additional steps to provide for some groups of characters which sound alike. This was one of the first attempts to consider the phonetic context of characters. However, only a very limited set of Anglo-Saxon homophone character groups are covered and, as with the original Soundex, the requirement that the first letters of the names are the same prevents many good matches from being identified.

As well as suffering from poor recall, Soundex is also a very imprecise method for matching names. Its restriction to three digits leads to the erroneous matching of longer names that start with the same basic sound pattern but finish very differently. For example, the names *Winters*, *Winterly*, *Winterson* and *Winterman* all share the Soundex code W536.

Soundex also ignores all vowels that don't appear as the initial character of the name. This is one of the reasons why *Kennedy*, *Kant*, *Knuth* and *Komet* all match using Soundex. This limitation is perhaps the most disruptive to the matching process in the case of Chinese names, many of which tend to consist of only one syllable. For example, *Za*, *Zai*, *Zao*, *Ze*, *Zei*, *Zi*, *Zou*, *Zu*, *Zui* and *Zuo* are all Hanyu Pinyin transcriptions for different Chinese names but have the same Soundex similarity key (Z000). As discussed in Chapter 3, a large part of the Chinese population shares just a few family names, and many names differ only in their tone rather than the way that they are spelt when transcribed. These factors are inherently a challenge in the matching process. If, in addition, the matching process is unable to differentiate between names that are actually transcribed differently, huge numbers of false positive results can be expected.

The disregard for the impact of vowels on the pronunciation of a name also leads to false positive matches in names of Arabic origin. Many different Arabic names differ in their transcriptions only in the vowels used to separate the consonants. *Muhammad* and *Mahmud* are two different Arabic names that share the same Soundex similarity key (M530) for this reason, as are *Hassan* and *Hussein*, which share the key H250.

There is, however, a beneficial side effect of Soundex's disregard for vowels in the case of Arabic names. As discussed in Chapter 4, often transcription variants of the same Arabic name will differ only in vowel usage and the use of double consonants. As Soundex ignores both of these features, it may match transcription variants which other G1 Methods would not. This is the case, for example, with many of the common transcription variants of the Arabic name محمد, including

Muhammad, Mohamed and *Mouhammad,* all of which share the Soundex code M530. However, this effect is achieved by accident rather than by design and is far from amounting to a comprehensive coverage of Arabic transcription variants.

Like the other G1 Methods discussed so far, Soundex also offers no solution for the matching of particular onomastic phenomena such as hypocorisms (for example matching *Bill* with *William*) or abbreviations (for example matching *limited* with *Ltd*), and it also has no solution for the matching of names with ambiguous word borders, such as *Hans Peter* and *Hanspeter,* or *Alinejad* and *Ali Nejad.* The last category of matching methods discussed in this chapter, the use of thesauri, is the only G1 Method to introduce consideration of some of these phenomena.

8.5 Thesaurus-Based Matching Methods

8.5.1 Dictionaries of Name Variations

In some matching processes, electronic catalogues of name variations are used to identify relationships between names that should be matched. These thesauri may contain several different classes of name variants, including:

- transcription variants, such as *Yeltsin, Jelzin* and *Eltsine*
- homophones, such as *Thomson, Thompson* and *Tomsen*
- hypocorisms, such as *Will, Bill,* and *Billy* (for *William*)
- common abbreviations, such as *Ltd* for *Limited*
- common acronyms, such as *Plc* for *Public Limited Company*
- translations, such as *Society, Société* and *Sociedad*

A comprehensive database of all these classes of variation would provide a near-perfect solution to the identity matching challenge. However, it is not easy to find a commercially available and economically viable thesaurus that focuses on proper names with sufficient coverage to provide adequate recall in a global name matching system. This is hardly surprising given the depth of linguistic and onomastic knowledge that would be required in order to compile such a database, particularly if it should include the names of non-natural persons. In addition to the very specific expertise required, the comprehensive, global research of proper names requires access to a large body of media articles, official records and other information as well as the means to extract the names from the surrounding text. Such a combination of skills and resources may be considered prohibitively expensive for a commercial product.

As a result, the quality of the proper name catalogues on the market varies widely and many are little more than auxiliary look-up tables containing hypocorisms and variants of the most common names. Many also focus heavily on names from Western cultures. Such tables are an effective way of matching the name variants they contain but often lack the depth of coverage necessary to avoid the risks associated with false negative results.

There are a number of options for integrating thesauri into the matching process. One common approach is to expand the query submitted to the database with all recorded variants of the search name. The query name *William Thompson* could be expanded to read:

(*William* OR *Will* OR *Bill* OR *Billy*) AND (*Thompson* OR *Thomson* OR *Tomsen*).

Such a query would then return hits on database profiles such as *William Thompson, Bill Thomson, Billy Tomsen, Will Tomsen*, etc.

8.5.2 The Application of Proper Name Thesauri for Name Matching

Thesauri of name variants are conceptually simple, easy to implement and, from a technical perspective, simple to maintain. Unlike other G1 Methods, for the most part they have a positive effect on the recall of a system without unduly affecting its precision. Thesauri are also one of the most effective ways of dealing with name variations such as hypocorisms and abbreviations, which are not addressed at all by any of the other G1 Methods.

There are some conditions to be considered when implementing thesauri, such as the application of hypocorisms only to given names and not to family names, so that *Richard Miller* can be matched with *Rick Miller* without *Clare Richard* being matched to *Clare Rick*. Though this is essentially a simple requirement, it can cause problems when searching databases with rigid name structures. As discussed in Chapter 3, the typical "first name, middle name, last name" structure makes it difficult to predict which parts of non-Western names will be contained in each field.

However, in most cases it is the lack of comprehensive coverage which is of most concern when using onomastic thesauri as a primary method for matching names. It is not realistic to expect that any database of names could ever cover all the family names used globally. Apart from the enormous effort that would be entailed in compiling such a database, the availability of research materials means that coverage will always be greatest for those names used in regions more widely covered in electronic media. For this reason, less common names and names from regions less well electronically documented may be under-represented in onomastic thesauri. In addition, the names of companies, organisations and other legal persons are traditionally less predictable and may also be subject to poor coverage in such catalogues.

Not only is the coverage of names extremely variable in onomastic databases, but it is difficult to see how such a catalogue could ever cover all variants of each of these names. There can be hundreds of valid transcription variants for some non-Western names, and the number of matching homophones may be even greater. At best, these databases usually only contain the most popular variants of each name.

A further issue is that such databases are often employed by identifying direct matches between the search name and the variants they contain. Clearly, it would not be feasible to add all variants containing typos to the thesaurus. This means that typing errors in either the search query or the database profile would prevent a match between variants from being identified.

The considerations discussed above suggest that onomastic thesauri are not the most efficient or effective form of matching proper names that differ through transcription, phonetics or cultural variations. They do, however, have an invaluable role to play in matching name variants that differ for other reasons, such as hypocorisms, translations and abbreviations. Their use for this purpose is discussed further in Chapter 10.

8.6 Summary of the Application of First Generation Name Matching Methods

None of the G1 Methods discussed in this chapter individually claim to be able to cover all sources of variation in names in a comprehensive manner. In addition, given the widely accepted limitations of these methods when used for matching names, it is clear that these methods could not reliably match all kinds of name variants even if packaged together. However, G1 Methods still feature heavily in today's name matching processes, despite the improvements available in the form of the second generation methods discussed in the next chapter.

The relative performance of different types of G1 Methods, as applied to the four key sources of variation in names, are considered in the following charts. The name variations considered are:

- **transcription variants**, such as *Yeltsin*, *Jelzin* and *Eltsine* (see Chapter 4)
- **derivative names**, such as *Joseph*, *Joe*, *José* and *Yosef* (see Chapter 5)
- **homophones**, such as *Thomson*, *Thompson* and *Tomsen* (see Chapter 6)
- **non-linguistic spelling errors**, such as typos and OCR errors (see Chapter 7)

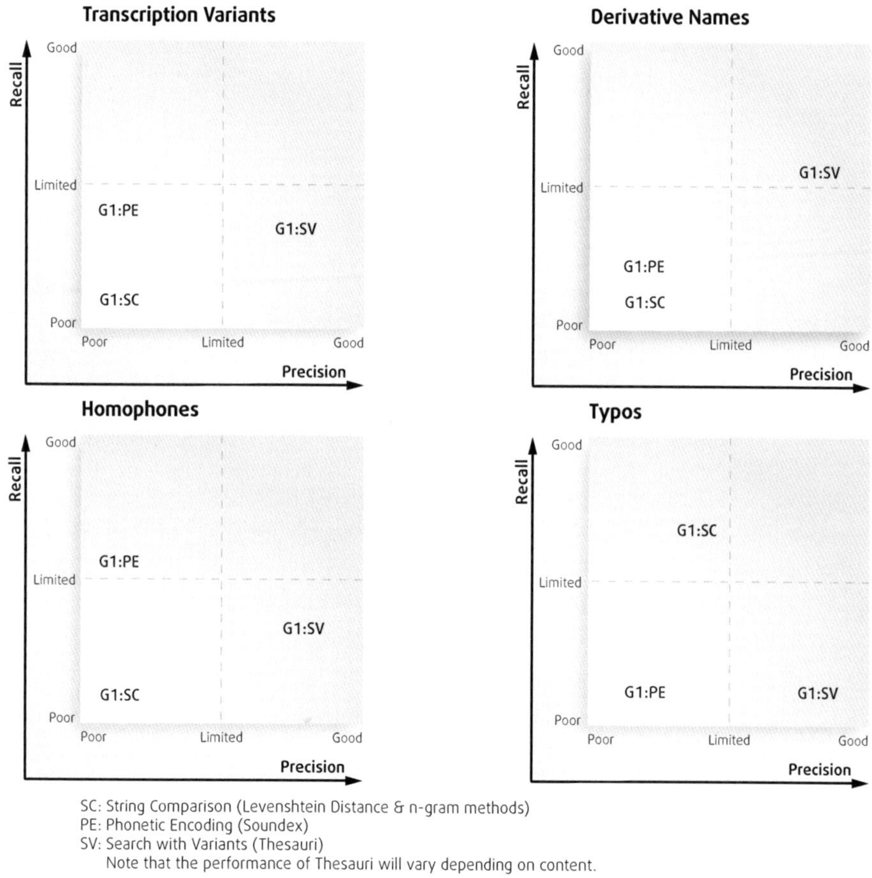

Figure 8.1: Relative performance of G1 Methods when matching each of the four main classes of variations in names.

The charts show the recall and precision of each technique when used to match each of the four key classes of variation in names. Note that several methods can be implemented in different ways to influence their performance, for example by altering the tolerated edit distance or by dedicating more or fewer resources to compiling a thesaurus. These charts are provided as a simple indicator of the typical performance achieved in practice.

String comparison methods such as Levenshtein Distance and n-gram methods are unable to match many transcription variations because the use of different romanisation standards can result in name variants that differ by multiple characters and even in the number of "words" each variant contains. For example, the character difference between *Abd al-Rahman* and *Abdurrachman* is significant. The same applies to name derivatives such as hypocorisms which are often quite different from the original name in terms of the characters they contain. However, both methods perform well at matching names containing random spelling errors, which is not surprising given the text comparison role for which they were created. They do, however, almost always suffer from problems with precision.

Soundex may provide acceptable results when matching some transcription variants. Essentially, it performs well when matching transcription variants that happen to be phonetically equivalent using Anglo-Saxon pronunciation. It may also match transcription variants that differ only in their vowels, though for the same reason it may suffer from poor precision when matching transcription variants of distinct names in which only the vowels differ.

Soundex generally performs poorly when matching name derivatives as, with the exception of some translated variants, they generally have a different sound pattern to their original form. The algorithm is targeted at phonetically similar names and it does match Anglo-Saxon homophones to the extent that their pronunciation is not significantly affected by the context of each character. However, Soundex provides poor recall when matching homophones from other languages and does not match a significant number of English homophones, such as *Lee* and *Leigh* or *Catherine* and *Kathryn*, due to its disregard for the phonetic context of each character and insistence on the initial character of each name being identical. In addition, the simplicity of the Soundex algorithm together with the fact that it only takes the first few characters of each name into consideration means that its precision is extremely poor.

Thesaurus-based methods, on the other hand, generally provide relatively good precision, as they focus on selected, researched variants of each name. The precision suffers if the use of the thesaurus is not appropriately bounded, for example if hypocorisms derived from given names are applied to family names. The recall of thesaurus-based methods is highly dependent on the amount of research that has been put into creating the onomastic database. Here, the recall has been assumed to be limited, as it is unlikely that all transcription variants, homophones, derivatives and other variations for all names could be comprehensively captured, particularly given the fact that the cultural use of names in many countries is still evolving. Clearly, however, the larger and better researched databases will provide better recall than smaller ones, though less common names, names from communities that are difficult to research, and the names of groups and organisations will always remain a particular challenge.

In summary, it is clear that the isolated use of any individual G1 Method to match global names would be inappropriate. Combining these methods into a packaged solution is also unlikely to produce satisfactory results, given the lack of sophistication in the way most of them treat linguistically-motivated variations. Even if the tolerance levels were set so widely as to generate many false positive results, it is unlikely that the transcription variants and homophones used globally could be reliably matched by a system of combined G1 Methods.

8.7 Reasons for the Continued Application of First Generation Methods

Some G1 Methods undoubtedly still have a role to play in modern identity matching systems. String comparison algorithms such as Levenshtein Distance and n-gram methods produce reasonable results when dealing with random typing errors, and thesaurus-based methods are still the most appropriate method for dealing with derivative names and abbreviations.

However, the most significant classes of variation in names are those resulting from linguistic sources such as transcription standards and phonetics. G1 Methods are less well equipped for dealing with these. Despite this, identity matching solutions that rely solely on G1 Methods have achieved a surprising depth of market penetration over the last decade and can still be found in key business processes today.

8.7.1 Name Matching as a Secondary Consideration

One reason for the continued use of G1 Methods is that they are available as technically mature components that can be easily integrated into standard technological infrastructure. Software built on these methods often fulfils many of the non-functional requirements for name matching technologies such as stability and short response times. Leaving the functional requirement of actually matching names aside, there is much to be said for G1 Methods, in that they are well-known, technically mature and inexpensive.

Beyond these considerations, a key driver for the wide-spread use of G1 Methods is their incorporation into many packaged solutions. Identity matching tools are often not shipped as separate modules but packaged as part of a particular technology solution. Solutions that are often shipped with a name matching component include:

- **compliance solutions** for use in AML processes in the financial services industry
- **CRM solutions** for the optimisation of client service processes
- **database systems** for the effective management of structured data
- **enterprise search platforms** for the integration of all business search processes

Often, the ability to match names is only one of many criteria evaluated by the purchasers of such systems. Other criteria, such as the integrated and user-friendly support for the relevant business process, often play a more significant role in the purchasing decision. The ability to match international names is frequently a secondary consideration. This is particularly so given the lack of standards or regulatory guidance on identity matching requirements, which leaves organisations with little to go on when defining system expectations.

Software vendors often focus their resources on developing those features of their solutions that play the most significant role in the purchasing decision. This may explain why some vendors continue to package outdated name matching technology with otherwise efficient business software. However, in most technology areas, a few pioneering developers will push through innovative changes that will eventually force their competitors to follow suit. It is worth considering why this effect has been more muted in the area of identity matching, making it one of the few technology areas where some of the methods still commonly used were first made popular several decades ago.

8.7.2 Typical Structure of Technology Vendors

One reason for the relative lack of recent innovation in identity matching technology is that the concepts that need to be introduced at this stage are linguistic rather than technological. As discussed in Part 1, the biggest challenges faced by the modern name matching system are the transcription and phonetic considerations that can only be addressed with solid linguistic and onomastic research.

Software vendors often understand name matching as a technical task that can be solved by technically trained software architects and developers using logical algorithms. This technology-oriented understanding is reflected in their organisational structures and affects the communication and decision making that takes place throughout the product development cycle.

Software vendors wishing to address the modern requirements for identity matching systems have to challenge the traditional understanding of name matching as a technical process and create the conditions necessary to appropriately address the linguistic considerations. The primary requirement for this is the creation of interdisciplinary teams in which regionally specialised linguists can define requirements in terms of transcription, phonetics and other onomastic concerns. These requirements can then be worked on by developers to produce solutions that address these criteria without compromising the non-functional requirements such as stability and response time. A central role in this process has to be reserved for computational linguists, who are skilled in communicating on both a linguistic and a software development level.

Given the efforts, structural changes and associated costs required in order to pioneer true linguistic identity matching solutions, it is not surprising that few software manufacturers have so far gone down this path. However, as pressure for effective identity matching systems rises, it is likely that more vendors will consider the necessary investment to be worth the risk in the future.

8.7.3 Buyer Sophistication

A further reason for the continued development and supply of solutions employing G1 Methods is the lack of concrete demand for more effective tools. This is the case even in industries such as the financial sector, where the risks associated with ineffective matching technology can be severe, partly due to the lack of published standards and regulatory guidance on minimum search requirements, but also to the sheer complexity of effectively evaluating a name matching solution.

At the most basic level, the requirements for a name matching system are that it must produce a minimum of false negative results (it must maximise recall) and a minimum of false positive results (it must maximise precision) as well as having a means to prioritise results based on linguistic criteria. In a modern context, these requirements must be applied equally to names originating in any writing system (particularly the main Arabic, Cyrillic, Chinese, Korean or Japanese systems) regardless of the standard used to transcribe them (focusing on the key English, Spanish, French, German, Italian and Portuguese variants).

It takes a considerable amount of linguistic and onomastic knowledge to assess whether apparently dissimilar names that have been matched might be different transcription variants of the same name, and a considerable amount of careful analysis to identify names that should have matched but did not. Generally speaking, such specific skills and resources are often not available to those charged with evaluating software with a name matching component.

Most Western software evaluators would not be able to recognise that *I*, *Lee*, *Yi*, *Rey* and *Rhee* may all be transcription variants of the same Korean name 이. Similarly, many would not be sufficiently confident to identify that *Zou*, *Zhou*, *Zhuo* and *Zhu* represent totally different Chinese names and should not be matched. Many will know that *Bill* is a nickname for *William* and *Bob* a nickname for *Robert*, but most will not be aware of many of the hypocorisms common in regions other than their own. Few native English speakers, for example, would recognise *Vovan* as a nickname for *Vladimir*, *Shurka* for *Aleksandr*, *Pepe* for *José* or *Paco* for *Francisco*, and fewer still would be able to identify nicknames from more culturally or geographically distant communities.

Given this, a name matching tool with very high recall that matches all these variants could easily be mistakenly rated as imprecise because relevant matches are incorrectly assessed as false positive hits. Conversely, false negatives often remain undetected as, for example, testers may not question the lack of hits when searching for *Fransisco*, even if they are aware that *Paco* is in the database, because they do not recognise the connection between the two names.

In many cases, negative results may be overlooked altogether in the evaluation process as purchasing organisations may limit their evaluation to an examination of true and false positive hits. The inherent invisibility of false negative results and the obvious nuisance of false positive results (real or perceived) have lead many organisations to shy away from any kind of fuzzy matching technology, despite the risks involved in under-matching.

Evaluating the way identity matches are prioritised on a hit list also requires linguistic knowledge, as names that are linguistically related should be ranked more highly than their spelling might suggest. As a good identity matching system should combine the strength of the name match with the strength of matches in other identity characteristics to calculate a rating for the overall identity match, the evaluation of hit prioritisation requires both linguistic and mathematical expertise. However, the evaluation is rarely extended to the ranking of each hit in the hit lists, despite the impact that this can have on the efficiency of resources used to review each match.

This topic is discussed further in Chapter 13, which provides some practical advice on the evaluation of identity matching solutions.

8.7.4 Lack of Standards and Guidance

A final key reason for the continued use of G1 Methods is the lack of visible incentive to upgrade. As previously mentioned, there is no accepted standard for the requirements of name matching systems, and regulators have been markedly reluctant to offer any guidance on what is expected. As a result, those tools which are widely used have become the market-standard, often providing their users with a level of comfort that is not supported by their actual performance.

The situation is particularly unclear in the financial services sector, where stringent penalties may be applied for negligently undertaking transactions with sanctioned or otherwise high-risk parties but no guidance exists as to how name matching should be implemented in order to avoid these penalties. While it is clear to most financial institutions that an exact match is insufficient, few have the resources to scrutinise the long hit lists resulting from excessively fuzzy matching, and where exactly the line should be drawn is left to the discretion of the individual organisations.

While regulators remain reticent about sufficient standards of matching and the only industry standard is based on legacy purchasing decisions, there is little immediate incentive for many organisations to re-evaluate their name matching tools. This is particularly so in the light of the financial situation of recent years and the resource implications that this will have for several years to come.

Though regulators have so far declined to provide advice on the minimum standard of matching required, they have been quick to criticise organisations in cases where they believe the minimum standard has not been met. Some level of guidance would undoubtedly be useful before penalties are incurred. Chapter 14 returns to this topic and introduces the concept of a Linguistic Search Standard.

Chapter 9: Second Generation Name Matching Methods

9.1 Introduction

Second generation name matching methods (G2 Methods) are direct progressions from G1 Methods. They have solved some of the most obvious problems of their predecessors and, as a result, provide marked improvements in both precision and recall. For the most part, they represent relatively recent developments and so have been designed with more modern technological capabilities in mind. Overall, they provide clear advantages over G1 Methods, but the market has not adopted them as enthusiastically as might have been expected.

One reason for this may be that the advent of G2 Methods cannot really be seen as a conceptual revolution in identity matching theory. In much the same way as the early tweaking of the original G1 Methods, G2 Methods represent a technology-driven optimisation of existing solutions; neither linguistics nor onomastic research feature strongly in their design. Examples of their benefits are usually given with reference to familiar examples from the Anglo-Saxon community, while the true global context of international name matching continues to be held at arm's length.

That said, G2 Methods do offer considerable improvements over the original techniques. The following sections describe how G2 Methods have evolved from their predecessors and discuss the practical implications of these advancements for name matching processes.

9.2 G2 Pattern Matching: Advancements of Edit Distance and N-Gram Methods

9.2.1 Advancements on the Original Pattern Matching Metrics

The Damerau-Levenshtein Distance is a widely adopted modification of the original Levenshtein Distance metric that extends the basic edit operations to include character transpositions. It recognises that the transposition of two adjacent characters is a common typing error and is therefore of less significance than the two basic edit operations that the original Levenshtein Distance metric considers it to be. This improves recall by extending the classes of typo covered at each edit distance tolerance level. Looked at another way, it also enhances precision by allowing the tolerance to be set at a lower level than would otherwise be necessary to cover transposition errors.

Other enhancements to Edit Distance metrics have addressed one of the key drawbacks of using the Levenshtein Distance algorithm for matching names: the lack of discrimination between various types of character differences. These advancements have allowed for flexible edit costs based on the characteristics of the letters involved. Some algorithms weight character replacements based on their visual similarity; for example, the replacement of a *g* with a *q*, or an *i* with an *l*, might be downgraded based on the fact that these characters look similar in some fonts. Such techniques are particularly useful when matching data sourced from poor quality document images. Other enhancements, known as Keyboard or Typewriter Distance metrics, weight character operations based on the keyboard position of the letters involved. Enhancement in this way significantly improves the precision of the edit distance metric by recognising that the probability of most typing errors can be predicted based on the layout of the keyboard being used. A lower edit distance is calculated for character differences that are more likely to result from inaccurate keyboard use.

Other techniques have addressed the presence or absence of spaces. This can be helpful in dealing with linguistic variants of compound names, such as *Hans Peter/Hanspeter* or *Abdul Rahman/Abdul-Rahman*, and non-linguistic typos, such as *Lawson/Law son*.

Some other extensions to traditional edit distance metrics have incorporated the phonetic capabilities of Soundex-type methods to reflect the phonetic similarity of the characters involved in spelling variations. For example, Editex calculates a lower distance for a replacement if the replaced characters are pronounced in a similar way, so that *Allsop* and *Allsob* show a higher congruence than *Allsop* and *Allsos* because *b* and *p* belong to the same phonetic class. Other efforts have taken this concept further by comparing words and names based on the syllables they contain rather than the individual characters involved.

However, most of these methods use limited phonetic rules similar to those described in Chapter 8 for the original Soundex algorithm. As a result, though phonetically enhanced string comparison algorithms represent a clear improvement over standard pattern matching techniques, many of the limitations described for Soundex also apply to these methods.

N-gram methods have also been used as the basis for a number of G2 techniques. An example of this is the Positional n-gram metric, which takes into account the position of matching n-grams within the name as a whole; n-grams are only considered congruent if they occur at similar positions within the name.

To some extent, the Jaro-Winkler Distance also takes into account the position of congruent characters. Based on the statistical finding that typos are less likely to occur at the beginning of a word, it considers all of the congruent characters within two names and applies a higher weighting to matching characters at the start of a name than to those at the end. This method also recognises the effect of transpositions, thereby improving recall as a reduced penalty is applied for transposed characters. However, using this algorithm, a transposition is often defined as two characters transposed anywhere within the name, as opposed to two adjacent transposed characters. This broader definition of character transposition has a negative effect on precision when applied to the matching of proper names.

9.2.2 The Effectiveness of G2 Pattern Matching Methods in Name Matching

The extensions that have developed from the original pattern matching metrics can be categorised into two classes: those which seek to optimise the distance metrics for dealing with typos and other non-linguistic spelling errors, and those which seek to introduce some element of phonetic tolerance into the metrics.

The measures that have sought to optimise the handling of typing errors and other non-linguistically driven spelling variations have done so in the following ways:

- by allowing a more appropriate treatment for transposed characters
- by allowing for the presence of absence of spaces in names
- by considering the visual similarity of the deviating characters
- by considering the effects of keyboard layout on the occurrence of typos
- by considering the significance of the position of character deviation within names

These enhancements have clearly improved the ability to match names containing non-linguistically driven spelling variations and have done so without disproportionately increasing the complexity of the edit distance concept.

The second class of enhancements, those which seek to introduce an element of phonetic matching to the edit distance metrics can be viewed in different ways. On the one hand, the introduction of phonetic tolerance is undoubtedly a step forward. It is far preferable to ignoring the phonetic similarities that make some characters much more likely to be confused than others. In the absence of other phonetic matching techniques, these enhancements provide significant advantages over their G1 counterparts. However, advancements in this direction can only be taken so far, given the limited possibility to take into account the phonetic context of each character without making the metric unworkably complex.

This greatly restricts the potential of these methods, as the context of each character is of crucial importance in determining the pronunciation of a name and cannot be ignored when attempting to identify phonetically similar names. For example, the homophone names *Fenleigh* and *Phenlea* require several edit operations in order to be matched. These could be:

- the replacement of *f* with *p*
- the addition of *h* and *a*
- the removal of *i*, *g* and *h*

Tolerance for the same edit operations without consideration of context would also match *Tegilforth* with *Thelporta*, names which are clearly not phonetically similar.

An edit distance metric that could match transcription variants would require an even more detailed consideration of context. This can be demonstrated using variants of the name of the last president of the Soviet Union. In English transcription, he is mostly referred to as *Gorbachev*, while German texts are likely to show his name as *Gorbatschow*. The edit operations required to match these two variants are:

- the elimination of *t*
- the elimination of *s*
- the replacement of *o* with *e*
- the replacement of *w* with *v*

If a metric were designed that downgraded these operations so that *Gorbachev* and *Gorbatschow* could be matched, it would also match many names that are unrelated, such as *Montewis* and *Menevi*. In order to avoid this reduction in precision, the context of each character needs to be taken into consideration. For example, the *t* and *s* should only be eliminated when forming part of the substring *tsch* and only when matching names from particular linguistic origins.

However, if such detailed context consideration were to be included in an edit distance metric, it would lose its two most attractive characteristics: its simplicity and its transparency. In addition, the technical implications of increasing the complexity of an edit distance metric in this way make it unlikely that appropriate performance could be achieved in terms of speed and efficiency of resource utilisation. For these reasons, it seems appropriate to leave string comparison metrics to what they do best – the handling of non-linguistically driven spelling variations – and to seek alternative methods for handling transcription variants and phonetically similar names.

9.3 G2 Phonetic Encoding: Advancements on Soundex

9.3.1 The Advancements of Recent Decades

Chapter 8 described Soundex as an early attempt to generate phonetic codes representing the pronunciation of names. Its shortcomings have long been recognised and many variations have been produced, some of which introduced a limited consideration of character context. For example, using the NYSIIS Soundex method, *Kn* at the start of a name becomes *Nn,* in recognition of the fact that the *K* is silent in this context, and the prefix *Mac* becomes *Mcc,* in recognition of the common spelling variation *Mac/Mc.*

The genealogists Daitch and Mokotoff developed the D-M Soundex algorithm in 1985 after having found the traditional Soundex method to be poor at matching names of Jewish or Slavic origin. The algorithm introduced several advancements, including the extension of the code to 6 characters to increase its precision and the encoding of the previously fixed initial character. Importantly, the algorithm also allowed the generation of multiple similarity keys per name, to account for multiple alternative pronunciations.

Many other variants of the original Soundex algorithm have been developed for specific practical applications, including the Kölner Phonetik algorithm, which focuses on phonetic similarities in German names. However, none of the Soundex variants that have been developed over the years effectively address the significant precision issues faced by all Soundex-type algorithms.

9.3.2 Metaphone and Double Metaphone

The Metaphone algorithm was developed by Lawrence Phillips in the early nineties and consisted of more numerous and specific simplification rules than the earlier phonetic encoding systems. It recognised 16 different consonant sounds and introduced some important considerations of character context. For example, a *c* may be equated with an *s* if followed by an *h* or a relevant vowel combination. Similarly, a *d* may be equated with a *j* if followed by a *g* and a relevant vowel. Though far from comprehensive, the phonetic rules incorporated in the Metaphone algorithm represented a significant step forward in phonetic encoding techniques. Despite the advantages of Metaphone over earlier methods, its author soon recognised a number of drawbacks and later created the more flexible Double-Metaphone algorithm.

Double-Metaphone is so-called owing to its use of an optional secondary similarity key. For each name, the standard American pronunciation is considered in the primary key and an alternative key may be produced to represent the most common alternative pronunciation in the US. It is frequently names derived from outside the Anglo-Saxon community that generate this optional key, which usually reflects an approximation of the native pronunciation. For example, the name *Kuczewski* has two common pronunciations in the US, *Kuh-zoo-ski* and *Kut-chef-ski* (approximated using common English phonetic conventions), so it returns keys representing both of these possible pronunciations.

Despite its considerable advantages, the Double Metaphone algorithm also has some important limitations. Although the first character is not fixed as it is under Soundex, all initial vowel sounds are represented with an *A* and others are largely ignored, so that *Alice*, *Elsa* and *Ullos* all yield the code *ALS* despite their lack of phonetic similarity.

In addition, the restriction to pronunciation prevalent in the US means that it is of limited use in matching names not widely used in the US population. For example, the French homophones *Bodins* and *Baudaint* would not match, as *Bodins* produces the code PTNS, while *Baudaint* is represented as PTNT. This last is the same code generated by *Padanot*, which is clearly not phonetically similar using either French or English pronunciation.

There is a common misconception in the market that Double Metaphone can be used to match transcription variants. Though improvements over Soundex' performance in this area are evident, they are largely the result of improved phonetic capabilities coupled with the fact that some transcription variants also happen to be phonetically similar. For example, Double Metaphone identifies the phonetic similarity between *Yeltsin* and *Eltsine* (ALTS) but does not recognise the connection to *Jelzin* (which has the primary code JLSN) because this transcription variant is not phonetically similar using Anglo-Saxon conventions. The secondary code for *Jelzin* is ALSN, which does recognise the alternative pronunciation of the *j* in some languages as a sound similar to the English *y* but ignores the harder *ts*-like sound of the German *z*. Transcription variants of many names do not match at all using Double Metaphone, including *Gorbachev* (KRPX / KRPK) and *Gorbatschow* (KRPT), *Jamal* (JML / AML) and *Djamal* (TJML), and *Zedong* (STNK) and *Tsetung* (TSTN).

9.3.3 The Effectiveness of G2 Phonetic Encoding in Name Matching

Double-Metaphone is the most popular and sophisticated of the G2 phonetic encoding techniques and so forms the basis for this discussion of the suitability of such methods for modern name matching processes. It has improved on the original phonetic algorithms in three areas.

In the first place, its ability to generate a secondary code provides a greater flexibility in dealing with alternative pronunciations than is possible with single phonetic codes. That said, its limitation to two possible alternative pronunciations restricts this flexibility and reflects a continued focus on pronunciation used in the US population.

The second area in which Double-Metaphone represents an improvement over techniques such as Soundex is in its consideration of pronunciation other than the Anglo-Saxon. However, the name variants considered in the development of the Double-Metaphone algorithm have been largely restricted to those from cultures with significant populations in the US, and the phonetic variants accounted for are mostly those prevalent in American speech (though in some cases the alternative pronunciation key may approximate one of the native pronunciations). Given the demographics of the US, relatively less consideration has been afforded to variants of names from African and Asian languages, and many phonetic features of European languages are also not fully covered. As a result, Double Metaphone cannot be said to be a truly international phonetic matching algorithm, despite its consideration of some non-Anglo-Saxon phonetic conventions.

Lastly, Double-Metaphone's enhancements include further consideration of the context of each individual character when generating the phonetic codes. Though the enhancements in this area represent a marked improvement over the original phonetic encoding techniques, they cannot be described as a complete phonetic matching solution. This would require a much wider consideration of character context as well as a more in-depth coverage of a larger number of languages.

Extending the algorithm to cover transcription variants would require a broader consideration of character context still, to account for the multiple combinations of possible source and target languages, as well as a flexible treatment of word borders to allow the matching of transcription variants such as *Abdurrahman* and *Abdul Rahman*.

Overall, there is no doubt that Double-Metaphone represents a significant improvement over early phonetic algorithms, though its restricted language focus continues to limit its performance as a method for matching homophones in a global context. In addition, it does not intentionally target transcription variants so its performance when matching these is limited to matching variants which would be pronounced similarly using the phonetic conventions on which it is based.

Double-Metaphone's ability to match derivative names and non-linguistic spelling errors is similarly limited to those that happen to be pronounced the same way in the US. As a result, although it is often perceived to be a substantially complete name matching algorithm, Double-Metaphone actually only partly covers phonetically similar names and any coverage of the other three major classes of variation in names occurs more by chance than by design. It is a very popular algorithm and outperforms many of its contemporary methods in the matching of homophones prevalent in the US, but it should be borne in mind that these represent only a small proportion of the variations that may be seen in proper names globally.

9.4 Generative Algorithms for Name Variants

9.4.1 The Theory Behind the Generation of Name Variants

The onomastic thesauri used in G1 matching methods were compiled by researching recognised name variants of more commonly used names. An improvement on this method is the use of generative algorithms to automatically generate variations of names. This is based on the theory that it is possible to define rules that will generate valid linguistic variants for a specified name. The rules are created based on an analysis of the underlying causes of variations in names and must contain both an analytic element, to check whether the conditions required for the generation of a specific variation are present, and a generative element, to produce the prescribed variations.

Generative algorithms can be applied to the name matching process in two ways. In the first, they can be used to automatically generate variations of names present in a pre-existing thesaurus. The variants are then used to expand the search query in the same way as those manually collected under G1 Methods. The disadvantage of this method of application is that the thesaurus is completed horizontally but not vertically: additional variants are generated for names captured through manual research, but no variants for new, unresearched names are generated.

The alternative method of application addresses this. The generative algorithms are embedded directly into the matching process so that the search profile can be expanded with variants of the name entered without recourse to a thesaurus. In this way, the variants considered in the search are not limited to variants of names that have been collected in a thesaurus. Whichever method of application is chosen, it is relatively simple to combine the use of generative algorithms with other search techniques, such as pattern matching or phonetic encoding, in order to realise a more flexible search. There may, however, be some impact on performance, depending on the number of variants generated.

9.4.2 Application Examples

The name *Müller* provides a simple example of linguistic variation. There are two common transcriptions for the German umlaut (indicated by a trema over a vowel, as in *ä*, *ö* or *ü*). In a data system that is unable to accept the trema, the diacritic may be replaced by inserting an *e* after the vowel so that *ä*, *ö* and *ü* become *ae*, *oe* and *ue*. Frequently, though less correctly, the umlaut diacritic is simply omitted, so that *ä*, *ö* and *ü* become *a*, *o* and *u*. A simple algorithm can be designed based on these alternatives and can be used without consideration of character context as no alternative treatments apply. The algorithm would generate the variants *Mueller* and *Muller* for *Müller*.

As soon as a name contains more than one characteristic for which variation is possible, the number of potential variants increases rapidly. This is because particular characteristics that can be the subject of variation are usually not mutually dependent, so variants must be generated for each possible combination of variation characteristics. The consequences of this can be demonstrated using the Arabic name *Abdurrahman* (عبد الرحمن). The table below describes the eight most important transcription phenomena when transcribing this name into the Latin script. Each of these could be used to derive a separate generative rule.

The right-hand column shows the number of variants that would be generated by the isolated application of each rule. Although no individual rule generates more than five variations, the total number of variants that could be generated by considering all possible combinations of the transcription characteristics listed here is 6,480.

Variation Characteristic	**Number of Variants**	
The *A* in the string *Abd* is sometimes preceded with an apostrophe, indicating that the underlying Arabic letter is an Ayn (ع) rather than, for example, an Alif (ا).	**2**	*Abdurrahman* *'Abdurrahman*
The *u*-sound between two consonants is commonly represented as a *u* but can also be expressed as *ou* (mostly in a francophone context) or as an *oo* (which is more common in an anglophone context). In the context of the *Abd-al-* construction, the sound is also often represented using *e* or *a*.	**5**	*Abdul Rahman* *Abdoul Rahman* *Abdool Rahman* *Abdel Rahman* *Abdal Rahman*
The Arabic equivalent of *R* in *Rahman* is a solar letter and as such has an effect on the pronunciation of the preceding article *al*. The *l* in *al* is not pronounced and the solar letter is doubled. This phonetic particularity is not reflected in the (unvocalised) Arabic spelling. In transcription it may be ignored (so that the *l* and *r* both remain), fully reflected (leaving a double *r*) or partly reflected (by the simple omission of the *l* without the doubling of the *r*).	**3**	*Abdulrahman* *Abdurrahman* *Abdurahman*
The Arabic letter ح is most often transcribed as *h* but may also be transcribed as *kh* or *ch*.	**3**	*Abdurrahman* *Abdurrakhman* *Abdurrachman*
The first and/or the last *a* in *Rahman* is sometimes omitted, as it has no representation in the (unvocalised) Arabic standard writing.	**4**	*Abdurrahman* *Abdurrhman* *Abdurrahmn* *Abdurrhmn*
An *e* may be added to the end of the name to indicate that the substring is not to be pronounced as a nasal vowel. This occurs mainly in a francophone context.	**2**	*Abdurrahman* *Abdurrahmane*

Continued ...

Variation Characteristic	Number of Variants	
The first and the second name elements, *Abd al*, can be written together or may be separated by a hyphen or a space.	3	*Abdalrahman* *Abd-Alrahman* *Abd Alrahman*
The same applies to the second and third name elements, *al Rahman*, which can also be written together or separated by a hyphen or space.	3	*Abdulrahman* *Abdul-Rahman* *Abdul Rahman*
Total possible combinations: 2 x 5 x 3 x 3 x 4 x 2 x 3 x 3 = 6,480		

Table 9.1: Eight generative rules for the example name Abdurrahman (عبد الرحمن), showing the number of variants generated per rule and in total.

The total of 6,480 variations is the result of multiplying all possible variations per rule. Although not all of these variations are used with the same probability or frequency in real life, they each represent a plausible transcription variant of the same name. In addition, the above table greatly simplifies the transcription possibilities for the name عبد الرحمن and the 6,480 variants generated by these rules would not cover all possible transcription variants. Variants that are common in Sub-Saharan Africa, such as *Abdirrahman*, or in Iranian language areas, such as *Abdorrahman*, or the Central Asian variants that have been transcribed via an extra loop through Cyrillic, such as *Abduraxman* or *Abdurakhmanov*, are not covered. Possible variants combining the name with standard Arabic name tags, such as *Abuabdurrahman* or *Binabdurrahman* are also not covered.

To further complicate matters, *Abdurrahman* is often just one element of a name that contains several parts, each of which can be transcribed in multiple ways. If all combinations of all variants for each part are considered the potential number of full name variants can be vast. And therein lies the difficulty with the generative algorithm model for global name matching; the sheer volume of variants that would be generated by truly comprehensive rule sets would have a significant negative impact on system performance. It is not so much the generation of the variants that causes the problem, but rather the expansion of the search with all the additional name variants generated. This applies both to the use of thesauri containing automatically generated variants and to the expansion of the search profile by generating variants of the search name.

The simple example of *Müller* and the more complex *Abdurrahman* example provide an indication of the possibilities and limitations of using generative algorithms for matching linguistic name variants. Theoretically, such algorithms can also be used for matching non-linguistic variations, but this could only realistically be done for very simple spelling errors. For the average name, attempting to cover variations with an edit distance of more than one would result in the generation of an impractical number of variants to be searched.

That said, it would be technically possible to cover the more specific classes of typing error using this method. For any name, the number of variants containing simple character transpositions is one less than the number of characters in the original name. The eight letter name *Thompson*, for example, contains the seven transposition variants *Htompson*, *Tohmpson*, *Thmopson*, *Thopmson*, *Thomspon*, *Thomposn* and *Thompsno*. The number of simple omissions is the number of characters in the name: eight in the example of Thompson. However, introducing character replacements or insertions greatly increases the number of variants to be generated.

The number of simple replacements is 25 times the number of characters in the name if replacements are limited to the 26 basic letters in the Latin alphabet. This would generate 200 replacement variants for the name *Thompson*. The number of character insertions is higher still. There are nine possible insertion positions in the name *Thompson* and 26 characters that could be inserted, assuming the same restriction to the basic Latin alphabet. This would generate 226 insertion variants for the name *Thompson* (not quite 9 x 26 as some insertions would result in the same variant; for example, inserting an *s* between the *p* and the *s* would give the same variant, *Thompsson*, as inserting an *s* between the *s* and the *o*).

The advantage of covering non-linguistic spelling errors using generative algorithms is that the variants generated can easily be combined with techniques designed to cover linguistic variants. This would, for example, allow the matching of transcription variants containing basic typing errors. For example, the name *Gorbachev* should match to the transcription variant *Gorbatschow*. Using generative algorithms to match character transpositions would allow *Gorbachev* to be matched to transcription variants containing transposed characters, such as *Gorbastchow*, relatively easily.

Clearly, however, there is a limit to the number of typo classes which can be accounted for in this way. Though the time taken to match one name in most modern matching systems is now measured in milliseconds, very large numbers of variants are likely to have a noticeable impact on performance. Realistically, an edit distance of one is at the limit of what could be covered this way in most matching processes. Chapter 10 looks more closely at the possibilities for using generative algorithms to match non-linguistic variations and considers the impact of restricting the classes of error to be covered based on keyboard layout and other factors.

In more time-sensitive processes, such as the real-time screening of banking transactions, even extending the search time by a matter of milliseconds may have a marked impact on overall performance. However, depending on the risks involved, it may not be considered appropriate to extend the fuzziness of the search in real-time processes to cover combined linguistic and non-linguistic variations, such as *Yeltsin* and *Jezlin* (a transcription variant with a character transposition). Building such tolerances into high-volume processes is only appropriate in situations where the risk of missing a broader match outweighs the costs associated with the increased need for manual hit review and the additional time added to the process as a whole.

At this point it is also worth mentioning that, although modern technology allows searches on large databases to be carried out in a fraction of a second, in practice many search applications do not achieve this speed. There are many reasons for this, including poor system design, insufficient hardware capabilities, network limitations and the need for compatibility with related legacy systems. Any system that struggles to carry out an identity search in the expected time frame would suffer greater performance impairment if large numbers of variants were used to expand the search.

9.4.3 The Effectiveness of G2 Generative Algorithms in Name Matching

The basic concept of using generative algorithms to expand name searches is functionally sound and has the important advantage that it can be used without complication in conjunction with other name matching techniques. The quality of the results provided by this type of search is directly related to the quality of the rule sets used to generate the variants. Quality, in this sense, is defined by two factors, the first being how comprehensively the rule sets cover all relevant linguistic and onomastic phenomena. Unfortunately, with substantially comprehensive rule sets there is a danger of generating unnecessary name variants and thereby producing excessive amounts of false positive results. The rule sets would need to contain thousands of rules in order to cover the most significant linguistic phenomena and could only be practically employed in conjunction with strict analytical conditions controlling their application.

This ability to apply the appropriate linguistic treatment in a targeted manner is the second aspect that defines the quality of the rule sets and can be more clearly explained using an example. There are many cases where *j* can be replaced with *y*, or *u* can be replaced with *o*, to create valid linguistic variants, as in *Jan/Yan*, *Yeltsin/Jelzin*, *Mohamad/Muhamad* or *Hossein/Hussein*. However, such generative rules must be controlled by a strict analytical component that prevents them being applied, for example, to match the Spanish name *Juan* with the Chinese name *Yuan* or the English name *Joan*. This is particularly important when very common names are involved; it may be appropriate for the analytical component to employ a thesaurus containing name distribution information so that this aspect can be considered.

As a result of the complexities involved in generating all appropriate variants while avoiding unnecessary ones, the skills required to create and maintain the rule sets are considerable. The tuning of both the analytical and generative components is particularly challenging and requires the close cooperation of regionally specialised linguists, computational linguists and technical specialists. Without this close cooperation, it is not possible to transform the detailed linguistic and onomastic concepts into functional rule sets.

Creating these rule sets is therefore a time-consuming and costly process and, even with the support of such skilled technicians, the complexities of global names and the huge number of ways in which they can vary mean that there is a practical limit to the reliability and precision that can be achieved in a matching system designed this way. In addition, the large numbers of variants generated may cause performance issues, another factor that has dampened market enthusiasm for such techniques. As a result, matching systems based on generative algorithms are not as widely available in the market as some of their less sophisticated counterparts.

9.5 Summary of the Application of Second Generation Matching Methods

This chapter has discussed methods that represent a clear progression from G1 Methods. Despite their advantages, G2 Methods have largely failed to gain the market share that might be expected for such theoretically improved techniques.

One reason for this is the ongoing popularity of the more conceptually simple G1 Methods, as was discussed in section 8.7.

However, a further reason for the limited adoption of G2 Methods is the fact that they do not represent a real breakthrough in the way names are matched. Identity matching components are often embedded into complex software suites and switching costs can be high. In many cases, it could be considered that the advantages afforded by G2 Methods are simply not sufficient to warrant the cost of embedding new techniques. The charts below show that, despite improved matching capabilities, no G2 Method is able to consistently match transcription variants, name derivatives or phonetically similar names in a reliable way.

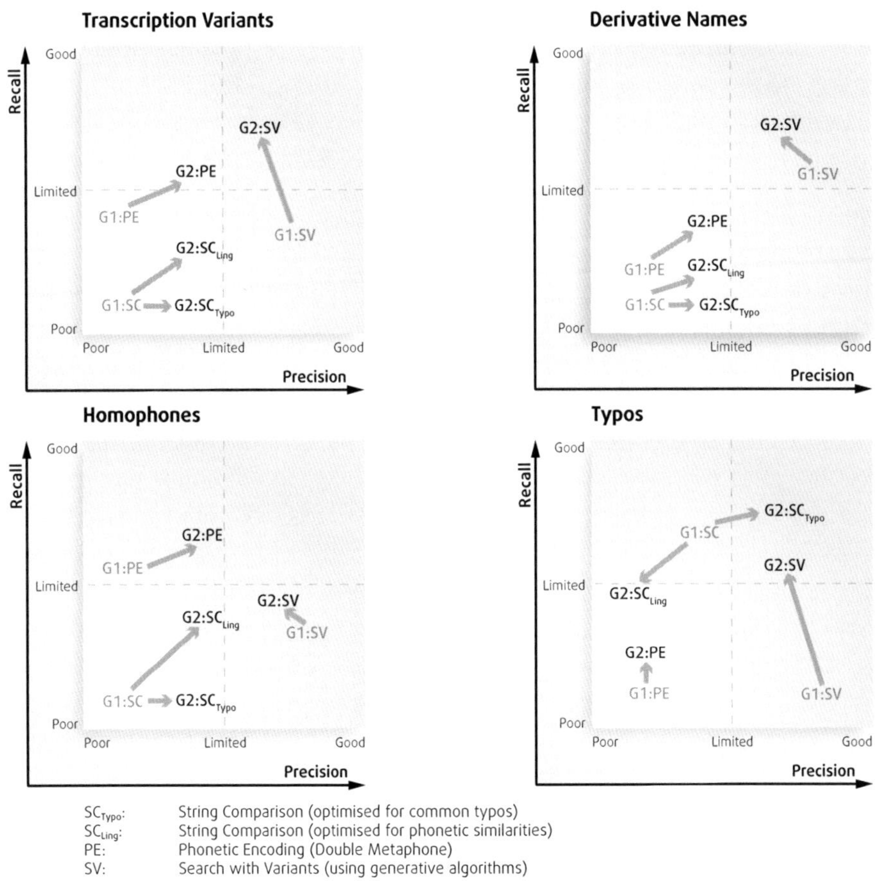

Figure 9.1: Relative performance of G2 Methods when matching each of the four main classes of variations in names.

The optimisation of string comparison methods for matching non-linguistic spelling variations has been relatively successful in matching non-linguistic variations. However, their phonetic enhancement has had a more muted effect in matching homophones owing to the restricted phonetic intelligence on which they are based and, in particular, the lack of consideration of the context of each character. Improvements in the matching of transcription variants are largely due to the fact that many variants of this type are also phonetically similar, as no consistent efforts have been made to cover transcription variants in the algorithms.

Phonetic encoding with Double-Metaphone has been more successful at matching phonetically similar names, but the results are still unsatisfactory in a truly global context as a result of the limited linguistic focus of the algorithm, which is broadly based on pronunciation standards in the US. The coverage of transcription variants is also not a specific focus of the Double-Metaphone algorithm, though it has achieved some success with the more phonetically similar transcription variants. Phonetic encoding systems in general are not designed to deal with non-linguistically motivated spelling errors and their performance in matching this kind of variation is relatively poor.

The performance of generative algorithms is heavily dependent on the quality and linguistic coverage of the rules used to generate the name variants. Assuming that these have been developed with appropriate input from language specialists and computational linguists, these methods have the potential to significantly improve recall when matching linguistically-motivated variations, though some impairment in precision is inevitable as compared to the use of G1 Thesauri. The improvement in recall is more marked when the generated variants are used to expand the search profile than when they are used to expand a name variant thesaurus. However, many of the generative tools available on the market have been developed with limited linguistic input, so the potential improvement in recall of these methods is not often achieved in practice. Even if this were not the case, the vast number of potential transcription variants and phonetically similar names makes it unlikely that linguistically motivated variants could ever be covered in a truly performant way using these techniques. For similar reasons, only a limited selection of non-linguistically motivated spelling errors can be effectively covered using generative algorithms, though this approach does have the technical advantage of being easy to combine with other matching methods.

9.6 Conclusion: Three Decades of Name Matching

The computer-based matching of international identity data has been carried out on a large scale since the 1980s. Since then many different methods have been suggested, tested and enhanced, and over the last decade, automated name matching techniques have been incorporated into ever-increasing numbers of business processes.

All of the methods discussed so far address some of the requirements of global name matching and all of them feature a number of weaknesses. Some of the original limitations have been the subject of significant conceptual improvements over the years, but no real revolution has been achieved in terms of addressing linguistically driven variations in names. Overall, it seems that name matching science has gone as far as it can go through the incremental adjustment of the techniques currently in use. This is not necessarily surprising, given that none of the G1 or G2 Methods were designed based on a comprehensive analysis of the types of variations that exist within global names. Some were not even designed with the matching of name data in mind.

From this perspective the situation can be compared with that of children playing football with an old tin can. The game can be enjoyed for a while, and from time to time a really good shot may be played, but there is no getting away from the fact that the can was designed for another purpose. Major improvements can only be achieved by switching to a real ball, designed with scoring goals in mind. Using this analogy, the next chapter kicks away the individual methods that have served their purpose until now and looks at the requirements for a comprehensive, purpose-built solution.

Chapter 10: Third Generation Name Matching Methods

10.1 Introduction

The previous chapters have demonstrated that none of the main sources of variation in names can be comprehensively covered by any combination of G1 or G2 Methods. Nowhere is this more apparent than in the coverage of linguistic variations, particularly those caused by the use of different transcription standards. This is to be expected, given the limited role that linguistics and onomastics played in the development of the original matching methods and the fact that many G2 Methods represent technology-driven enhancements of their earlier counterparts.

Name matching solutions of the third generation (G3 Solutions) differ from G2 Methods in that they do not simply build on an existing matching technique. Instead, the starting point for G3 Solutions is a careful examination of all the different classes of variation within names. This is the core of the paradigm shift which sets G3 Solutions apart from their predecessors: the solution design follows a comprehensive analysis of the causes of variation in spelling.

As a result, G3 Solutions focus on ensuring that all major sources of variation are each addressed in the most effective way. For the most part, these different variation sources are rooted in linguistic phenomena: in the idiosyncrasies of the languages, writing systems and naming conventions of the world. A core focus on these international cultural and linguistic aspects is a defining characteristic of G3 Solutions.

Much work has been carried out to assess the various advantages and limitations of G1 and G2 name matching methods; this can be drawn upon to help identify those methods that effectively cover particular types of variation and thereby deserve a role in G3 Solutions. There is no doubt that G1 and G2 Methods have contributed some promising approaches to the matching of proper names and, owing to their long-standing prevalence in the market, considerable experience has been gained in their use. However, given the well-documented limitations of these traditional techniques, the new generation of matching solutions must also include some new ideas to cover the variation phenomena that earlier methods have not effectively addressed. The paradigm shift therefore reflects a move away from individual matching methods towards a search for the optimum blend of traditional techniques and innovative solutions that is equipped for handling all sources of variation in names.

This chapter starts by taking a step back from the individual methods of the earlier generations to examine the principal requirements for a G3 Solution. It goes on to introduce the use of linguistic similarity keys for matching transcription variants and phonetically similar names before looking at the ways in which matching methods from earlier generations can best be harnessed to cover the remaining sources of variation.

10.2 Principle Requirements for G3 Solutions

To be worthy of the G3 label, a matching solution should meet certain principal requirements. These can be split between the general requirements, valid for any search solution, and the specific requirements, designed to ensure that the particular linguistic challenges of matching identity data are addressed.

The overview given below describes these requirements in qualitative terms, as in any practical application, the quantitative parameters must be defined against the specific context of the overall business process. Similarly, for the purposes of evaluating a particular matching system, each requirement must be quantified based on the risks and costs involved in the relevant process. Methods for evaluating different search tools are discussed in Chapter 13.

10.2.1 General Requirements

The general requirements for G3 Solutions are valid for any data-searching situation. They are derived from practical experience and reflect the minimum expectations that users typically have of their search tools.

Reliability, precision and performance with regard to all relevant classes of variation

A search solution should be able to match data that features any or all of the relevant classes of variation, either in the search term or in the data to be searched.

The term "fuzzy matching" has become unpopular in recent years as it has come to be associated with over-matching and the increased effort involved in dealing with excessive false positive results. However, it is widely recognised that simply performing an exact match is rarely sufficient to manage the relevant risks. Where exactly the line should be drawn between these two considerations depends on the particular circumstances of each business process. The relevant variation classes must be dealt with as efficiently as possible, effectively identifying the appropriate records while minimising false positive results. The performance of the system should be optimised so that the required recall and precision are achieved within an acceptable time frame.

Primacy of recall

In general, methods that improve recall at the expense of significantly poorer precision should be avoided. However, in cases of conflict, recall should generally be afforded the highest priority. A solution which generates a limited number of irrelevant hits can be tolerated, but one which fails to identify the appropriate records will rightly never reach acceptance as a G3 Solution. This requirement points away from the use of thesauri as a primary matching method as, however carefully researched, they are unlikely to contain all variants of all names. This is particularly the case given the number of names that are relatively rare and the huge vocabulary that can be involved in the names of legal entities and other groups. Thesauri can be an invaluable complement to G3 Solutions, to cover the matching of derivative name forms or to provide statistics on name distribution, but carefully designed linguistic rules better fulfil the requirement to prioritise recall as they are able to deal with any search name, whether or not it has previously been researched.

Fully flexible configurability

A high degree of configurability is crucial for a matching solution to be deployable across a wide range of business processes, enterprises, industries and countries. Different scenarios will each have characteristics that will determine the way the functions and data components in a matching solution should most appropriately be configured. The goals of each process, the risks involved and the intensity of its usage will vary, and with these the tolerance for false negative and false positive results. The expertise of users and the resources available for the review of results will also vary, as will the data to be matched, for example in its volume or degree of standardisation. All these features highlight the need for full configurability and an adjustable search accuracy to ensure that costs and risks can be appropriately balanced in any business area.

Consistent rating of hit quality

A search system should provide a consistent way for the hits it produces to be identified and prioritised. A good match should always produce a score above the threshold required for it to appear on a hit list, regardless of the particular names involved or the data fields that are used to search for it. The comparability of match scores across different searches is an important prerequisite for being able pinpoint a certain match score the a cut-off point, below which matches will not be returned as hits. All good matches should consistently appear above this threshold.

To ensure consistency across different data sets, each element of the match score calculation should also be fully configurable. For example, the weight given to each part of the name or penalties applied for different types of variation should be configurable based on data quality. This concept is discussed further in Chapter 12.

10.2.2 Specific Requirements

For an application to be described as a linguistic identity matching solution, it should also meet some more specific requirements. These are derived from an understanding that the key sources of variation in names are essentially linguistic in nature and must be addressed with specific linguistic matching methods.

It is worth noting at this point that the linguistic capabilities used in multilingual full text searches have little in common with the linguistic intelligence required for the matching of proper names. A full text search uses structured information about the semantic and syntactic aspects of the relevant languages, which has effectively no role to play in identity matching. Conversely transcription, a key consideration in the matching of proper names, is largely irrelevant for full text searches. This is because text is mostly translated from one language to another rather than transcribed from one script to another as proper names often are. Even a fully comprehensive multilingual text search application would be unlikely to provide sufficient linguistic capabilities for the reliable matching of proper names in a global context.

Global linguistic coverage

The rules and thesauri employed in a linguistic identity matching solution should be able to match variations of names from all relevant languages and cultural areas of the world. A solution that, for example, deals with European names and names from Eastern Asia but fails to match variants from India or names of Arabic origin is clearly not sufficient for the challenges of today's identity matching processes. A realistic target coverage could be based on the roughly 70 languages that are spoken by at least 10 million people worldwide, perhaps adding some of the less-widely spoken European and Central Asian languages. Coverage of these languages would inherently allow for the matching of names from all major writing systems, which is an important precondition for the matching of transcription variants. In addition, allowing for the variation phenomena in these key languages would provide partial coverage for less widely spoken languages that share some of the same characteristics.

Matching of key romanised variants

The importance of transcription variants in the identity matching process has been emphasised a number of times. Given the prominent role of the Latin script in many identity matching processes, any G3 Solution should be able to match the most significant romanised variants of non-Latin names. These are generally the variants converted using well-established English, Spanish, French, German, Portuguese or Italian transcription standards. Thus *Yeltsin*, *Eltsine*, *Jelzin*, *Iéltsin* and *Elcin* should all match to each other. This capability is often confused with cross-script matching (discussed below) but is one of the most significant requirements for G3 Solutions in its own right.

The ability to match non-Latin script names that have been transcribed into other non-Latin scripts plays a less significant role in many of today's identity matching procedures and so has a lower priority in most matching systems than the ability to match romanised variants.

Cross-script matching capabilities

The ability to match names across different writing systems is important, partly because many organisations maintain records in a non-Latin script, but also because many watch-list issuing bodies are starting to realise that providing the original script version of listed names is the best way to support effective screening. Again, given the prominence of the Latin script in many identity matching processes, the highest priority should be afforded to the matching of names in non-Latin scripts to their romanised counterparts. In order to maintain appropriate recall, this requirement dictates that non-Latin script names should match not only to one romanisation, but to all relevant romanised variants. Thus Ельцин must match not only with *Yeltsin*, but also with *Eltsine*, *Jelzin*, *Iéltsin* and *Elcin*.

Language-specific configurability

Match methods and their options, as well as the integration of rule sets and thesauri, should be configurable based on the cultural origin of the names being matched. This allows for the fact that names of different cultural and linguistic origin display structurally different variation phenomena. Chinese names, for example, need to be handled very differently from names of French origin; a large number of irrelevant hits would result if identical matching methods were applied to both. For this reason, an important analytical function of linguistic rule sets is to determine which variation phenomena might be present, based on the likely cultural and linguistic origin of the names involved.

Field-specific configurability

Match methods, options, rule sets and thesauri should also be configurable separately for each data field so that different settings can be applied to data representing each identity characteristic. Some variation phenomena apply only to certain characteristics and it is important that match methods designed to handle these phenomena are not applied too widely. For example, thesauri designed to match hypocorisms should not be applied to family names so that *Clare Bill* is matched to *Clare William*. Similarly, it may be possible to allow for a wider range of typos in country-related data than is efficient when matching proper names since the number of possible country names and their related adjectives is limited. A partial match in country information is therefore likely to be more significant than a technically similar match in a name.

Matching of names with multiple variations

An identity matching system should be able to match names that contain more than one source of variation. For example, if it is accepted that transcription variants, such as *Yeltsin* and *Jelzin*, should match and that names containing transposed characters, as in *Yeltsin* and *Yetlsin*, should match, then it could also be expected that transcription variants containing transposition errors should match.

The system should therefore be able to match *Yetlsin* with *Jelzin*, albeit with an appropriately downgraded match score.

Linguistically-driven match scoring

The match score that rates the quality of each hit should be based on linguistically defined criteria. The comparison of each separate identity characteristic, or part thereof, should be assigned scores based on two essential factors: significance and congruence.

The significance of a particular characteristic comparison represents its information weight, or how distinctive the characteristics involved are. In linguistic terms, the significance of a particular comparison is low if it involves less distinctive elements, such as common given or family names, or abbreviated elements like initials. The significance is higher if it involves more distinguishing characteristics such as a rare family name. The use of thesauri for determining the rareness of particular name elements is less problematic than their use in the core matching process; if the name is not present in a well-researched thesaurus it can be assumed to be relatively uncommon.

In most cases, a name match can be said to be more significant than a matching nationality or year of birth, though this may also depend on the distinctiveness of the name. For example, a match in Vietnamese data on the surname *Nguyễn* is less significant than a birth-year match as this surname is shared by approximately 40% of the population.

The congruence of a particular name element comparison reflects the similarity of the two elements being compared and the consistency of their placement within the identity record as a whole. For example, *Stephen* and *Steven* might be considered highly congruent in themselves, but slightly less so if one is recorded as a "first" name while the other appears as a "middle" name. The congruence score should also be defined in linguistic terms, so that transcription variants are considered more highly congruent than names that are simply phonetically similar. For example, transcription variants could be considered to be a 90% match, while homophones might represent a 75% match or derivative names an 80% match.

The final match score should be defined in terms of the significance and congruence ratings of each characteristic comparison that forms part of the overall identity match. In this way, the scores for given name matches are mathematically combined with those for family name matches to give a complete name match score, which is then combined with the scores obtained from comparing other identity characteristics to give one overall identity match score.

10.3 Linguistic Similarity Keys for Transcription and Homophones

The biggest weakness of G1 and G2 Methods has been shown to lie in the matching of linguistically-driven variations, and in particular in their handling of transcription variants and non-Anglo-Saxon homophones. String comparison techniques demand a high price in terms of precision for any improvements in recall so the degree of tolerance required to match linguistic variations in this way would result in many false positive results. Thesauri and generative algorithms also struggle to provide appropriate reliability due to the high number of rare names in use and the sheer volume of transcription variants and homophones that exist for many names. Even if all variants of all names could be included in a thesaurus or generated via algorithms, the number of possible variants would be too many to provide an efficient search solution.

Similarity keys are therefore the most efficient and effective way to reliably match transcription variants and homophones. Performance issues are avoided by comparing similarity keys rather than attempting to match the many linguistic variants of a name. In addition, by not relying on a finite catalogue of name information, similarity keys offer a more reliable solution for handling rarer names and less-common variants of other names.

The concept behind the use of similarity keys is that related name variants should produce the same similarity key. Thus if the name *Yeltsin* generates the code XZ12345, then *Jelzin*, *Eltsine* and the other transcription variants of this name should also generate the same code. In order to facilitate the provision of different levels of search accuracy, multiple similarity keys should be generated from each name. For example, if XZ12345 is the precise match level key for *Yeltsin*, then *Yeltsene* should perhaps produce a different similarity key at the precise level, but *Yeltsin* and *Yeltsene* should generate the same code (for example, XZ135) at a broader match level. This is discussed in more detail in section 10.3.3 below.

The use of similarity keys is fundamentally similar to the concept on which earlier phonetic encoding techniques were based. However, as previously discussed, the earlier methods have not been entirely successful at matching linguistic variations. Despite their central role in global identity matching processes, transcription variants have never been a core focus for phonetic encoding techniques and attempts to improve the matching of phonetically similar names have had limited success due to the variety and complexity of phonetic phenomena evident in global proper names. It therefore seems unlikely that further enhancements to the original algorithms could effectively cover all phonetic similarities and additionally cover transcription phenomena.

Though the heart of the G3 approach to linguistic matching has similarities with the concept of phonetic encoding, it makes far greater use of linguistic and onomastic knowledge. The linguistic rule sets used in G3 Solutions are much more detailed than the earlier phonetic algorithms. They include a more extensive consideration of the linguistic context of each character and cover transcription as well as phonetic phenomena. Crucially, there is no attempt to combine the rules derived from multiple languages into a single algorithm, as it is recognised that the rules necessary to match variations in names from one language are not necessarily compatible with those required to match names from other origins. Different rule sets, and therefore different similarity keys, are generated for each language group. This allows a much more exact and precisely targeted application of the rules than was possible with earlier algorithms.

Aside from the vital inclusion of transcription as well as phonetic phenomena, the three key factors which place linguistic rule sets apart from earlier encoding techniques are:

- the separate treatment of phenomena from different language groups
- the more detailed consideration of the context of each character
- the generation of similarity keys for different levels of similarity

These three aspects are discussed in more detail below, with a view to highlighting the complexity that is necessary in order to match all classes of linguistic variation with both high precision and high recall.

10.3.1 Recognition of Different Language Groups

A key strength of the G3 approach to linguistic similarity keys is its recognition that it is not possible to cover variation phenomena associated with all relevant languages and scripts in one single rule set.

The specific requirements for G3 Solutions listed in section 10.2.2 above suggested that approximately 70 languages should be handled by a linguistic name matching solution: essentially those spoken by over 10 million people world-wide. As different languages display different variation phenomena, some of which may contradict one another, it is necessary to separate these out into groups of languages that display consistent variation characteristics.

Around 40 of the most prominent languages world-wide are written using systems other than the Latin alphabet. The requirement to match name variants transcribed from these 40 source languages into the six specified target languages (English, French, German, Spanish, Portuguese and Italian) provides 240 constellations of conditions for the transcription of names that must be covered by a linguistic matching solution. As transcription phenomena in the various constellations partly overlap, far fewer than 240 rule sets are required, but each constellation must be individually researched to determine the applicable rules from the variations observed.

The total number of rules in each rule set will vary depending on the rule syntax and the complexity with which the rules are interrelated, but in total, the coverage of these 240 transcription conditions will require dozens of rule sets containing thousands of rules. The challenges involved in accurately creating these rule sets are significant and can only be addressed with the expert input of language specialists and computational linguists.

Similar conditions apply for the creation of rule sets that match homophones in each language, as these must cover the phonetic phenomena of all 70 relevant languages. These rules partly overlap with those for matching transcription variants. Again, it may be possible to group languages so that fewer than 70 phonetic rule sets are required, but the phonetic features of each language must be individually examined in order to define these groups.

10.3.2 Consideration of Character Context

The importance of taking into consideration the context of a character when matching linguistic variants has been highlighted several times throughout the last few chapters. In looking at phonetic variants, it has been noted that the *p* in *Thompson* is effectively silent due to its position between an *m* and an *s*, just as the *c* in *Eckerhof* has no significant effect on pronunciation because it is followed by a *k*. In the context of transcription, it has been pointed out that a *ts* may be ignored in a name transcribed from Cyrillic if it is followed by *ch*, as in *Gorbatschow* (the German equivalent of the English *Gorbachev*).

G3 Solutions expand the definition of character context to consider the position of each character from several perspectives: between other characters, within a syllable, within a name part and as part of the full name. This makes the rule sets involved in generating G3 similarity keys extremely detailed, to the point where they have little in common with the simple mapping tables used by Soundex or even the relatively more sophisticated rules of Double Metaphone.

In most languages there are some letters that are pronounced in some character settings but fulfil a controlling function for the pronunciation of adjacent characters in others. In English, the *H* in *Henry* is pronounced as an aspirate, while the letter *h* takes on a controlling role in names such as *Charles*, *Alisha* or *Philip*. In names such as *Thomas* or *Christian* it has effectively no impact on pronunciation at all. These are simple examples using just one character and the contextual effects become even more involved when groups of characters are considered.

The context of a character is defined not only by the preceding and succeeding characters (and character sequences), but also by word and syllable borders. For example, in some Western languages, the combination *ph* is pronounced like an *f*. However, this does not apply if the *p* and the *h* are separated across two syllables, as in *Stopham*. The identification of word and syllable borders is therefore a vital analytical feature of linguistic rule sets. If word and syllable borders are not clearly identifiable, the generation of similarity keys becomes more of a challenge. This is the case, for example, in Thai names, as Thai is written without spaces between words and names.

Sophisticated linguistic identity matching solutions also take into account the context of each name element as part of the full name in order to determine the most appropriate treatment for each character. This can be particularly useful in resolving ambiguous word borders. For example, the alternative compositions of the *Abd-al* naming construction (discussed in section 9.4.2) only apply to names of Arabic origin. While *Abdul Rahman* could be broken down into *Abd ul Rahman*, *Abdul Miller* would not normally be split out into *Abd ul Miller*. Similarly *Wang Susan* could alternatively be transcribed as *Wang Su San*, but *Susan Miller* should most likely not be broken down into *Su San Miller*.

The consideration of the full name as context for each element also helps in assessing the linguistic origin of each name part, which in turn defines the linguistic rules and other techniques that should be applied to the name. For example, the common Korean family name *Kim* should match with its alternative transcriptions of *Gim* and *Ghim*, while the Western given name *Kim* should match as a hypocorism of *Kimberly*.

Where a name is of truly ambiguous origin, the similarity keys generated by all language rule sets can be compared in the search. However, one analytical function of a G3 Solution is, as far as is prudently possible, to narrow down the number of linguistic rule sets that should be applied to each part of a name. The automated classification of name origin is a task that requires careful handling, but when approached as the selective exclusion of unlikely origins rather than the prediction of certain origin, can be an effective way to improve the precision of a matching system. In a very simple example, it could be assumed that a name consisting of three multisyllabic parts, with the middle name ending in *-evich* and the family name ending in *-ev* (for example, *Dmitry Anatolyevich Medvedev*) may not need to be matched using rules derived from Japanese or Chinese languages. In some cases, onomastic thesauri enriched with global name distribution information may be used to enhance the classification process. Care must be taken to consider the likely origin of each name part as well as the name as a whole in order to account for names such as *Sarah Wang* or *Katarzyna McDonald*.

10.3.3 Multiple Search Accuracy Levels

The ability to use linguistic rule sets to define different search accuracy levels is extremely useful in practical application. Similarity keys are generated by progressively flattening various differences in the spelling of names until related names generate the same similarity keys. The more differences are levelled, the broader the search results become. By creating rule sets which flatten different classes of variation, it is possible to construct different levels of search accuracy.

This can be demonstrated with a simple phonetic example. Three different levels of phonetic similarity could be defined as follows:

- Precisely phonetically related: the phonetic properties of the name are exactly the same, as in *Carlsberg* and *Karlsberg*.
- Closely phonetically related: differences are flattened between characters whose sounds differ only in whether they are voiced or voiceless, such as *b* and *p*, *d* and *t*, *s* and *z* or *g* and *k*. At this level, *Carlsberg* would match with *Garlsperk*.
- Remotely phonetically related: all vowels are reduced to a standard sound, so that any differences between, for example, *e* and *a*, or *o* and *u* would be flattened. This level of tolerance would allow *Carlsberg* to be matched with *Garlspark*.

Using this simple example, some possible similarity keys could be generated, as shown below. The letters in these example similarity keys represent classes of sounds rather than the sounds that are traditionally associated with each character and are used to equalise the differences at the three levels rather than to approximate the names' pronunciation.

	Original Name	Carlsberg	Karlsberg	Garlsperk	Garlspark
Similarity Keys	**Precise**	karlsberg	karlsberg	garlsperk	garlspark
	Close	karlsperk	karlsperk	karlsperk	karlspark
	Remote	karlspark	karlspark	karlspark	karlspark

At each level, keys that match are shaded.

Table 10.1: Simplified example of the use of similarity keys for 4 names on 3 phonetic search accuracy levels.

The table above shows that names that match on one level also match at all the lower accuracy levels. The highest level on which an identical key is found corresponds to the level on which the two names match. In this example, *Carlsberg* matches to *Karlsberg* at the phonetically precise level, and is considered closely phonetically related to *Garlsperk* and remotely phonetically related to *Garlspark*. The implementation of the similarity keys must ensure that keys are only compared with other keys of the same search accuracy level.

The above example is obviously greatly simplified and it is a huge task to ensure that all names that should not match have distinct similarity keys while those that should match generate the same keys at the correct search accuracy levels.

10.4 Thesauri for Derivative Names and Special Cases

Linguistically generated similarity keys may be complex to produce, but they are the most efficient and reliable method for matching transcription variants and homophones. There are, however, other classes of variation in names that similarity keys are less well equipped to handle. Though there may be some identifiable patterns in the creation of hypocorisms and other derivative name forms, these patterns are not consistent and, for the most part, cannot be turned into reliable linguistic rules. Fortunately, as compared to the vast number of transcription variants and homophones, there are a relatively limited number of hypocorisms and other derivative versions for each name. This means that, with sufficient research, appropriate coverage of derivative names can be reflected in an onomastic thesaurus.

These thesauri often have a very simple structure, recording only the original name and the derivative versions related to it. They may also record the relationship between the names, such as "hypocorism of" or "translation of". The most comprehensive thesauri also include other information, such as the countries or languages in which the derivative version is found, or the degree of interchangeability of the names in different situations (identity documents, media articles, chat messages, etc). Technically, such thesauri are easy to integrate into the matching process, requiring only a look-up function and the option to expand the search with the relevant variants. Any effect that query expansion has on performance is likely to be tolerable, as the population of derivatives of each name is limited.

In addition to derivative forms of given names, G3 thesauri should contain standard abbreviations (such as *Ltd* for *Limited* or *Jnr* for *Junior*) and variations on the usage of symbols and numbers (such as *1, I, 1st, First*). It may also be appropriate to include translations of standard terms (such as *bank, banque, banco* or *society, societé, sociadad*). Covering these special cases with a thesaurus has the same advantages as the use of thesauri for given name derivatives; it improves recall without creating a significant risk of poor precision. It is also technically easy to combine with other methods, though the amount of research necessary to cover all relevant derivatives, abbreviations and other special cases on a global scale should not be underestimated.

10.5 Generative Algorithms for Covering Simple Typos

Having dealt with transcription variants, homophones and derivative forms of names, only the truly non-linguistic spelling errors remain to be addressed. In most practical identity matching scenarios, these account for only a small proportion of the variations in names that must be considered. For this reason, linguistic matching solutions generally assign a lower priority to the handling of non-linguistically motivated typos, though there will clearly be some situations where typos are more important, depending on the source and quality of the data to be matched.

In some situations it may even be appropriate to disregard non-linguistic spelling errors altogether, provided that all other classes of variation are appropriately covered, as methods for addressing them can be expensive: not in terms of development or licencing costs, but in terms of the effect they may have on performance and precision, and the resources required to review additional false positive results. However, in most matching processes, it will be appropriate to allow for at least the most common classes of typing errors.

The basic rule still holds: match methods that increase recall only at the expense of significantly worse precision should be avoided. In identity matching terms, this includes very simple string comparison techniques such as the unmodified Levenshtein Distance. It is always worth investing a little more in the implementation of a technique to improve precision, provided that the proposed enhancements are appropriate for the particular matching scenario. For example, modifications focused on OCR errors will bring minimal results if the data does not derive from scanned documents, and optimising a technique for the most common typing errors made on a QWERTY keyboard will be less effective if the data was created using the AZERTY keyboard system.

That said, in many cases it would be valid to assume that the accidental striking of a key adjacent to the intended key, either together with or instead of the key itself, form some of the most common classes of typing errors. This being the case, an algorithm which takes this into account will provide better precision than the unmodified Levenshtein Distance metric, which treats all character insertions or replacements equally. The algorithm could be further refined, for example, to exclude insertions or replacements involving numbers or punctuation, if it is assumed that such errors would be more likely to be noticed and corrected by the typist. The same principle could potentially also be used to exclude errors involving the first character of a name.

A further supportable assumption is that transpositions are most likely to happen between characters found on different sides of the keyboard, due to the motor skills required to coordinate the left and right hands when typing. Transpositions are less likely between keys that are typically struck with fingers of the same hand. Applying string comparison techniques adapted for such specific assumptions is likely to increase the recall of the system without unduly affecting precision.

However, the potential improvement in recall that could be obtained by dealing with less common types of non-linguistic spelling error may not warrant the price that would have to be paid in reduced precision.

In this scenario, where only a limited number of typo classes are to be covered by the matching system, it may be most appropriate to use generative algorithms to cover non-linguistic variations. This means that the search will be expanded by selected typo variants of the name searched for. The query expansion will not be excessive provided that only the most likely classes of typo are included. For example, the transposition variants of the name *Weston* are *Ewston*, *Wseton*, *Wetson*, *Wesotn* and *Westno*. If the assumption that transpositions only occur between the two different halves of the keyboard is applied, only the single variant *Wesotn* need be included. This method covers transposition errors both in the data to be searched and in the search term, as if *Wesotn* is searched by accident, *Weston* is one of the variants generated.

One benefit of using generative algorithms, as opposed to modified string comparison techniques, is that they can more easily be integrated into the matching solution as a whole, so that common classes of typos in transcription variants, homophones and derivative names are also covered. However, given the performance effects of radically expanding the query, it is clear that only some classes of typos can be efficiently dealt with in this way.

The following table uses the example name *Weston* to demonstrate the number of variants that would have to be generated in order to cover different classes of typing errors. This simple example shows that some classes of typos are associated with very large numbers of potential variants and demonstrates the extent to which the number of variants can be reduced if some plausible assumptions are applied. It is, for example, perfectly reasonable to assume that typos only rarely affect the first character of a word, or that any typos involving non-alphabetic characters are more likely to have been spotted and corrected by the typist.

Typo Class	Restrictions	Example Variant of Weston	Variants
Single transposition	None	Ewston, Wseton, Wetson, Wesotn, Westno	**5**
	First character excluded. Only transpositions between characters typed with different hands	Wesotn	**1**
Single omission	First character excluded	Wston, Weton, Weson, Westn, Westo	**5**
Single replacement	Alphabetic characters only	Aeston, Beston, Ceston, Deston ... Westow, Westox, Westoy, Westoz	**150**
	First character excluded. Replacement only with an adjacent alphabetic character.	Wwston, Wrston, Wdston, Wsston ... Westob, Westom, Westoh, Westoj	**22**
Single Insertion	Alphabetic characters only	Aweston, Bweston, Cweston, Dweston ... Westonw, Westonx, Westony, Westonz	**176**
	No insertion before first character. Insertion of any alphabetic character adjacent to (or the same as) one of the characters it is inserted between / after.	Wweston, Wqeston, Weeston, Waeston ... Westonb, Westonm, Westonh, Westonj	**47**
Double Replacement	Alphabetic characters only	Aaston, Abston, Acston, Adston ... Westzw, Westzx, Westzy, Westzz	**9,375**
	First character excluded. Replacement with adjacent alphabetic character only	Wdaton, Wddton, Wdeton, Wdwton ... Westpb, Westph, Westpj, Westpm	**192**

Table 10.2: Typo variants of the name Weston, demonstrating the effects of limiting the allowed variations to the most common typos. In all cases, the use of a QWERTY keyboard is assumed.

When dealing with longer names it may be desirable to allow for more than one edit operation, though it is still recommended that the types of character difference allowed are limited in order to maintain acceptable levels of precision. For example, it may be appropriate to allow for two edit operations so that *Featherstone* matches with *Feahterston*. Limiting the classes of typo allowed, as described above, would prevent *Leatherstore* from also being considered a match, despite it containing the same number of edit differences.

If it is decided that broader typo classes should be covered in an identity matching process, it is not really feasible to match these using generative algorithms to expand the search query. Even an edit distance of one is at the limit of what could practically be implemented without some fairly strong assumptions being made as to the nature of the typos that might be present. If large numbers of potential typos are to be covered, string comparison techniques such as n-gram methods could be used: preferably those that take into account the position of each character on a keyboard or are otherwise modified based on the quality of the data to be matched.

10.6 Integration of Methods

G3 Solutions are a linguistically focused mix of techniques designed to include the most suitable methods for matching each of the key sources of variation in names.

- The majority of variations in proper names are typically either transcription variants or homophones. The most effective way of matching these is to generate similarity keys using detailed linguistic rule sets.
- Onomastic thesauri provide the best option for covering derivative names and other special cases.
- Simple classes of typos can be dealt with using generative algorithms.
- If required, wider classes of typos can be addressed using string comparison techniques.

Each of the methods employed should be configured to reflect the specific needs of each matching process. Where appropriate, it should also be possible to apply these methods in combination to account for names which contain more than one class of variation.

The combination of the various match methods may be carried out as part of the definition of various search accuracy levels. The following table provides a simplified example defining four possible search accuracy levels: Exact, Precise, Close and Broad.

	Similarity Keys	Thesauri	Generative Algorithms	N-Gram Based Methods
Exact				
Variants with and without diacritical marks	✓			
Precise				
Transcription variants	✓			
Frequently exchanged name derivatives		✓		
Transcription variants of common derivative names	✓	✓		
Close				
Homophone names	✓			
Less-common derivative names		✓		
Homophones of derivative names	✓	✓		
Transcription variants containing common typos	✓		✓	

Continued...

	Similarity Keys	Thesauri	Generative Algorithms	N-Gram Based Methods
Frequent name derivatives containing common typos		✓	✓	
Names with any single typo / multiple common typos in longer names				✓
Broad				
Homophone names containing common typos	✓		✓	
Less common derivative names containing common typos		✓	✓	
Less closely phonetically-related names	✓			
Wider classes of typos				✓

Table 10.3: Example integration of match methods into search accuracy levels.

Where a proper name includes more than one source of variation, it may do so in two ways.

- Type 1 combinations include only one source of variation in each element of the name. For example *Boris Jelzin* and *Borid Yeltsin* (typo in given name, transcription variant of family name) or *Bill Stuart* and *William Stewart* (hypocorism and homophone family names).
- Type 2 combinations involve single name elements that include more than one type of variation, as in *Jekzin* and *Yeltsin* (a typo in a transcription variant), or *Bill* and *Willyam* (a given name derivative and homophone).

The following table provides some examples of names containing multiple classes of variations and shows the search accuracy levels that they might be allocated to.

Search Accuracy	Examples of type 1 combinations	Examples of type 2 combinations
Exact	*(No combination possible as only one match method applies)*	
Precise	Asja Kuznetsova and Anastassija Kusnezowa (Given name derivative, family names are transcription variants of the same name)	The derivative name Asya matches with Anastasia via a Thesaurus entry and then with the transcription variant Anastassija
Close	William Stuart and Wililam Stewart (Given name with transposition, family names are homophones)	The derivative name Bill matches with William via a Thesaurus entry and then with Willima based on a transposition
Broad	Steven Carlsberg and Stevne Karlsburg (Given name with transposition, phonetically similar family name)	Carlsberg matches with the homophone Karlsburg and then with Karlsbrug based on a transposition.

Table 10.4: Examples for name matches containing multiple classes of variation

Implementing combined match methods to account for Type 1 combinations is relatively simple. Each name should be split into its component elements prior to matching. This can be done by considering the position of spaces and hyphens, or by using linguistic rules to detect less clearly defined word borders, such as those between the 4th and 5th characters of *Hanspeter*, or between the 3rd and 4th characters of *Alinezhad*. Once this is done, the matching system can match the names using the different methods appropriate for the selected search accuracy level.

The implementation of match methods to identify different sources of variation present in the same name element is more complex as the match methods need to be performed simultaneously. Methods based on similarity keys can relatively easily be combined, even if they cover different variation classes, due to the flexibility in the definition of the rule sets. For example, the rules for matching transcription variants and homophones in a particular language could be combined into one rule set that flattens the variations in both sources.

Similarity keys can also be relatively easily combined with the use of thesauri and generative variants. Keys can be created not only from the original search term, but also from the additional variants found in the thesauri or generated by algorithms. For example, a search for *Anastasia* may trigger a thesaurus look-up and find the hypocorism *Asya*. The similarity key for *Asya* would match the similarity key for its transcription variant *Asja*. Combining these methods allows *Anastasia* to be matched with both its derivative *Asya* and the alternative transcription *Asja*.

Thus similarity key based methods can be combined with thesauri and generative algorithms without significant difficulties. There will likely be some reduction in performance as compared with the individual methods when used in isolation, but provided the number of variants generated is limited and the system is implemented in an efficient manner, any performance impairment should be tolerable and should be more than compensated by improvements in recall.

Thesauri and generative algorithms are also easy to combine with n-gram based string comparison methods. Again, this is simply a case of matching the additional variants as well as the name originally searched for. Only the combination of string comparison techniques with similarity keys poses difficulties in implementation. This is one reason why it is hard to find a practical solution which fully combines rule-based methods with tolerance for wider classes of typos. However, such a system would likely generate a wider range of hits than would be efficient to review in most processes, including transcription variants and homophones containing wider classes of typo. This may be another reason why such systems are not typically found in practice.

10.7 Conclusion

This chapter began by setting out the general and specific requirements for a G3 Solution and ended by demonstrating that it is quite possible for these requirements to be met by carefully combining the techniques most suited to addressing each variation type.

The technical design of a G3 Solution is considerably more complex than the that of either the G1 or G2 Methods. The effort required to design and implement a G3

Solution is significant, partly due to the inclusion of multiple matching methods, which must be optimised to produce the desired results both in isolation and in combination with each other. However, the additional technical complexity is probably not the main reason why many vendors continue to go to market with applications using G1 and G2 Methods. The real driver of the effort involved in producing G3 Solutions is the required linguistic and onomastic research.

The linguistic rules that generate similarity keys and the complementary thesauri used in G3 Solutions have to reliably cover transcription standards, phonetic characteristics and naming conventions from all relevant languages and writing systems world-wide. The research needed to collect this information and the expertise required to convert it into efficient rule sets and modules is significant. That said, the additional technical and linguistic efforts involved in the creation of G3 Solutions have a marked effect on the quality of the results that can be expected, and G3 Solutions are likely to continue to grow in popularity as users recognise the reductions in both cost and risk that can be achieved.

The following charts show that the individual components of a G3 Solution could be expected to provide both strong recall and high precision when matching the particular class of name variation for which they are designed. An efficiently integrated G3 Solution should provide similarly strong results when dealing with all classes of variation.

This assessment has been made based on theoretical considerations and the lessons that have been learned from decades of experience with G1 and G2 Methods. In order to test this hypothetical assessment, a simple benchmark study has been compiled to compare the recall and precision of the most important G1, G2 and G3 techniques. The results of this study are discussed in the next chapter.

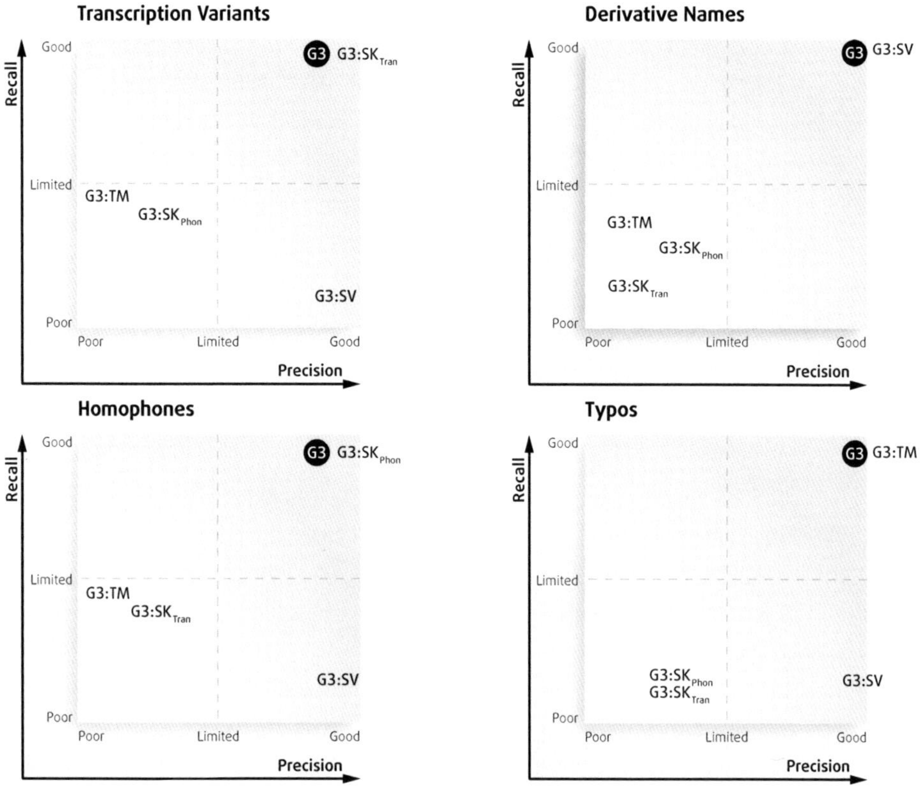

SK_{Tran}: Similarity Keys (for transcription variants)
SK_{Phon}: Similarity Keys (for phonetically similar names)
SV: Search with Variants (complementary Thesauri)
TM: Typo Methods (n-gram methods and generative algorithms)
In each chart, the darker disc represents the performance of the fully integrated G3 Solution.

Figure 10.1: Relative performance of G3 Methods when matching each of the four main classes of variations in names.

Chapter 11: Benchmark Study

11.1 Introduction

Earlier chapters theorised about the performance of G1, G2 and G3 Methods and commented on their potential contribution to identity matching systems. This chapter presents the findings of a simple, practical study that has been conducted to demonstrate the relative performance of selected methods.

The test reflects a simplified version of the benchmark studies that should be carried out prior to any investment in identity matching technology. Full application evaluations are designed to test a variety of technical and functional criteria, and are discussed further in Chapter 13. The assessment described here has been stripped to its core in order to highlight the recall and precision that can be achieved with each of the selected match methods when matching the major classes of variation in names.

11.2 Match Methods to be Assessed

A range of G1 and G2 Methods were selected for inclusion in this study based on their relative popularity and prevalence in the market. Levenshtein Distance (using four different tolerance levels) and Soundex were selected as the G1 Methods to be investigated. The five G1 test conditions were, therefore:

- Levenshtein Distance 1
- Levenshtein Distance 2
- Levenshtein Distance 3
- Levenshtein Distance 4
- Soundex

From the possible G2 Methods, Jaro-Winkler, Editex, Kölner Phonetik, Metaphone and Double Metaphone were selected for assessment. Jaro-Winkler and Editex were each tested using four similarity levels, resulting in a total of 11 G2 test conditions:

- Jaro-Winkler 0.9
- Jaro-Winkler 0.8
- Jaro-Winkler 0.7
- Jaro-Winkler 0.6
- Editex 2
- Editex 3
- Editex 4
- Editex 5
- Kölner Phonetik
- Metaphone
- Double Metaphone

The similarity levels tested for Jaro-Winkler and Editex were selected to extend either side of the parameters that could be expected to produce optimum recall and precision, based on a review of the technical literature. Both methods were tested using standard, basic implementations. The Jaro-Winkler method was implemented for this study with the common prefix length set to 4 and weighted with a factor of 0.1.

The Editex score represents the adjusted edit distance between two strings (where phonetically similar character differences are awarded half the weight of phonetically different character operations). A low Jaro-Winkler score indicates less similar names, conversely to the increasing similarity indicated by reductions in the Editex and Levenshtein Distances. A Jaro-Winkler score of 1 reflects a perfect match, while a score of 0 indicates that the two names share no common characters.

Program code for the G1 and G2 Methods is freely available and was implemented in its standard form for the purposes of this assessment. This is not the case for the more complex modules of G3 Solutions so this assessment has had to include a commercial tool. The tool Traphoty (Rel. 1.0) from Linguistic Search Solutions AG was selected as its conceptual design fulfils the requirements for a linguistic search tool set out in Chapter 10. In addition, its modular architecture allows the four components relevant to this study to be assessed both individually and as an integrated solution.

The final five test conditions are, therefore:

- Traphoty Transcriptions
- Traphoty Phonetics
- Traphoty Name Forms
- Traphoty Typos
- Integrated Traphoty Solution

11.3 Methodology and Findings

The aim of this exercise was to assess the recall and precision achieved by each method when matching different classes of variation in names. In order to isolate these measures, simplified queries have been run against a test data set and the results compared with those expected. No comment has been made as to the technical performance of each method, as this is very much determined by factors specific to each individual implementation.

The study was carried out using a publicly available list that is commonly screened in the financial services industry: the consolidated list of persons, groups and entities subject to financial sanctions by the European Union. The version selected for this study was issued in November 2009 and contains 1,436 profiles relating to natural persons. For the sake of simplicity, profiles relating to legal entities and other groups were excluded, as including these name types would have required additional search configuration.

The searches submitted comprised a set of 120 test names, which was compiled by identity matching experts to reflect the four most important categories of variation in names: transcription variants, homophones, derivative names and non-linguistic spelling errors. Thirty test names were included for each of these classes of variation. Each test name consists of only one name element, such as a given or family name. This is to ensure that the test results directly reflect the performance of each match method and are not complicated by the combination of multiple name elements. Given the relatively small size of the test data, single-element test names were also necessary to ensure sufficient hits were obtained to provide meaningful results. That said, some of the test names do contain multiple sub-elements, as in *Abd al-Rahman*.

As a final selection criterion, test names were chosen that were expected to generate matches under at least one of the match methods being tested. Test names that produced no hits using any of the match methods would have been of little use in demonstrating the differences in performance of the individual methods.

The test names used in this study are shown below.

Transcription variants of Arabic and Russian names
1. Hussein 2. Houssayn 3. Hussain
4. Abdurrahman 5. Abd al-Rahman 6. Abdul Rahman
7. Muhammad 8. Mohamed 9. Mohammad
10. Mahmud 11. Mahmoud 12. Mehmood
13. Nor Eldin 14. Noureddine 15. Nureddin
16. Nikolaevich 17. Nikolajewitsch 18. Nikolaievitch
19. Vasilyevich 20. Wassiljewitsch 21. Vassilievitch
22. Basayev 23. Bassajew 24. Basaiev
25. Aleksandr 26. Alexander 27. Aleksander
28. Evgeny 29. Yevgeniy 30. Jewgeni

Western homophones
31. Dumont 32. Dumon 33. Du Mont
34. Lavilla 35. Lavila 36. La Villa
37. Taylor 38. Tailor 39. Tayler
40. Brighton 41. Brighten 42. Bryton
43. Fritz 44. Friz 45. Frits
46. Schneider 47. Schnayder 48. Shneyder
49. Shiri 50. Schiri 51. Shiry
52. Joshua 53. Yoshua 54. Joschua
55. Christopher 56. Kristopher 57. Christoffer
58. Yeaten 59. Yeeten 60. Yeaton

Given name derivatives
61. George 62. Jorge 63. Giorgio 64. Georg 65. Georges 66. Juri
67. Joseph 68. Jose 69. Giuseppe 70. Josef 71. Joe 72. Yusef
73. Richard 74. Dick 75. Riccardo 76. Ricardo 77. Ricky 78. Richie

Continued ...

	79. Stephen 80. Stefan 81. Stephane 82. Steven 83. Stefano 84. Esteban
	85. Michael 86. Mike 87. Mikhail 88. Michele 89. Miguel 90. Michel
Typos	
	91. Goerge 92. Geogre 93. Gorge 94. Geortge 95. Geirge 96. Geeorge
	97. Jsoeph 98. Jospeh 99. Jseph 100. Joserph 101. Joaeph 102. Jooseph
	103. Rcihard 104. Ricahrd 105. Rchard 106. Richjard 107. Rixhard 108. Riichard
	109. Setphen 110. Stehpen 111. Sephen 112. Stepühen 113. Stwphen 114. Sttephen
	115. Mcihael 116. Micahel 117. Mchael 118. Michjael 119. Mixhael 120. Miichael

Table 11.1: The 120 test names used in the benchmark study.

11.3.1 Calculation of recall and precision

This study measured recall and precision by comparing the results achieved using each match method with the expected, correct results. In order to define the expected search results, each of the 1,436 profiles in the test database were classified as either relevant or not relevant with regard to each of the 120 test names. This allowed the performance of each match method to be viewed in terms of the relevant and irrelevant profiles that were matched to each test name, as well as the relevant profiles that were not identified.

Recall and precision have, therefore, been calculated as functions of three metrics: good matches identified by each method (True Positives = TP), good matches overlooked by each method (False Negatives = FN) and irrelevant profiles matched by each method (False Positives = FP).

Recall = relevant profiles identified / all relevant profiles

= TP / (TP + FN)

Precision = relevant profiles identified / all profiles identified

= TP / (TP + FP)

An important feature of this study is the separate assessment of each method when used to match different kinds of variation in names. The recall and precision of each method have therefore been separately quantified for transcription variants, homophones, derivative names and typos, using the total numbers of true and false positive matches and false negative results for all the test names in each variation class.

An overall performance rating has then been calculated for each match method by considering its performance in matching all classes of variation. Rather than simply taking the average of the four scores for the different variation classes, this rating has been calculated using the total numbers of actual and expected matches and false positive results across all searches. This differs from the simple average of the four class ratings as the test data used in this study contains more expected matches for transcription variants than for the other classes of variation. For example, the data contains 25 profiles that are expected to hit on the name *Hussain* as part of the testing of transcription variants but only 5 profiles that are expected to match the homophone test name *Taylor*. This could be seen as typical for international data sets such as that used in this study; other distribution patterns might be expected with more localised databases. As a result, the "overall" results presented here are slightly closer to those reported for the matching of transcription variants than the simple average would be.

Depending on the context, there are advantages and disadvantages to either method of assessing the overall performance. For the purposes of this study, the overall scores have been calculated using the total results figures across all search queries because, in many matching processes, the total number of false positive results provides the best indication of the effort required to review irrelevant matches, and the total number of false negative results is an important indicator of the level of risk inherent in the matching process. However, the prevailing pattern of results and the relative performance reported for each of the different methods is not significantly affected by the choice of averaging method.

Studies of this nature often report information retrieval performance using the F-Score: a measure that combines the results for precision and recall (with the option to apply different weights to each). The F-Score has not been reported here as it is considered important to assess the two performance ratings separately. This is because, in most identity matching scenarios, there is a minimum acceptable recall and minimum precision that should be achieved. Though many processes currently compromise between recall and precision, there are limits to the trade-offs that can be tolerated. Excellent levels of precision can never compensate for very poor recall and, in practical terms, it is very unlikely that very low levels of precision could be tolerated, even if perfect recall could be achieved by doing so. The recall and precision scores have been reported separately to provide a fuller picture of the performance of each method.

11.3.2 G1 Methods

The following table shows the consolidated recall and precision of each G1 Method when used to match names containing each class of variation.

	Transcription		Homophones		Derivative Names		Typos		Overall	
	Rec.	Prec.	Rec.	Prec.	Rec.	Prec.	Rec.	Prec.	Rec.	Prec.
LD 1	54	99	77	90	20	47	67	100	50	91
LD 2	77	85	94	37	43	21	100	91	73	61
LD 3	89	59	96	3	65	5	100	20	85	16
LD 4	91	23	96	0	85	2	100	2	91	4
Soundex	88	36	83	37	41	47	67	45	77	37

LD x = Levenshtein Distance with a distance tolerance of x.

Table 11.2: Recall and Precision values of selected G1 Methods (as percentages) split by variation source and as an overall score.

As might be expected, the overall recall increases with the Levenshtein Distance tolerance (from 50% to 91%) but this is paid for by a significant fall in precision (from 91% down to 4%). This means that even if a Levenshtein Distance of 4 were to be tolerated (and, in practical terms, around 25 irrelevant hits for each relevant hit) not all of the relevant profiles would be identified. As expected, Levenshtein Distance only displays a satisfactory recall when used to match non-linguistic spelling errors. Here, a recall of 100% was achieved using a distance tolerance of just 2. Surprisingly, the precision achieved when matching typos using this tolerance level is also relatively good, at 91%. However, this may be a consequence of the selection of Western names for assessing the handling of typos, given the relatively lower concentration of Western names in the test data and their general lack of similarity with names from other cultures.

Overall, Soundex provided limited recall for relatively poor precision. As a phonetic algorithm, it could be expected to perform best in matching homophones. However, in this test it did not match homophones as well as Levenshtein Distance, offering a recall of just 83% and extremely poor precision, at 37% (a Levenshtein Distance of 2 provided recall of 94% for the same level of precision). In practical terms, one in five homophones was not detected by Soundex in this test. In addition, the results show that for every homophone correctly identified as a match, two names that are not phonetically similar were also included in the results.

11.3.3 G2 Methods

The following table shows the average recall and precision of each of the eleven G2 test conditions for each variation source.

	Transcription		Homophones		Derivative Names		Typos		Overall	
	Rec.	Prec.	Rec.	Prec.	Rec.	Prec.	Rec.	Prec.	Rec.	Prec.
JW 0.9	73	93	85	98	30	84	94	88	67	92
JW 0.8	91	52	96	22	54	47	100	35	85	46
JW 0.7	93	21	96	3	74	9	100	5	90	12
JW 0.6	93	8	96	0	85	2	100	1	92	3
Editex 2	83	83	94	85	28	41	78	94	72	78
Editex 3	88	47	94	24	42	23	78	79	79	42
Editex 4	88	37	96	5	57	10	100	32	84	22
Editex 5	89	28	96	1	84	5	100	9	89	10
Kölner	88	31	94	11	48	24	60	34	78	28
Metaphone	88	82	79	63	27	67	40	78	72	79
Double MP	88	81	90	39	36	32	33	38	74	65

JW x = Jaro-Winkler implemented using a distance of x
Editex x = Editex implemented with a distance tolerance of x
Kölner = Kölner Phonetik
Double MP = Double Metaphone

Table 11.3: Recall and Precision values of selected G2 Methods (as percentages) split by variation source and as an overall score.

The results obtained using the Jaro-Winkler and Editex methods demonstrate the known negative correlation between recall and precision for such metrics. The two measures display a similar correlation between recall and precision, with improvements in the recall of both methods being paid for by significantly reduced precision. In order to obtain a 90% recall (a level which would not be sufficient in many practical identity matching processes) approximately 10 irrelevant hits must be reviewed for each relevant hit. Only when matching typos could a 100% recall level be obtained using these methods, and then only by accepting a relatively low precision.

The three phonetic algorithms tested as part of the assessment of G2 Methods displayed similar levels of recall overall (between 72% and 78%) to those produced using Soundex. However, Metaphone and Double Metaphone both provided significantly better overall precision than either Kölner Phonetik or Soundex. As would be expected, the results obtained when matching homophones, and to some extent also transcription variants, were considerably stronger than the results for matching name derivatives or typos. However, the recall of these methods when matching homophones still left room for improvement and the precision was often poor. Only the Kölner Phonetik algorithm provided recall of over 90%, and this was achieved at the expense of a precision of just 11%. Arguably, the strongest results when matching homophones were provided by Double Metaphone, which achieved 90% recall for 39% precision, though such performance figures would be considered far from ideal in a practical matching application.

11.3.4 G3 Methods

The table below shows the recall and precision values obtained for each of the four Traphoty components (Transcription, Phonetics, Name Forms and Typos) together with the results obtained using the integrated system.

	Transcription		Homophones		Derivative Names		Typos		Overall	
	Rec.	Prec.	Rec.	Prec.	Rec.	Prec.	Rec.	Prec.	Rec.	Prec.
Traphoty Transcript.	100	100	40	100	17	97	2	100	74	100
Traphoty Phonetics	32	100	100	100	21	100	22	100	32	100

Continued …

	Transcription		Homophones		Derivative Names		Typos		Overall	
	Rec.	Prec.	Rec.	Prec.	Rec.	Prec.	Rec.	Prec.	Rec.	Prec.
Traphoty Name Forms	32	100	42	100	100	100	0	100	42	100
Traphoty Typos	59	99	79	100	18	100	100	100	55	100
Traphoty Integrated	100	99	100	80	100	97	100	95	100	98

Table 11.4: Recall and precision values of the G3 Tool Traphoty (Traphoty Integrated) and its components (Transcription, Phonetics, Name Forms and Typos).

Each Traphoty component achieved maximum recall when used to match the variation source that it was designed to address. Recall of 100% might seem surprising but could reflect the fact that only relatively common variations were included in the test names. As might be expected, recall scores when used to address other variation sources were considerably lower. Very high precision was achieved in these scenarios, and though that can hardly be said to compensate for such poor recall, it is a promising indicator of the precision that could be expected from the combined solution.

The results indicate a relatively weak relationship between the matching of transcription variants and phonetic matching. The Transcription module achieves recall of 100% when matching transcription variants but only 40% when used to match homophones. Similarly, the Phonetics module was only able to match 32% of transcription variants. This demonstrates the different effects that transcription standards and phonetic characteristics have on spelling. For this reason, a single method designed to cover both effects would be likely to suffer from weaker precision than the individual targeted modules.

However, the effect on precision is far less significant when modules specifically focusing on one variation source are integrated into a complete solution. The integrated Traphoty solution maintained a recall of 100% in this test without substantially compromising precision. At 98% its precision is higher than that achieved by many of the G1 and G2 Methods.

11.3.5 Limitations to this Exercise

The findings of this benchmark study are consistent with the expectations identified during the theoretical discussions of the individual methods in Chapters 8, 9 and 10. However, this study was carried out as a simple test of these expectations and, from a scientific point of view, has a number of limitations that must be recognised.

The study was designed to assess the recall and precision of each method in matching specific types of variation in names. While appropriate for this purpose, some features of the test design limit the extent to which the results can be said to be truly representative of those likely to be achieved in a practical identity matching process. For example, the base data set of around 1,500 profiles is not particularly large and, as a result, is only partly representative of larger international identity databases. It is also likely that the nature of the data set, an international sanctions list, has affected the overall results. As noted above, the relatively higher proportion of names originating in non-Latin script languages may have resulted in slightly stronger overall performance being reported for those methods that performed well when matching transcription variants.

In addition, the test names have not been empirically collected, but compiled by experts with the aim of covering all key sources of variation equally. In practice, some classes of variation are likely to be more significant than others, depending on the nature of the search process and quality of the data. The structure of the test names has also been simplified as compared to those generally searched for in identity matching processes. While most search processes look for full proper names, for the purposes of simplicity the test names used in this study have been restricted to individual name elements. Had full names been used, it could be expected that precision results might have been higher than those achieved here.

The design of this study focused on the core function of matching variations in names. Many features of practical identity matching processes, including the use of wildcard characters and the matching of initials, were not included in the test. Similarly, the matching of data using varying name structures and the matching of non-name identity characteristics were not included. The study has also been restricted to the use of the Latin alphabet. The ability to match names presented in a script other than Latin, or across different scripts, was outside the scope of this assessment.

The G1 and G2 Methods assessed are commonly used in practice and, as a result, reasonably representative. However, some of the methods can be implemented in different ways and this has only partly been accounted for with the testing of the Levenshtein Distance, Jaro-Winkler and Editex methods at different tolerance levels. In general, the methods were implemented in their basic forms, as is common in practice, but it must be recognised that a more sophisticated implementation may have been better able to deal with some specific variation phenomena. In particular, a more sophisticated implementation of some of the G1 and G2 Methods could have yielded stronger results where test names consisted of multiple sub-elements, such as *Nor Aldin*.

The results of this study have been reported in a straight-forward, descriptive manner; no attempt has been made to base the findings using inferential statistics. This is appropriate for a simple demonstration of relative performance in a practical text on identity matching but is a further factor limiting the scientific nature of this study. Though this test has served its purpose in demonstrating the abilities of the assessed match methods in addressing the key sources of variation in names, it would be interesting to see it re-performed on a larger scale and under more conventional scientific conditions. A more scientific assessment of the performance of G3 Solutions would be particularly of interest, as they have yet to be widely discussed in the technical literature available.

11.4 Conclusion

Notwithstanding the limitations discussed above, this study has demonstrated that non-linguistic matching techniques consistently provide poor results when matching some of the most important classes of variation in names. In particular, it is striking that not one of the G1 or G2 Methods is able to effectively match names from non-Latin scripts that have been transcribed in different ways.

The highest level of recall achieved by a G1 or G2 Method when matching transcription variants was 93%. This was achieved using the Jaro-Winkler method with a tolerance of 0.7, but only at the expense of precision of just 21% (or 12% across all classes of variation). Even if such poor levels of precision could be accepted, it should be noted that recall of 93% for transcription variants is often not sufficient to manage the risks involved in identity matching processes. In addition, the transcription variants used as test names in this study reflect only the most common transcription phenomena; the G1 and G2 Methods might have experienced even lower recall if less widely used transcription variants had been included.

Results for the matching of homophones using G1 and G2 Methods displayed even weaker precision at high levels of recall. The highest level of recall achieved (using various tolerance levels of the Levenshtein Distance, Jaro-Winkler and Editex methods) was 96%, and always with precision levels of 22% or less. This highlights the complexity of international phonetic phenomena and the difficulties of covering them all in a single algorithm. Interestingly, in this study, the Double Metaphone method did not perform as well as some of its less popular counterparts. This could be due to the inclusion in this test of homophones from languages that are not emphasised in the Double Metaphone algorithm, but it would be interesting to see if this finding held up in larger studies.

Given the challenges of achieving strong recall using the selected G1 and G2 Methods, it seems unlikely that it would be possible to combine these techniques into a packaged solution that provides appropriate recall, though this has not been specifically tested as part of this study.

By comparison, the results obtained using the G3 Solution are far more promising. The single components all yielded maximum recall when used to match the variation source for which they were designed. Such a result may appear surprising at first sight, but can be explained by two important factors. The first is the flexibility of linguistic rule sets, as compared to the mathematical algorithms of the G1 and G2 Methods, and the associated increased potential to take account of the linguistic context of each character. The second is a feature of this study itself; only the most common types of variation phenomena were included in the test names, and only one source of variation was included per name. Whether or not maximum recall could also be achieved when matching less common variations, or matching names that include combinations of different types of variation, was not investigated. Nevertheless, the same test conditions were applied to the assessment of G1 and G2 Methods and the improvements in the G3 results are marked.

Of particular interest are the results obtained using the integrated G3 Solution. Under the specified test conditions it was possible to maintain a 100% recall for all classes of variation, while a precision of 98% was achieved. Though the test conditions are relatively specific, the enhancements provided by G3 Solutions appear promising.

The following chart shows the overall results for those methods that yielded a recall of greater than 70%.

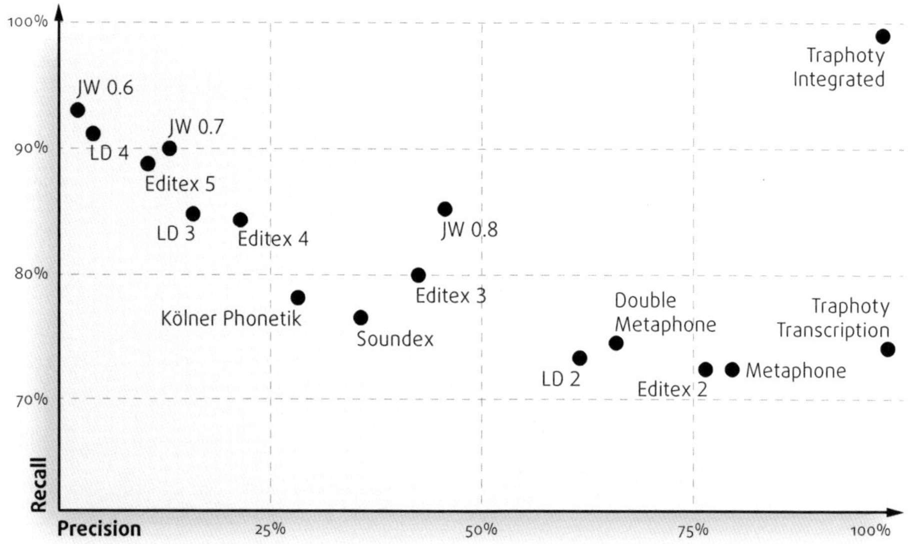

Figure 11.1: Overview of recall and precision for all methods yielding an overall recall of at least 70% for all classes of variation.

The chart demonstrates that the incremental improvement of G1 Methods to create the G2 Methods has not had a significant impact on the quality of the results when matching global names. The improvement in results seen here is perhaps even less than might have been predicted following the theoretical discussions in Chapter 9.

The dramatic improvement demonstrated by the G3 Solution shows the possibilities that have opened up as a result of the paradigm shift towards linguistic identity matching. The 100% recall experienced in this study is likely due to the relatively basic variations included in the selected test names, and in practice there will always be some relevant profiles that prove more elusive than others. However, the improvement in the results shown by the G3 Solution in comparison to those produced using the G1 and G2 Methods is significant and indicates the cost saving and risk management potential of this new approach to identity matching.

Part III:
Into the New Paradigm

Part III: Into the New Paradigm

Part II discussed the concepts and methods underlying the linguistic identity matching paradigm and demonstrated the potential that this new understanding has for revolutionising identity matching processes. The new paradigm relies on the art of linguistics, and in particular its onomastic sub-discipline, as well as more traditional information retrieval methods to address all the major sources of variation in person names.

The key to the power of this third generation of matching solutions is in identifying the appropriate blend of methods and parameters to ensure that each type of name variation is dealt with in the most effective manner. This targeted approach provides enormous improvements over the results offered by first and second generation methods, in terms of both recall and precision. Risks related to missing a relevant match are greatly reduced, as is the cost of manually reviewing matched names as false positive results are minimised.

The final chapters of this book are intended to help leverage these benefits in a practical identity matching system. Chapter 12 describes the expansion of name matching to full identity matching and considers different methods for calculating an overall identity match score. In doing so, it looks at factors that need to be born in mind when matching non-name identity characteristics such as the date of birth, nationality or address.

Chapter 13 offers some practical advice for the challenging and much underestimated task of assessing the performance of commercial identity matching products. A number of factors have combined to create a situation where an identity matching application's relative market popularity may not be as indicative of its performance as might be expected. An effective product evaluation can therefore be invaluable in ensuring that investments in identity matching technology achieve their full potential.

Once a strong solution has been selected it must still be appropriately configured to ensure that the most relevant hits are identified and are correctly prioritised. Chapter 14 introduces a Linguistic Search Standard to offer guidance on the minimum criteria that could be applied when defining expected results and configuring search parameters to meet these expectations.

Chapter 12: Name Matching and Identity Matching

The matching of proper names plays a key role in any identity matching process; in many cases, the name may be the only criterion entered into the search. Name matching is also the one element of identity matching that is most directly affected by the paradigm shift towards linguistic matching, which is why this text has so far focused on the way that names are matched. However, a person's name is only one feature of their identity and many identity matching processes allow for a broad range of search attributes. This chapter looks at the non-name characteristics that are most frequently included in the search profile and introduces the additional requirements that they bring to the design of a comprehensive identity search solution.

Identity characteristics other than the name can be grouped into classes of attributes that share similar features. The most important attribute classes are:

- **space-related attributes**
  including address, place of birth and nationality
- **time-related attributes**
  including date of birth (or incorporation for legal entities)
- **classifying attributes**
  including gender (or the legal form of legal entities)
- **identification codes**
  including tax reference, passport number or social security number

These attributes are often used to complement name information in an identity search but may also be used alone (for example when a search is based on a social security number). The match methods most appropriate for these non-name attributes may differ significantly from those that have proven most useful for matching proper names. However, while some attributes may demand the use of greatly modified match methods, others can be dealt with using methods borrowed from the name matching techniques previously discussed.

The following sections look more closely at the attribute classes listed above. The final part of this chapter considers the possible methods for combining the search of all these different attributes with a proper name search to assess an overall identity match.

12.1 Space-Related Identity Attributes

For matching data related to natural persons, the most relevant space-related identity attributes are nationality, country of birth, place of birth and the addresses of residence, correspondence and tax domicile. For legal entities, the key space-related identifiers are the country of incorporation and the addresses of headquarters, subsidiaries, branches and legal advisors. All these features may vary in the way they are represented and, as with proper names, it is important to understand the sources of potential variation in order to determine the most appropriate matching methods.

12.1.1 Nationality, Country of Birth and Country of Incorporation

The range of possible nationalities and countries of birth (or incorporation) is largely defined by the set of nation states, though on occasion an individual may be "stateless" or consider their nationality to be a country that is not internationally recognised. Many identity matching systems use a drop down list based on the internationally recognised ISO codes for the entry of country-related search criteria. Each recognised state is allocated both a two and a three digit code under this system. Where the data to be searched has been mapped to these ISO codes, and search entry is limited to a drop-down list containing these values, most sources of variation can be controlled.

However, errors can arise if the ISO country codes are confused, either in the underlying data or in the search query. For example, the ISO code for *Iran*, *IR*, could be mistaken to mean *Ireland*, which is assigned the two digit code *IE*. Other problems may arise if it is not clear which standard has been used to assign the country codes. While many databases use the ISO standard codes, other systems may be appropriate for different purposes, and there is scope for confusion between the two. For example, the international vehicle registration code for cars registered in *Liechtenstein* is *FL* but the ISO code for *Liechtenstein* is *LI*, while *FL* may mistakenly be thought to represent *Finland*. Such confusion can be avoided if the drop-down list used for data entry displays full country names rather than the standardised codes, but the codes are often used in order to save space on the user interface.

Misunderstandings can also occur in the use of full country names. For example, someone entering data from an official record that cites the place of birth as *East Pakistan* may enter the country as *Pakistan* instead of the modern day independent nation of *Bangladesh*, as the former *East Pakistan* is now known. If the data being searched is known to contain such errors, simple adjustments can be made to the matching process to allow for this.

If the input of data, either to the underlying database or to the search profile, is not limited to selection from a drop down list and allows free-text entry, several different types of variation may be introduced. Many of these are similar to those that have been discussed when looking at proper names. These include:

- **Translated country names**
  such as *Germany / Deutschland / Allemagne*
- **Multiple names within a language**
  such as *Ceylon / Sri Lanka* or *Burma / Myanmar*
- **Abbreviations**
  such as *GB / GBR / Great Britain* or *UK / United Kingdom*
- **Optional elements**
  as in *People's Republic of China / China*
- **Homophonic spelling errors**
  such as *Kenya / Kenia* or *Thailand / Tailand*
- **Non-linguistic typos**
  such as transpositions, as in *Beligum / Belgium*

One variation source which does not exist in the names of people and organisations stems from the emergence and decline of different countries. At the end of the 20th Century, the *Soviet Union*, the *German Democratic Republic* (*GDR*) and *Yugoslavia* ceased to exist as nation states or federations. New states emerged from the *Soviet Union* and *Yugoslavia*, while the *GDR* became part of the *Federal Republic of Germany*. Without special measures to address these relationships, errors may be made in the matching process. The three examples given below show the different ways in which this could happen:

- A person born in *Belgrade* in the 1980's would have had their country of birth registered as *Yugoslavia* (or *YU* under the two-digit ISO system). Since the breakup of the former *Yugoslavia*, *Belgrade* has been the capital of *Serbia* (with the ISO code *RS*). If a search is submitted using *Serbia* as the country of birth, the query may well fail to find a matching profile showing the birth country as *Yugoslavia*.

- A database may use the separate codes *DD* (the code for the former *German Democratic Republic* or *East Germany*) and *DE* (the code for the *Federal Republic of Germany*, formerly *West Germany*) for the countries of birth for persons born between 1949 and 1990. Many search tools use a drop-down list containing only current ISO country codes for entering the search profile. To allow for this, they may include a reference table that directs searches for current states to include all their predecessor states. In this case, the search with the code *DE* would also find profiles with the country code *DD*, thus avoiding the situation in the example above where the matching profile is potentially not identified. However, this improved recall comes at the expense of precision, as it is not possible to restrict a search to persons born in *East Germany*, or to those known to have been born in the West.
- If two data sets relating to the former *Soviet Union* are merged, it may be challenging to reconcile the way that the different modern states have been recognised, particularly if data has been collected at different points in time. In this case, the data will likely reflect the different stages of the dissolution of the *Soviet Union*. Some entries may refer to the *Soviet Union*, while others may list its successor states, such as the *Russian Federation*, *Georgia*, *Ukraine*, *Armenia* or *Uzbekistan*. Owing to the difficulties of separating out the records that refer to the *Soviet Union* into the correct former Soviet states, the consolidated database may convert all such records to refer to *Former Soviet Republics*. Though this avoids the obvious false negative problem, it is another way in which precision may be compromised, as the information previously recorded in the more specific records is lost to the matching process.

This situation is not purely of historical relevance. Recognised territories continue to break apart and new states continue to declare independence. For example, the break-away territory of *Kosovo* began to issue its nationals with passports in 2008, and though not every state officially recognises its independence from *Serbia*, many accept its passports as valid travel documents. As Kosovo's declaration of independence has only partially been accepted by the international community, at the time of writing it has yet to be issued with a distinct ISO code and many databases still classify *Kosovo* under the Serbian code *RS*. Other databases may use their own codes to refer to such disputed territories. These codes should be replaced with an official ISO country code if Kosovo's international recognition reaches the required level.

A good matching system will include a heuristic method for dealing with such fluctuations in geographical borders and will be updated with the ebb and flow of international recognition. However, this would seem to be the exception rather than the rule in most matching applications, not because an appropriate solution would be technically complex or expensive to implement, but more likely because the issue has been overlooked.

12.1.2 Names of Districts, Towns, Villages and Other Places

While country information is often stored in a database (or entered into a search) with the help of a drop-down reference, this is rarely the case for other space-related attributes. Even if spelling variations are not considered, in most cases the number of place names that could potentially need to be entered is simply too high to be comprehensively covered in a drop-down list. Such information is therefore often entered as free-text and the possible variants that can be introduced are similar to those that occur in free-text country information. These include:

- **Names in translation**
  such as *Munich* (in English or French), *München* (German), *Munique* (Portuguese), *Monaco di Baviera* (Italian) or *Münih* (Turkish)
- **Different transcriptions of place names from non-Latin scripts**
  For example, although the Chinese name (北京) for *Peking* has not changed, it is now more common for it to be referred to in English as *Beijing*, following the Pinyin standard of romanisation.
- **Multiple names within the same language**
  such as *Mumbai/Bombay*, *Harare/Salisbury* or *St Petersburg/Leningrad*
- **Abbreviations and acronyms**
  including *NYC* for *New York City* or *LA* for *Los Angeles*
- **Optional name elements**
  as in *Stratford* (*-upon-Avon*), (*St.*) *Petersburg* or *Frankfurt* (*am Main*)
- **Homophonic spelling variants**
  such as *Edinburgh/Edinborough*, *Bangkok/ Bankok* or *Melbourne/Melburn*
- **Non-linguistic typos**
  including transpositions, such as *Lodnon* instead of *London* or *Manchetser* instead of *Manchester*

The examples above show that, where place names are searched for in an identity matching system, it is important that derivatives of these can be recognised. Derivative variants of place names are arguably more common than those for country names, which, on the whole, have been subject to greater standardisation efforts. Place names in their native language (endonyms such as *Milano*) may be used interchangeably with their corresponding exonyms (such as *Milan* or *Mailand*) and towns and cities often change their names as a result of regime changes, movement of national borders or changes to the local language.

In Germany, many place names were altered as a result of the 1996 national spelling reform. Examples include *Haßberg*, which became *Hassberg*, *Rauhkopf*, which became *Raukopf* and *Gemsenberg*, which became *Gämsenberg*. Nevertheless, the earlier spelling variants are still often used.

Like countries, other places may change their form through the process of amalgamation and separation of villages or towns. Thesauri can be used to ensure that the search correctly identifies current and former names of related places. Similarly, thesauri should be used to incorporate information on geographical hierarchy; *Islington* is part of *London* just as *Kreuzberg* is part of *Berlin* or *Manhattan* a part of *New York*. This information can be kept in a reference table so that a search, for example, for *Westminster* could identify records that list a location simply as *London*.

Complications may arise from the fact that a place name is not necessarily distinctive, with many places sharing the same name. In English-speaking countries, there are many places called *Newtown* (or variants such as *New Town* or *Newton*). The same logical naming pattern can be seen in other language areas, with *Villeneuve* (or *Neuville*) in French-speaking areas, *Neustadt* (or *Neuenstadt*) in German-language regions, *Villanova* (or *Cittanova*) in Italian-speaking areas and *Novograd* (or *Novgorod*) in East Slavic language areas such as Russia and the Ukraine. In addition, many new settlements were traditionally named after historic cities; the United States alone contains dozens of places named *London*, *Birmingham* or *Manchester* and dozens more named *Berlin*, *Paris* or *Amsterdam*.

Even connecting a place name with a state or region within a country may not be enough to uniquely identify the place. For example, the US state of Wisconsin contains two towns and a city all called *Berlin*. The use of postal codes can alleviate this problem significantly, but these are often omitted and may be entered only in part or in varying formats. In some parts of the world they may not even be used. That said, depending on the context, a matching place name in itself may provide significant corroboration for a name match or match on other identity characteristics.

12.1.3 Addresses

Many of the considerations discussed above apply also to the matching of more detailed address information. The full address can take many forms, from one single free-text field to multiple structured data elements. Besides town and country information, an address may include elements such as postal codes, street names and house names or numbers. They may also include additional information in the form of prefixes such as *c/o* or *FAO*. Any of the component elements may be omitted and the order of the remaining parts varies according to the standards used in different postal regions. For example, many continental countries place the house number after the street name rather than before, as is more common in English-speaking countries, while Japanese addresses typically do not include a street name at all.

A street name, or hodonym, usually consists of a specific name part (such as *Fleet*, *Harley*, *Station*, *King George*, etc) and a generic name part (such as *Street*, *Road*, *Avenue*, etc). Variations in the specific part of a street name are similar to those seen in the names of people and organisations (particularly in cases where a street has been named after one of these). Many streets are named after their destination, so that the variations seen in place names also exist in names of streets. The most common variations in the generic part of a street name are abbreviations. There may be one standard abbreviation in use, such as *St.* for *Street*, or several possible abbreviations, such as *Bd*, *Bvd* or *Bvld* for *Boulevard*. In some circumstances, errors may be more likely in the generic part of the street name than in its specific core. For example, *Churchill Street* may be more likely to be a mistaken reference to *Churchill Avenue* than to *Carnaby Street*.

International influences play a strong role in the matching of global address data. The thesaurus of abbreviations for the generic parts of street names must consider abbreviations in all major languages, such as the German *Str.* for *Strasse*, or the French *Ch.* for *Chemin*. There may also be variation sources that are specific to particular languages. For example, the specific and generic parts of German street names may be written together or apart, as in *Neuheimer Weg*, *Neuheimer-Weg* or *Neuheimerweg*. Other typical variations seen in German street names include differences in conjunctive elements as in *Friedrichgasse* and *Friedrichsgasse*, or *Sonnweg* and *Sonnenweg*.

Though street names are usually fairly static, depending on the country involved and the time at which the data was collected, potential name changes may also need to be considered in the matching process. Streets may be re-named en masse at times of regime change or changes to the national languages, particularly if former colonies gain independence or borders between neighbouring countries are shifted. If the data to be searched is likely to be affected by such factors, a reference table linking the old and new street names could be incorporated into the matching routine.

A final possible source of variation stems from the data collection and storage process. Address element labels such as "Post Code" or "Town" may be stored as text with the related data so the matching routine needs to be able to screen out these standard terms in all relevant languages.

Once a match or mismatch in address information has been determined, it is important to consider the way in which this should affect the rating of the overall identity match. While a matching address is highly likely to confirm a match in the name, a mismatched address may be less significant. Given the transient nature of address information, a mismatch in this data does not necessarily indicate that a matched name is a false positive result. The relevant significance of matches and mismatches in each identity characteristic is considered further at the end of this chapter.

12.2 Time-Related Identity Attributes

Time-related identity attributes include the date of birth of a natural person or the incorporation date of a legal entity. Other time-related attributes may relate to the date of marriage or death. In some cases, time-related attributes may add detail to other identity characteristics, as with the dates that show the duration of residence at a specified address or the length of employment in a particular position.

Dates are usually stored in a database as a date data-type. Though this may seem obvious, it is often not the most appropriate way to store dates that may be used in an identity matching process. One reason for this is that the date data-type is not able to store partial date information. In many countries it is not uncommon for an individual to know only their year of birth (e.g. 1978). In such cases, the date of birth may be arbitrarily completed as *01-Jan-1978*. Depending on the search logic in place, a search with the date *27-Nov-1978* may not find the related profile, despite the year (the only certain part of the date) being correctly matched. In other processes, other parts of the date may be missing. For example, recruitment data in some jurisdictions may record only the day and month of the date of birth in order to prevent age discrimination. This kind of information is typically entered to a comment field in databases that require a full date for the date of birth, and so may be excluded from the matching process altogether.

Another reason why a single date data-type field may not be sufficient for storing identity data is that dates are frequently only known within a certain range. For example, if a media report gives the age of an individual as 37 at the time of his conviction on *01-Jun-2010* then his date of birth could be assumed to be *between 02-Jun-1972 and 01-Jun-1973*. In such situations, date of birth information is frequently entered into a comment field, perhaps in the form of an approximate age. In other cases, an approximate date of birth may be entered or, if the system allows, two dates of birth may be entered. The most flexible way of storing date information for identity matching purposes is to use a date range stored as a "date from" and "date to", with both of these dates split into separate numeric fields for day, month and year. This method of storing dates, however, is the exception rather than the rule.

The splitting of day, month and year information also helps to avoid one of the key sources of variation in dates in the Anglophone world: the swapping of the month and the day in the US and UK date formats. In the UK *02/08/73* would be read as the *2nd of August*, while in the US it is likely to be understood as *February 8th*. However, the fact that dates are stored and entered to a search system as separate day, month and year values does not rule out the possibility that the day and month values were swapped at some point before they were entered to the database, so it is always important that the matching system is able to account for such errors.

The least structured method of storing date information is in a free-text field. This has the advantage that additional information such as circa or approx. or comments such as *age 37 as at 1 June 2010* can be added, which may be helpful if the record is manually reviewed. However, such information is of limited use in an automated search situation and this method of storage allows typos and other variations to be introduced. These include simple spelling errors (such as *Jannuary* instead of *January*), abbreviations (such as *Jan.* for *January*), translations (such as *Janvier*, *Januar*, *Gennaio* or *Enero*) and abbreviations for translations (such as *Janv.* for *Janvier*). Other variations may be introduced in the use of digits or symbols and the order of the date parts. For example, free-text date entries could include *5/1*, *5. Jan*, *fifth January*, *January fifth* or *5th January*. Transposition errors may also alter the way digits are entered, turning *12-Jan* into *21-Jan*, or *1974* into *1947*. All these classes of variations can typically be dealt with using string comparison techniques and / or a thesaurus-type reference table.

There are generally two ways in which a fuzzy search can be realised with time-related attributes and it may be appropriate to implement them both.

Time-span as a measure of fuzziness

The time-span fuzziness is a measure of the length of time between the two dates being compared. Using this concept, *31-Dec-99* and *1-Jan-00* are closer than *1-Jan-00* and *3-Jan-00* (one day apart as opposed to 2 days apart), despite the very different composition of the day, month and year elements. Similarly, *12-May-47* and *7-Jul-1950* are closer under this method than *12-May-47* and *12-May-74*, despite the similarities in the component date parts of the latter pair.

Element-congruence as a measure of fuzziness

The element-based fuzziness is defined by the degree of congruence between the individual date elements. Using this method *31-Dec-99* and *1-Jan-00* would not match as none of the individual date elements match. *1-Jan-00* and *3-Jan-00* would be considered a stronger match. Similarly, using this method *12-May-47* and *12-May-74* are a good match, despite the 27 years that separate them, as the day and month match and the year is also matched if transpositions are considered.

If appropriate, the two fuzziness models can be combined with relatively little conceptual or technical difficulty.

In most matching processes, the element-based congruence is of most relevance. It may be refined to allow for date elements to be swapped, for example to facilitate the matching of dates using the US and UK formats, or to allow the matching of dates from calendars other than the Gregorian. For example, some Islamic countries use the Hijri calendar to date official documents, so it may be desirable to allow Gregorian dates to be matched to their Hijri counterparts. For a number of reasons, including different methods for determining the start of a lunar month, the fact that Islamic dates start at sunset rather than midnight, and differences in conversion algorithms, the translation of Gregorian dates may result in varying Islamic dates. The Gregorian date 2-Oct-56 may, for example, be converted to 26 Safar 1376 (٢٦ صفر ١٣٧٦) or to 27 Safar 1376 (٢٧ صفر ١٣٧٦).

Such factors need to be taken into consideration if more than one calendar type is to be accommodated.

12.3 Classifying Attributes

In the context of this book, classifying attributes are those characteristics of a person that are neither directly related to space or time, nor individually assigned like identification numbers and other reference codes. The highest level of classification attribute defines the type of person that the record relates to, such as *natural person*, *legal entity* or *unofficial organisation*. Additional classifying attributes may be used to further describe the person's characteristics, such as the gender, distinguishing features such as eye colour, qualifications or occupation of natural persons, and the legal form and industry sector of other entities.

It is beneficial for these attributes to be captured using pre-defined categories that allow for a simple, unambiguous and error free selection of the appropriate value. The required reference tables can be compiled relatively easily in the case of simple attributes such as gender. However, the compilation of an unambiguous catalogue of values that comprehensively reflects other classifications, such as industry, is much more complex. Even outwardly simple characteristics like legal form can pose challenges when looked at in a global context. This is because the legal forms used in each jurisdiction are defined and delimited by different criteria; the forms used in one country are often not directly comparable to those used in other areas. The creation of a systematic and practical reference system that covers all legal forms in use globally is therefore a complex task.

Where identity data includes these classifying attributes, they can be used to filter or weight search hits, as described in section 12.5 below. In some cases, however, identity data may include little information beyond the person's name. Advanced identity matching systems have introduced methods for inferring some classifying attributes from different aspects of the name. For example, a profile bearing a name that includes the terms *Limited*, *Inc*, *GmbH* or *Trust* most likely refers to a legal entity. This information can be used to filter the profile out of the hits on a search for a natural person.

Though far less straightforward, similar techniques can be used to infer a likely gender for the profiles of natural persons. The use of inferred gender information can be particularly useful in matching names based on initials. For example, it may be appropriate to match *Alan Smith* with *John A. Smith*, but a match to

Clare A. Smith would most likely be a false positive result and could either be filtered out or downgraded based on the inferred gender mismatch. In a global context, this is a much more complicated task than it may at first appear, as the onomastic influences of all languages and cultural areas need to be taken into account.

In the Western world, the given name is often indicative of the individual's gender, though there are obviously exceptions to this rule (such as the name *Ashley*, which can be given to both males and females). However, different language areas frequently associate the same names with different genders. In English, *Andrea*, *Simone* and *Nicola* are typically female names, while in Italy they are more likely to refer to men, just as the name *Anne* is generally given to females in the Anglophone world but may be a man's name in the Netherlands. In Spanish and Portuguese-speaking communities it is not uncommon for a man to have *Maria* as the second part of a compound given name, as in *José Maria* and it is important that such culturally specific features are incorporated into any kind of gender inference process.

Even within English language areas there are inconsistencies. As described in section 3.3, the naming system in the US provides for children to take their mother's maiden name as a form of matronymic middle name. As many common given names can also be found as family names (and therefore maiden names) it is perfectly possible for a person in the US to have a middle name that is typically a given name for the opposite sex. Thus a woman may have *Stewart*, *Gilbert* or *Martin* as a middle name if one of these was her mother's maiden name. Given the ambiguities involved, it may be more appropriate, when dealing with Western names, to infer that a profile is simply more or less likely to refer to a person of a particular gender and to reflect this in the overall match score, rather than to filter the search results based on an assumed gender.

As in the Western naming system, the Russian given name is reasonably indicative of gender, with certain specific exceptions. However, in the Russian context, the patronym and family name are used in a different grammatical form for males and females (as described in section 3.5) and offer a clearer indication of gender. For example, if Ивановна Кузнецова *(Ivanovna Kuznetsova)* are the patronym and family name of a woman, Иванович Кузнецов (*Ivanovich Kuznetsov*) would be the related name parts of her brother.

However, while the original Cyrillic name is usually clear in this regard, the transcribed family name may be more ambiguous. Кузнецова, for example, may be correctly transcribed as *Kuznetsova* but is often transcribed in Western media as *Kuznetsov*. This use of the masculine version of family names is becoming more widespread, so that while *Kuznetsova* clearly refers to a woman, *Kuznetsov* may refer to either a man or a woman. In a well-known example, *Raisa Gorbachova* is frequently referred to in the West as *Raisa Gorbachev*, playing to the Western assumption that a wife's family name will match that of her husband. In such cases, the original script version of the family name (if available) may give a clearer indication of gender. Otherwise it should be recognised that while a "female" family name is very likely to belong to a woman, the gender of a person with a "male" romanised family name is less clear.

In the Arab name system (described in section 3.6), gender may be inferred from the Ism (similar to the way Western given names may indicate gender), from the Kunya (with *Abu* indicating a male and *Umm* used by females), from the Nasab (in which *Bin* indicates a male and *Bint* a female) and sometimes even from the Laqab (for example, the male name *Abdullah* and female name *Amatullah*). However, some ambiguity is introduced in the fact that these names may also appear in their male form as family names. In addition, there are cases where the *Bin* or *Bint* may be omitted from the Nasab construction, so that the clearly female *Bint Hasan* becomes the ostensibly male *Hasan*. In such cases there are often other name elements that can be used to infer gender. For example *Fatima Hasan Hussni* is likely to be the daughter of *Hasan*. This demonstrates that any routine designed to infer gender from a person's name must consider the name as a whole and not the individual elements in isolation.

These are just some examples from three important name systems; many more features can be found in the other naming systems in use around the world. Overall, there are certainly a number of starting points from which to infer gender from a name, particularly where the name element type is known. Some systems use this information to increase precision by filtering results based on the assumed gender. As the inference of gender from name is by no means an exact science, there will be some price to pay in terms of recall for the increased precision. A more risk averse but more complex strategy might be to use onomastic thesauri to assess the probability that a name refers to a particular gender and then to use this probability to adjust the overall match score accordingly.

12.4 Identification Codes

Identification codes such as passport numbers, social security numbers, tax references or customer IDs are some of the most distinctive identity characteristics. This is not surprising given that this was largely the reason for their creation. Their comparatively limited circulation is the only reason why they do not play a more central role in the identity matching process.

Identification codes have a relatively simple structure and are often optimised for automated processing. They are most appropriately referred to as identification codes rather than identification numbers as they often consist of alphabetic and selected punctuation characters as well as numerical digits. The typical variation sources differ from the key sources found in proper names as they are rarely transcribed and hardly ever pronounced (or mispronounced).

Non-linguistic typos are, however, relevant for the matching of identification codes, though in this context they may differ slightly in the most common types of error. As many identification codes include numbers and other special characters, the theory that a typo involving a non-alphabetic character is more likely to be spotted and corrected by the user does not apply. The assumption that typos are more likely to involve characters set closely together on the keyboard still holds but has to be modified to take into account that numbers may be entered either via the top row of a standard keyboard, via a separate numeric key pad, or through the use of standard alphabetic keys with the number lock turned on. The use, replacement or omission of non-alphanumeric characters also has to be considered. For example, *1234567* may also appear as *123-4567* or *123.4567*. Codes may also include optional prefixes and suffixes so in many cases partial matches should not be overlooked.

One of the most important considerations when matching identification codes is to ensure, where possible, that only codes of a like kind are compared; there is little benefit to be gained from comparing a passport number with a social security number. Where the type of code used is uncertain, this must be factored into the way the code match contributes to the overall identity match. In many cases a matching identity code is likely to indicate related profiles, as codes are usually specific enough for a random match to be unlikely, particularly if supported by other matching characteristics. However, a mismatched code is far less significant if it is not sure that the codes represent the same kind of identity attribute.

12.5 Integration of Single Attribute Comparisons

In an identity search involving multiple attributes, the results of the individual attribute comparisons must somehow be combined to determine the overall identity match rating. As with many aspects of identity matching, the most appropriate way to do this will depend on the particular circumstances of the process, taking into consideration the quality of the data being searched, the expertise of the users and the intended use of the search results. Essentially, there are two main methods of combining the individual attribute match scores to produce an overall identity match: the filter model and the weighting model.

12.5.1 The Filter Model

In its purest form, the filter model sets threshold limits for each of the identity characteristics, which all have to be passed if a profile is to appear in the search results. This is clearly quite a restrictive method, as just one mismatched characteristic would prevent a match being displayed in the search results even if a perfect match was present in all other attributes. To prevent the recall of the search being excessively compromised, it is necessary to set the threshold limits at a relatively low level, to apply broad fuzzy matching techniques and to ensure that absent characteristics (such as a missing date of birth) do not prevent the match from passing through the filter.

At first glance, it may seem that the filter model is of limited practical value. However, the users of identity search systems often want and expect the search to behave in this way. For example, if a search for a common name generates large numbers of hits, the user may expect to be able to add a nationality to the search and thereby remove all the profiles with a different nationality from the hit list. In simple terms, users often expect that with every additional attribute added to the search profile the number of hits generated will decrease (or at least will not increase). This effect is provided by the filter model but, as discussed below, cannot be reproduced using the weighting model.

The basic function of the filter model can be illustrated with a simple example.

A search is submitted with three criteria: name, date of birth and nationality. The thresholds for each of these three attributes are set at 60%. Any profile that does not match all of the characteristics with a score of at least 60% will not appear on the hit list.

Consider the following search and data profiles:

	Name	Date of Birth	Nationality
Search Profile	Jelzin	2-Jan-1930	Russian
Data Profile	Yeltsin	1-Jan-1931	Russian

A comparison of these two profiles could result in a congruence of, for example, 90% in the name (as they are valid transcription variants of the same name), 50% in the date of birth and 100% in the nationality. As the congruence of the date of birth is below the 60% threshold, the data profile would not be identified as a match to the search profile. Even if the name were a 100% match, the profile would still not meet the requirements for the profile to be shown on the hit list. Only lowering the date of birth threshold to 50% or removing the date of birth from the search profile could change this result.

12.5.2 The Weighting Model

The weighting model assigns weighting factors rather than threshold values to each identity attribute. The overall congruence of the identity profiles is calculated as a weighted average of the single attribute comparison scores. In simplified terms, this can be shown in the following formula:

$$\text{Match Score} = \frac{(W_{Name} \times C_{Name}) + (W_{DoB} \times C_{DoB}) + (W_{Nat.} \times C_{Nat.})}{W_{Name} + W_{DoB} + W_{Nat.}}$$

Where W_{Name}, W_{DoB} and $W_{Nat.}$ represent the weighting factors applied to the three attributes, and C_{Name}, C_{DoB} and $C_{Nat.}$ represent the congruence, or match scores, calculated by comparing the individual attributes.

Setting the weighting factors for name, date of birth and nationality to 10, 5 and 3 respectively, the *Yeltsin* example used above can be modified to demonstrate the application of the weighting model.

	Name	Date of Birth	Nationality
Search Profile	Jelzin	2-Jan-1930	Russian
Data Profile	Yeltsin	1-Jan-1931	Russian
Weighting Factor	10	5	3
Congruence	90%	50%	100%

In this example, the formula provides a match score of just over 80%.

$$\text{Match Score} = \frac{(10 \times 90\%) + (5 \times 50\%) + (3 \times 100\%)}{10 + 5 + 3} = 80.56\%$$

Unlike the filter model, which sets a threshold for the congruence of each individual characteristic, the threshold in the weighting model is set for the overall identity match score. If the overall threshold is set at 80%, then the *Yeltsin* profile would appear on the hit list in this example. With a threshold of 81% or higher, the profile would not be shown.

A popular advantage of the weighting model is that a low congruence in one identity attribute can be compensated for by a very close congruence in other characteristics. However, this is achieved at the expense of the filter-type effect that many users have come to expect from their search tools. Using this method, it is perfectly possible that adding additional criteria to the search profile could expand, rather than reduce, the number of hits produced.

For example, if a search based on name and date of birth produces a large number of hits, the user may try to reduce the hit list by additionally specifying the nationality in the search profile. Using the weighting model, some profiles may indeed drop off the hit list if they have a different nationality to that specified. However, profiles that produced identity match scores just below the required threshold in the original search may be added to the hit list if their overall match score is boosted by a matching nationality.

This effect can be demonstrated using the *Yeltsin* example from above:

Consider the search using just the name and date of birth:

	Name	Date of Birth	Nationality
Search Profile	Jelzin	2-Jan-1930	
Data Profile	Yeltsin	1-Jan-1931	Russian
Weighting Factor	10	5	3
Congruence	90%	50%	

The following score can be calculated:

$$\text{Match Score} = \frac{(10 \times 90\%) + (5 \times 50\%)}{10 + 5} = 76.67\%$$

If the overall threshold is set at 80%, the profile would not be shown on the search hit list. However, as demonstrated in the calculation above, adding the nationality to the search profile would raise the overall identity matching score to 80.56%: just enough to bring the profile on to the search hit list.

Thus, though the weighting model is perhaps more theoretically sound than the stricter filter model, it often does not meet the expectations of system users.

12.5.3 Combined Models

There are many ways in which the filter and weighting models can be combined or adapted to provide a more flexible search that more closely fits users' expectations. These include:

- Using some attributes as a filter, while others contribute to a weighted match score. For example, in some cases it may be appropriate to use gender or nationality as a filter, with other attributes combining to create the overall score.
- Using some attributes as a filter but taking a weighted average of all attributes to create an overall identity match score.
- Applying a minimum match threshold to certain attributes that they must reach in order to contribute to the overall identity score. For example, a

match score could be defined using a weighted average of all attributes, substituting zero for the score of any attribute that is not at least 40% congruent.

Though this chapter has focused on non-name identity attributes, it should not be forgotten that the name itself consists of multiple elements, such as the given and family names, that must be combined in order to arrive at an overall name match score. A combined approach could be used to consolidate the scores obtained from comparing each name element. For example, the filter model can be applied to stipulate that there must be at least some form of match in the family name field, while the weighting model can be applied to combine the element match scores into an overall name match.

12.5.4 Missing and Mismatched Attributes

The scoring methods described above are greatly simplified examples; in practice, a good matching system will modify the match score calculation in many ways. One common modification alters the way that mismatched attributes, and attributes that are missing from either the search or data profile, affect the match score. Again, the way in which this is done will depend on the particular circumstances of the matching process. Data quality is an important consideration. For example, if the middle name is missing from a data profile, does that mean that the individual really has no middle name or simply that it has been omitted from the data? If the data profile has no nationality recorded, is it certain that the person is stateless? Similarly, if the profile does have a nationality listed, is it certain that the individual does not hold additional nationalities that are not recorded?

A further consideration is the amount of time that has passed since the data was collected or last updated. If the search profiles and data profiles were collected at different times then mismatches in less stable attributes like the address will be far less significant than matches in these attributes. The weighting factor for these attributes therefore depends on whether each characteristic is matched or mismatched. This is similar to the example discussed above where identification codes of different types may be matched against each other. If it is sure that the codes represent the same identity attribute then a mismatch can be attributed a higher weight than if it is not certain which kind of identification codes are being compared. Conversely, matched identification codes can be allowed a relatively more significant weight, even if it is not certain that they refer to the same type of code, as accidental matches in different types of reference codes can be assumed to be relatively rare.

12.6 Conclusion

This chapter has put name matching (the core focus of this book) into the context of the overall identity match. The name is usually the most important aspect of a person's identity as names are both widely used and relatively distinctive. However, both recall and precision can often be significantly improved if additional identity attributes are added to the search.

Some of the principles discussed for matching names can also be applied to the matching of other identity characteristics. For all attributes, the principle holds that the most appropriate match methods can be identified by analysing the sources of variation that may be introduced in each case. Some of the methods appropriate for matching names will also be appropriate for matching other attributes. For example, the methods used to deal with transcription variants and homophones in the matching of person names can also be applied to the matching of place names. In other cases, for example when matching time-related attributes, new matching methods must be devised.

This chapter has also introduced the possibilities that exist when using name information to infer other characteristics, such as gender, legal form or industry. The potential of such methods is largely untapped in many popular matching systems but, when used within appropriate boundaries, they can have a significant impact on precision. For example, the names *J. Arthur Clarke* and *Julie A. Clarke* can potentially be excluded as matches, despite their matching initials, based on the gender inferred from the available given names. However, such techniques can lead to reductions in recall if not carried out with a truly global linguistic perspective, as which name elements are indicative of which gender varies across different languages and cultural regions. The research required to accurately implement gender inference may be one reason why many software vendors have so far shied away from this kind of enhancement despite the benefits it may yield if applied correctly.

The basic features of the filter and weighting models for integrating the results of single element comparisons have also been discussed. These models can be used to combine the scores from the comparison of different name elements into an overall name match score, as well as to bring together the name match score with the scores from other attribute comparisons to provide an overall identity match score.

The methods for calculating an overall identity match score that have been introduced in this chapter are an appropriate starting point for more sophisticated models. They incorporate the two main concepts on which match scores should be based: the significance of each attribute comparison and the congruence of the two attributes being matched (as discussed in section 10.2.2). These core concepts may then be extended with other factors. Modifications may include the application of attribute-specific parameters that weight matches and mismatches differently or determine the treatment of missing attributes.

The information presented in this chapter should help management to define the aspects of a match that they wish to be reflected in the overall identity match score. Formulas that comprehensively include a logical treatment of comparison scores for each individual attribute are inherently extremely complex. However, these more sophisticated formulas allow match scores to more closely reflect the overall similarity of the matched profiles, and therefore the expectations of system users.

Chapter 13: Evaluation of Identity Matching Software

13.1 Introduction

There are several commercially available tools designed to search identity data and many more software suites that contain an identity matching component. Assessing the matching performance of such products is no trivial task, requiring specialist expertise that is available in only a very few commercial or administrative organisations. In the absence of specialist identity matching resources, businesses often look to market position as an indicator of quality.

In many software areas this may be a reasonable approach, but in a market where many businesses are ill-equipped to evaluate the performance of identity matching components, this has lead to a situation where popularity begets wider popularity, with actual functionality often having a surprisingly low impact on this process. As a result, the matching performance of the most widely recognised search-related products often displays little correlation with their popularity in the market.

Anyone considering investing in software with an identity matching component would therefore be well advised to take the time to effectively test the functionality on offer. As this chapter will explain, simply typing in a sample of names and checking to see that the hit lists look reasonable is not sufficient. The test design requires a good degree of planning if it is to assess both recall and precision with regard to all classes of variation. Care taken at this stage will help to avoid poor investment decisions as well as additional operational and regulatory costs further down the line.

Most software purchase decisions require a careful evaluation phase, but there is one important difference in the evaluation of identity matching capabilities. Behind most software evaluations lies an existing business process, often in need of a replacement for a legacy system. Experienced users of the existing system (those with a good understanding of the functionality of the tool) are usually well positioned to define requirements for the new application and able, at least approximately, to determine how well the potential replacement system fulfils these requirements.

The difference with the assessment of identity matching software, and the reason that this chapter has been included in this text, lies in the definition and testing of the essential linguistic and onomastic requirements. Users of the existing system may be able to formulate requirements in the areas of usability, functional scope or technical performance, but are less likely to possess the required knowledge to set linguistic targets for recall and precision. It is in this area that organisations often lack the resources to accurately define what is required of an identity matching component and to design the test cases that will demonstrate how well these requirements are met. And yet it is performance in this area that truly matters; a linguistic assessment of recall and precision should be at the heart of every identity matching evaluation.

As discussed in section 8.7.3, the linguistic knowledge required to accurately identify transcription variants of the same name is considerable. The ability to recognise that, for example, *I*, *Lee*, *Yi*, *Rey* and *Rhee* should be regarded as good matches to one another (as transcription variants of the same name), while *Zou*, *Zhou*, *Zhuo* and *Zhu* are transcriptions of different names, is essential to the evaluation of identity matching applications. Corresponding knowledge of other variation sources, such as derivative names or homophones, is also vital and though this may appear to be less problematic, looked at in a global context, the challenges are significant.

If an assessment of matching capabilities is carried out without the required linguistic input, it can be expected that the results will tend to favour a more exact (less "fuzzy") search. More exact searches often provide seemingly good quality hit lists because each hit looks relevant (and usually is). However, it is actually only the precision of such searches that is strong, while their recall is often severely compromised. Crucially, this significant weakness is not directly visible in the search results, which by definition do not highlight the relevant profiles that have not been matched.

The considerations relevant to the preparation and execution of application evaluations in general would fill a book on their own and many texts are available on this subject. This chapter focuses on the aspects specific to the evaluation of identity matching tools and does not cover the more general requirements such as:

- **Technical criteria**, including platform requirements, response times, ease of integration and maintenance

- **User-focused criteria**, including usability, training requirements, available "help" functionality and documentation
- **Organisational criteria**, including budget, deferred payment requirements and the impact on existing supplier relationships
- **Vendor-related criteria**, including market position, financial stability, mid-term strategy and the quality of available support

It should not, therefore, be expected that the information contained in this chapter is sufficient in itself to allow the full evaluation of identity matching tools. However, together with the linguistic background provided in the rest of this text, it should allow those experienced in software testing to successfully evaluate tools in the unique area of identity matching.

This chapter focuses on the testing of identity matching software components rather than on-line identity search facilities. The effective testing of on-line services can be more challenging, but provided that the data being searched against is known and available for analysis (for example, a publicly available watch list), many of the principles discussed here can also be applied. Where this is not the case, it may be possible to obtain a reasonable assessment of precision through an on-line test, but recall will be more difficult to evaluate. Some approaches to assessing recall given an unknown data population are discussed in section 13.5.1.

13.2 Defining Requirements

The requirements for a new matching system should reflect the views of all relevant stakeholders within the organisation. It is particularly important to find out who intends to use the tool, for what purpose and in which way. This information forms the basis for the first draft requirements specification. This initial draft will generally require further clarification and is unlikely to cover all of the requirements from which evaluation criteria will eventually be drawn, but it provides a good starting point for more technical consideration.

Where a legacy system is to be replaced, key users of the existing system will often be able to provide useful input regarding both functional and non-functional criteria, and to assess the relative priority of each requirement. However, some users will be more able than others to think beyond the normal functions of the existing process. The ability to stand back from the status quo is important if the new application is to generate process improvements so it may be worth supplementing the users' comments with a more independent view.

The introduction to this chapter highlighted the fact that even experienced users will likely lack the linguistic and onomastic knowledge necessary to precisely define matching requirements. Some users may simply state that they only want to see relevant hits on a hit list. Such a generalised statement is of little use when gathering test criteria, but obtaining an exact definition of what is and is not relevant in the particular business process is likely to require further exploration. Users are often better able to describe their expectations when provided with specific examples. Asked about two potentially matching profiles, a user should be able not only to indicate whether they would expect these profiles to match, but also to explain these expectations. It is the explanations that form the basis for the more detailed requirement specification. Of course, it may be necessary to provide the user with relevant linguistic information to support their choices. For example, if the user states that *Sasha Jelzin* should not match with *Aleksandr Yeltsin*, it would be appropriate to ensure they are aware that *Jelzin* and *Yeltsin* are transcription variants of the same name, and that *Sasha* is a derivative of *Aleksandr*.

The benefit of a practical and interactive discussion between the system evaluator and the key users is demonstrated in the following example:

- Evaluator: If you search for *John Smith*, born *1941*, do you expect to find a profile for *John Smith* born *1970*?
- User: No, because the date of birth is different.
- Evaluator: How about if you were searching for *Jonathan Taylor-Hardcastle*, born *1975*? Would you expect to find a profile for *Jonathan Taylor-Hardcastle*, born *1957*?
- User: In that case I would like to see the match because the name is so distinctive that a transposition error in the date of birth should be allowed.

The objective of such discussions is the detection of the principles by which system users rate the congruence of data profiles in their particular business process. The principles gathered from the example conversation above suggest that:

- The distinctiveness of a name should affect the way other identity characteristics are treated.
- It should be possible to use fuzzy searching on date of birth information.

Clearly, the way in which the distinctiveness of names is to be assessed requires clarification, as does the nature of the tolerances that are to be applied to date of birth information. The final principles, from which the evaluation criteria will be determined, should be clear and specific in their intention.

The interactive nature of the discussion means that there is no standard questionnaire that can be used to identify system requirements. In general, however, the discussions will cover:

- Which of the four main classes of variation in names are to be considered?
- What degree of variation should be tolerated for each class? For example:
  - Which languages (source and target) are relevant for transcription variants and homophones?
  - Which languages are relevant for derivative names and what depth of coverage is required (only very common/officially used derivatives or all derivatives)?
  - Which kinds of non-linguistic spelling error should be covered?
- Which kinds of combinations of variation classes should be covered:
  - in each name part (for example, a derivative name containing transposed characters)?
  - in the full name (for example, a homophone given name with a transcription variant of the family name)?
- To what extent should the length and/or distinctiveness of each name part affect the tolerated variations?
- What allowances should be made for name elements appearing in a different order or in different data fields?
- Which kinds of variation should be tolerated in non-name identity characteristics?
- What degree of tolerance is to be allowed for each kind of variation for each identity characteristic?
- How should the distinctiveness of the name and/or the quality of the name match affect the variations that are tolerated in other identity characteristics?

- How should any of the above tolerances affect the priority (match score) allocated to each match?
- How should the above tolerances be combined to produce different levels of search accuracy (for example, to provide "exact", "close" or "broad" searches)?

These are complex considerations and the evaluator's role is to lead the user through the different options using practical examples.

The principles resulting from this evaluation should be fed back to the user group so that they can be clarified or corrected if necessary. It is important at this stage to highlight the consequences of the implementation of each principle. In this context, it is useful to provide examples of corner cases: complex or unusual examples that may be adversely affected by the implementation of a principle that appears to be beneficial in more standard cases. For example, a principle might be defined that says profiles should only be matched if they contain some kind of match in the family name. Such a principle would prevent *Michael John Brown*, born *1957*, from matching with *Michael John Farraday*, born *1957*. However, it would also prevent *Charlotte Helena Louise Brown*, born *3 March 1957*, from matching with *Charlotte Helena Louise Farraday*, born *3 March 1957*, despite the possibility of these profiles referring to the same woman before and after marriage.

Once the search requirements have been defined, it is worth considering how much of the required search logic, including search rules, algorithms and thesauri, should be delivered by the vendor. Several tools exist that contain no search capabilities at all but provide a framework that can be populated with search rules and dictionaries by the purchasing organisation. Though these template-type applications are often quite flexible, the time, effort and resources required to create the desired functionality is usually significant. In most cases, hundreds of rules will be required and fully accounting for the interaction between them is a hugely complex task in which errors can easily be made. A preprogrammed search engine with configurable parameters is often preferable, unless the organisation has both unique requirements and highly-skilled linguistic search analysts available to build the required capabilities.

13.3 Selecting Potential Candidates

In the early stages of any application selection process, a "long list" will be drawn up of vendors and products that are potential candidates for evaluation. Initially, the long list may be drawn from vendors that the company already has a relationship with, together with vendors recommended by peer organisations. However, particularly in the area of identity matching, it is always worth carrying out independent research to identify other suitable options, as new vendors are constantly appearing and existing vendors rapidly adjust their product portfolios. Twelve months is a long time in the identity matching market, especially in the current situation with a new paradigm about to emerge and new vendors competing with established players to bring this new approach to market.

Both general requirements, such as the technical, user-focused, organisational and vendor-related considerations mentioned above, and the more specific identity matching requirements will be used to filter the long list down to a short list of potentially suitable applications.

13.3.1 Request for Information

The vendors of the short-listed products will usually be sent a Request for Information (RFI). This is a catalogue of questions designed to determine how well each tool should theoretically fulfil the specified requirements. The wording of the questions is vital to the collection of meaningful information. A question starting "Is your product able to ..." is almost always answered in the affirmative. A more effective wording might be "In its standard delivery, how does your product treat ...". This wording provides two key advantages.

Firstly, it requires information on how a particular effect is achieved. This helps to avoid a situation where a vendor simply answers "yes" to each question in the hope of winning a place in the evaluation stage. It also helps to identify instances where the question has been misunderstood. For example, many vendors would respond positively to the question "Is your tool able to match transcription variants?" even if all their tool is actually able to do is match names in some non-Latin scripts with one romanised version (i.e. to match Ельцин to *Yeltsin*, but not *Yeltsin* to *Jelzin*, *Eltsine*, etc). Of course, a detailed description of the functionality of their product would be extremely time-consuming (and potentially commercially disadvantageous) for a vendor to provide, but even a few words, such as indicating that homophones are matched using the Soundex algorithm or that transcription variants are "covered" by the Double Metaphone algorithm, can help to determine the ranking of the product on the short list.

A second effect of the altered wording is that it focuses on the standard delivery of each product. Vendors may answer "yes" to all requirements on the basis that they could provide customised modifications given sufficient time and compensation. In the case of the template-type products mentioned earlier, the vendor may state that all requirements can be fulfilled because the purchasing organisation has, in theory, the possibility to design their own rules to create the desired results.

For each question, it may be beneficial to ask the vendors to state whether the relevant functionality:

- is part of the standard package
- could be designed by the purchaser using the framework provided
- is not part of the standard package but could be added by the vendor with minor effort (details of the additional work required should be provided)
- is not part of the standard package and would require significant effort to provide

Precise phrasing of each question is particularly important as the relevant terminology in the area of linguistic identity matching is not yet widely recognised and misunderstandings are common. For example, vendors may answer positively to the question "does your product provide linguistic matching functionality?" simply because they have incorporated the Double Metaphone algorithm, or because their user interface is able to accept search terms in non-Latin scripts. A good way to avoid this kind of misinformation is to use examples in the RFI.

- Is the ability to match transcription variants part of the standard package, and if so, how is this achieved? Examples of matching transcription variants include *Yeltsin / Jelzin*, *Abd Al-Rahman / Abdurrahman* and *Xu Diezhan / Hsu Chihchan*.

- Is the ability to match derivative names part of the standard package, and if so, how is this achieved? Examples of matching name derivatives include *Bob/Robert*, *Sasha / Aleksandr* and *Paco / Francisco*.

- Is the ability to match homophones part of the standard package, and if so, how is this achieved? Examples of matching homophones include *Stuart / Stewart*, *Maier / Meyer* and *Bodins / Baudaint*.

- Is the ability to match common typos part of the standard package, and if so, how is this achieved? Examples of such errors include *Clinton/ Clibton/ Clitnon*.

13.3.2 Selection of Candidates for Full Evaluation

The responses to the RFI are examined, together with other information gathered on each product, to identify those that are worth the effort and expense involved in a full product evaluation. It will often be necessary to go back to the vendors to clarify some points or to obtain further details where these have not been provided. It may also be useful to have some of the vendors demonstrate their products to put the responses to the RFI in context and to get a feel for the way the product works. It is important, though, that this takes the form of an interactive demonstration rather than a fixed presentation to avoid any potentially misleading pre-prepared examples. For the same reason, examples other than those used in the RFI should be chosen during the demonstration.

There are a number of techniques for grading the responses to the RFI. The requirements may be divided between the "must-haves" and the "nice-to-haves", with any vendor not meeting the must-have requirements being excluded from further evaluation. However, care should be taken to ensure that any requirement treated as a must-have is focused on the desired effect rather than a particular technique. There may be several ways to achieve the required results, and this should be borne in mind when assessing product information.

It is also possible to weight each requirement and grade every vendor's response. An overall rating for each vendor can then be obtained by summing the weighted grades for each requirement. Again, this approach should be used with care, as stronger performance in one area may mask important weaknesses in another. It is the overall picture of each product's capabilities that is important. It should also be borne in mind that in some circumstances, the best solution may be achieved by combining parts of different products.

13.4 Test Focus and Test Design

Following the initial selection process, it is necessary to evaluate which of the vendors' claims are borne out in a practical test. If the RFI has been correctly worded there should not be any major inaccuracies in the information collected, but linguistic identity matching is a complex and evolving topic so there will always be scope for particular terms or phrases to be understood in different ways. This is particularly the case if the RFI has been completed by a sales agent for the vendor rather than one of their technical specialists.

At this stage, the focus of the practical evaluation can be defined, based on the information collected so far together with knowledge of the business process and technical environment in which the new application is to be used. Leaving aside the more generic topics, such as speed and usability, the rest of this chapter assumes that the test is to evaluate the four aspects that play a significant role in any identity matching situation:

- Recall
- Precision
- Hit rating
- Configurability

Whatever other requirements are to be tested, these four aspects should form the heart of any identity matching tool evaluation.

Once the focus of the test has been set, the test design can commence. The test design specifies the test environment, the data to be used, the kind of queries that should be run and the different phases that the test will encompass. Full-scale tool evaluations are both expensive and time consuming; though the longer term costs of selecting an inappropriate tool far outweigh the cost of an effective evaluation, it makes sense to ensure that resources are targeted in the most efficient manner. If the information collection stage has indicated that more than one or two products are worth evaluating, it may be appropriate to test the most important requirements in an initial phase and to drop any non-performing products from later phases of the evaluation.

With the evaluation focused on recall, precision, hit rating and configurability, an effective test can be designed using multiple person queries in a before-and-after test. Essentially, a set of carefully selected search profiles are submitted against the test data in two separate test runs. After the first search, the results are reviewed and the search configuration modified to see if the results can be improved. As well as demonstrating the matching performance of the application, this approach allows an assessment of the ease with which the search configuration can be adjusted as well as the impact that the changes have on search results. It can also be useful in correcting any initial misunderstandings in the definition of relevant and irrelevant hits.

13.4.1 The Test Environment

It is helpful for the test environment to reproduce the proposed production environment as closely as possible, or at least for any differences to be controlled such that their effects on test results can be accounted for. This is important if technical performance and integration have been determined to be a key focus for the evaluation. However, such test environments often take time to construct and may incur additional hardware costs. If the main evaluation is to focus on the quality of matching results, or if the eventual production environment will depend on the tool selected, a different test environment can be designed and a separate technical assessment held later to ensure that the selected tool can be successfully integrated into the organisation's infrastructure.

A test environment that allows unrestricted querying of a static database ensures maximum flexibility in the analysis of search results as specific matches can be further analysed by submitting additional targeted queries without having to change the database or update the search index. Another reason for keeping query definition separate from the rest of the test design is to ensure independent results are obtained. Many search tools are complex to set up, making some level of vendor involvement in the creation of the test environment almost inevitable. The ability to define the search queries independently of this process is preferable to ensure that the test queries are not disclosed to the vendor prior to the assessment. This avoids a situation where a vendor might attempt to skew the performance of their product based on the test names being used, either by researching additional variants to enhance a thesaurus or by configuring different match methods in a targeted manner. Such actions would result in test results not being representative of the true capabilities of the tool.

Many identity matching evaluations are carried out through a front end similar to the one intended to be used in the live process. This has advantages in that the testers' experience is similar to the end-users' experience of the application. However, there are a number of ways in which a specially designed test application can speed up the evaluation and ensure results are accurately evaluated. For example, some test applications include a match analyser, which provides a breakdown of how the match score has been calculated for each match. This can be useful in analysing unexpected results and suggesting configurative changes.

Another useful feature of dedicated evaluation applications is the ability to highlight the impact of any alias names. Many modern watch lists provide alias names or alternative spellings for the profiles they contain. These may be transcription variants or alternative forms of the primary name, or full aliases that are completely different. Matching applications usually show only the primary name of each profile on the hit list, which can lead to confusion if the profile has been matched based on one of its alternative names. This is discussed further in section 13.5.1.

One of the most useful features of purpose-built test environments is the option to compare the results of different query runs, highlighting the differences in results caused by configurative changes or changes to the underlying data set. Using this feature, only the results of the first query run need to be fully analysed, with subsequent tests focusing on new hits or matches that have dropped off the hit lists since the last run. This feature can also be used to help assess recall in cases where the underlying data set is not fully known. An initial test can be run using very broad search parameters, and the results of subsequent, narrower searches can be examined to ensure that only less-relevant matches have been dropped from the hit lists.

13.4.2 Configuration

Configurability is a key requirement, particularly if the system is to be deployed across different business processes, on different databases or by different user groups. Configuration should be possible both on the system level and on the level of the individual query. At the system level, the configuration is carried out by the Search Administrator, who defines the standard settings for the search and determines which search parameters are fixed and which may be altered by the user.

Settings that the user is able to alter often include the search accuracy level to be used for each search as well as the way in which the search profile is entered (for example, by entering the full name as one text string or by splitting it into its component parts). In order to ensure that the search remains accessible to users at all levels, it may be appropriate to provide different search templates, such as a basic search template using standard settings and an advanced search template that allows the user greater flexibility in how the search is run.

The configuration of most modern identity search solutions is extremely complex and it is advisable to discuss the relevant parameters carefully with the vendor prior to starting the evaluation. The configuration parameters at the system level can easily run to hundreds. Some of the most important include:

- the attributes that may be included in the search profile

- the data profile attributes that each attribute of the search profile will be searched against
- the match methods used to compare the search profile attributes with the attributes of the data profiles (including the various options that may be applied to each)
- the relative weight applied to each attribute of the search profile (for example, the family name may be weighted more highly than the given name)
- the weight applied to each combination of search profile attribute and data profile attribute (for example, a match between the given name of the search profile and the given name in the data profile may be weighed more highly than a match between the given name of a search profile and the family name of a data profile)
- the number and definition of different search accuracy levels
- the definition of a hit, in terms of the conditions required for a data profile to appear on the result list for a specific query
- the relative contribution of different types of match elements to the match score

The required matching criteria will have been defined as part of the requirements specification stage. While the definition of true and false positive hits will depend heavily on the process in question there are certain minimum matching criteria that will be relevant in most matching scenarios. These are discussed in more detail in the next chapter and could form the basis for the initial configuration of the test environment.

13.4.3 Coordination with Product Vendors

An assessment of this nature should normally be carried out in coordination with the product vendor, to ensure that the application is set up and used in the most appropriate way. Ideally, the vendor needs to understand the focus of the test and the requirements being evaluated in order to provide the most effective assistance. In particular, it is important that the vendor understands how the organisation defines relevant and irrelevant matches. The definition of a good match varies so widely between different organisations that even an experienced vendor cannot be expected to guess an individual client's requirements.

In particular, the vendor needs to know:

- which variation sources should be covered, and to what extent
- how false negative and false positive hits are defined, and what the tolerance for each of these is
- how the hits should be rated and prioritised
- which search accuracy options should be available
- which aspects of the search should be configurable for the user

It is also useful to allow the vendor to analyse the quality of the base test data prior to configuring the test environment. As discussed in the next section, it is helpful if the base test data is representative of the data used in the live business process. Where the test data is of limited quality, the vendor may suggest cleansing it before completing the evaluation, but this is only appropriate if the opportunity to cleanse the live data also exists.

Experienced vendors are familiar with the kind of data quality issues that are likely to exist in identity information and will have different methods for dealing with them, though each data set will present these issues to differing degrees depending on data administration practices and maintenance routines. One option might be to tailor the search process to make allowances for anomalies present in the data. However, the vendor may also be able to configure the application such that the search index reflects a cleansed version of the data without actually altering the underlying records. Provided that all such measures could be re-performed in the live process, they form a valid part of the system configuration.

The vendor should also be able to advise on the best way to run the test queries: either uploaded as a batch job or entered manually with the help of a search screen. Either way, it is important that the exact details and results of each search are stored and made available for later analysis.

13.4.4 Base Test Data

The base test data is the core database of person profiles that will be searched in the evaluation and must be sufficiently large to produce meaningful results. Typical base data sets will, at a minimum, include tens of thousands of profiles. Testing based on a smaller data set may lead to identical results being produced by different tools and difficulties in isolating differences in their capabilities. Depending on the context, base data sets may contain over a million profiles, but it should be borne in mind that larger data sets typically lead to longer results lists, which may be time and resource-intensive to analyse.

The base test data should be representative of the type of data that the business process will deal with. Here, a longer-term view is helpful. For example, if the process currently focuses on customers in Anglophone areas but the organisation's strategy suggests significant expansion in Asia, then focusing on the current data set may lead to problems in the future. Given the global nature of many of today's markets and the international lists that many organisations are required to screen, a multi-language focus is almost always appropriate and is assumed in this chapter. It is recommended that the base data includes names from each of the most significant language areas of the world, including Anglophone, Francophone and Hispanic areas as well as Germany, Italy, Eastern Europe, China, Japan, Korea, India, the Middle East and Northern Africa. There may also be particular languages that should be included as a result of the organisation's different geographical activities.

Beyond the language origin of the names, the base test data should be representative in:

- its mix of natural persons, legal entities and other organisations
- its completeness, in terms of full names, date of birth information and other characteristics
- its presentation, in terms of scripts and formats used
- its quality, for example in terms of errors or noise introduced to the data

In all cases, consideration should be given to likely future changes in the above aspects, particularly if the tool evaluation is part of an overall process re-design that might alter the nature of the data being searched.

It may be necessary to supplement this base test data with additional profiles to ensure that all relevant variation phenomena are represented in the data profiles targeted by the test queries and that meaningful test results can be expected.

13.4.5 Test Queries

The set of test queries should cover the most common sources of variation and error in names originating in the most important languages globally. In practice, identity search systems are often tested by randomly searching for particular variations of different names. However, this method provides only a superficial view of matching quality. To obtain a complete picture of an application's performance, a more structured approach is required.

One useful approach is to select "core profiles" from the base data and then design a cluster of test queries around each of these. The core profiles should be selected to cover an array of different data features. In particular, they should reflect all major language origins as there are few business processes where a restricted linguistic focus would be appropriate in today's global economy. They should also be selected to include both common and less familiar name parts. The use of less familiar name parts tests the coverage of rules and thesauri, while including common name parts in test queries will help to highlight any problems that may exist with precision.

The test queries should contain characteristics from the core profile, partly accurately and partly containing variations.

Given the following characteristics from the core profile:

Family Name	First Name	Middle Name	D.o.B
Zhang	Chenyang	Thomas	1956

The following cluster of test queries could be defined

	Family Name	First Name	Middle Name	D.o.B	Note on Variation
1	Zhang	Chenyang	Thomas	1956	No variation

Continued...

	Family Name	First Name	Middle Name	D.o.B	Note on Variation
2	Zhang	Chen Yang	Thomas	1956	Splitting personal name and generation name
3	Zhang	Chenyang	Tom	1956	Hypocorism of "middle" name
4	Zoeng	Canjoeng	Thomas	1956	Jyutping transcription instead of Hanyu Pinyin
5	Zhang	Canjoeng	Thomas	1956	Mixture of Jyutping transcription and Hanyu Pinyin
6	Zhangf	Chenyang	Thomas	1956	Insertion typo in family name
7	Zhag	Chenyang	Thomas	1956	Omission typo in family name
8	Zjang	Chenyang	Thomas	1956	Replacement typo in family name
9	Zhang	Chenyang	Tomas	1956	Homophonic variation of Thomas
10		Chenyang	Thomas	1956	Family name missing
11	Zhang	Yang	Thomas	1956	Generation name missing
12	Zhang	Chen	Thomas	1956	Personal name missing
13	Zhang		Thomas	1956	Family name alone
14	Zhang	Chenyang		1956	"Middle" name missing
15	Chenyang	Zhang	Thomas	1956	Family and given name swapped
16	Zhang	Yangchen	Thomas	1956	Generation and personal name swapped
17	Thomas	Chenyang	Zhang	1956	Family and middle name swapped

Continued...

	Family Name	First Name	Middle Name	D.o.B	Note on Variation
18	Zhang	Thomas	Chenyang	1956	Given name and "middle" name swapped
19	Zhang Chenyang		Thomas	1956	Same field for all official name elements
20	Zhang Chenyang Thomas			1956	Same field for all name elements
21	Xiao	Chenyang	Thomas	1956	Different family name
22	Zhang	Chenlau	Thomas	1956	Different person name
23	Zhang	Chenyang	Christian	1956	Different "middle" name
24	Zhang	Chenyang	T	1956	"Middle" name as single-letter initial
25	Zhang	Chenyang	Th	1956	"Middle" name as double-letter initial
26	Zhang	Chenyang	Thomas	1955	Small date deviation
27	Zhang	Chenyang	Thomas	1982	Large date deviation
28	Zhang	Chenyang	Thomas	1965	Date with transposition

Table 13.1: Example cluster of test queries based on the profile Zhang Chenyang Thomas (1956)

This example cluster of 28 test queries contains variations involving transcription, derivative names, homophones, alternative fielding, typos, initials and name element discrepancies. The queries listed above each include only one type of variation. This eases the analysis of differences in the query results, but queries combining different types of variation should also be included as combined variations are important in practice, as described in section 10.6. Even if the matching of names containing multiple variation sources is not required of the new system, it is useful to include such examples in the test queries to verify that the results meet expectations.

Clearly, there are many more variations and combinations thereof that could have been included. It is not necessary to cover every possible variation in each cluster so long as the main combinations are covered across all the clusters that make up the full set of test queries. To get the broadest coverage of variations, it is recommended to use different types of each variation class in each cluster, for example different kinds of typo or different homophonic variations. It is also important to include some less familiar variations in the test queries, such as valid but less commonly used transcription variants or variants from less prominent source languages. This helps to assess the completeness of any thesauri used in the search and the coverage of linguistic rules. It may also be advisable to avoid using test names frequently cited in technical literature and media articles on identity matching, or at least to ensure that they are supplemented by more original examples, as vendors may have made special efforts to ensure that the most commonly discussed examples are covered.

It is useful to select the core profiles and compile the related query clusters such that several of the test queries are expected to hit on multiple profiles within the base data. This effect can be achieved, for example, through the inclusion of common names in the queries, or the omission of more distinctive data characteristics. This adds an explorative element to the test and may throw up unexpected findings beyond those that could be gleaned from analysing just one hit on each search. If necessary, supplementary data profiles that should match the test queries can be added to the base data set to ensure that this effect is achieved.

Evidently, the selection of the core profiles and definition of related query clusters requires significant linguistic and onomastic knowledge. Internet research may provide some useful suggestions, but it is often best to enlist the help of native speakers with knowledge of naming practices in the relevant regions. It is worth conducting the necessary research at this stage, as a poorly defined set of test queries can seriously reduce the value of investment in a practical evaluation.

13.5 Analysis of Results

The test focus defines what has to be analysed in both the before and after test results: in this case, recall, precision and hit rating as well as the effectiveness of configurative options.

13.5.1 Recall and Precision

In order to assess the recall and precision of the application, each hit on each result list should be reviewed to determine whether it is a true or false positive result. The same data profile may be a true positive hit on one search profile and a false positive result on another, even if the two queries belong to the same cluster. For example, two test queries, searching for *Bob Chamberlain* and *R. Chamberlain*, could be defined based on the core profile of *Robert Chamberlain*. The data profile for *Richard Chamberlain* would be a false positive hit if matched to *Bob Chamberlain* but a true positive when matched to *R. Chamberlain*.

As discussed in section 11.3.1, precision can be calculated by dividing the number of true positive hits by the total number of hits on each query. It may be useful to calculate separate precision ratings for each query, for each cluster, and for the test as a whole to obtain a full picture of the overall performance of the system. Any exceptional results, such as queries which have resulted in hit lists so long that they cannot realistically be reviewed, should be further analysed to determine whether configurative changes may help, or whether such results could be expected in operation. A search that produces very long lists of false positive matches misses the point of an automated search system, but there will always be some search conditions, such as the search for a very common name in a very large database, where longer hit lists are to be expected.

Assessing recall is more difficult, as unlike precision, it cannot be calculated based on the result lists alone; it is necessary to identify all relevant profiles within the database. If the base data set has been artificially generated for the purposes of the test, the calculation of recall should be possible with relatively little effort. In general, however, tool evaluations are carried out on existing data sets, the content of which is less certain. This makes the assessment of recall more problematic. Two methods can be adopted to make the recall of each search more apparent:

- One or more very broad queries can be added to each cluster; for example, by including very little information in the search profile, or by searching using a very broad search accuracy level. The long hit lists that these broader searches produce can then be used to help identify false negative results on the narrower queries in the same cluster.

- Additional queries, targeted to find variants of the search name that did not appear in the hit list, can be submitted. For example, if a search for *Abdurrahman* produced hits containing only this variant, targeted queries can be submitted for *Abd al-Rahman*, *Abdourahmane*, *Abdul Rahman*,

Abdar Rahman, etc. to determine whether any data profiles with these variants exist.

One factor which can complicate the assessment of both recall and precision is the presence of alias names in the data profiles. For example, a search for *John Brown* that hits on the profile of *Jason Bowen* may at first sight appear to be very imprecise. However, if *Jason Bowen* is recorded as also being known as *John Brown*, the hit is simply an exact match on this alias name. Conversely, if a search for *Abdurrahman* hits on a profile with the name *Abd al-Rahman*, it could be assumed that the search has correctly identified the transcription variant. However, if the data profile contains *Abdurrahman* as an alternative name, it cannot be concluded that the profile would also have been identified if it hadn't contained this additional alias name.

If the focus of the test is purely to assess the quality of linguistic name matching, it may be possible to exclude alias names from the search for the purposes of evaluation. However, if the handling of alias names is to be tested in the assessment, the review of each hit must include the potential impact of aliases. This is a useful point to consider when designing the test environment, as easy access to this additional information will significantly speed up the analysis work.

13.5.2 Hit Rating

A true assessment of the accuracy of hit rating requires the re-calculation of individual match scores. In general, only a sample of scores need be re-calculated, but this sample should cover a broad range of different variation types. Depending on the complexity of the model used to rate matches, this can be resource intensive if no auxiliary technology is available to help compute the expected score. Unfortunately, many vendors do not typically provide match analysis facilities.

A less accurate but far simpler method of assessing hit rating is to review each hit list to ensure that the relative ranking of each hit meets expectations. In order to gain a true picture of the effectiveness of the hit rating using this method, a much larger sample of hit lists must be reviewed and the reviewer will require a sound knowledge of linguistic variations. Any hit that is awarded an unexpected ranking must be analysed to identify the effects of any alias names or previously unrecognised variations, such as less common transcription variants.

Ideally, both of these methods will be applied as it is possible for match scores to be calculated correctly according to specification but not to result in an appropriate ranking of hits overall. It is the relative prioritisation of each hit that is the main function of a match score.

13.5.3 Configuration

For the "before" test, the parameters should be set such that optimal test results are expected. The results of this initial test often give reason to make some adjustments before the queries are re-submitted. Analysing the differences between the initial results and those obtained after the settings have been adjusted provides an indication of whether the configuration options work in the expected manner. Depending on the level of configurability required, it may be necessary to perform several "after" tests to assess the impact of changing various combinations of parameters.

When analysing the differences in results between various different search runs, it is important that each new (or dropped) match can be explained. A seemingly harmless but unexplained change in results could be a sign of a deeper problem.

13.6 Conclusion

More and more organisations are looking to upgrade their identity matching capabilities, particularly in the current environment as client bases are altered by globalisation, compliance requirements become more stringent, and organisations are forced to recognise the limitations of systems based on older technology. To maximise the potential of this investment, it is vital that a comprehensive and systematic evaluation is carried out prior to purchase. The evaluation of identity matching tools poses some specific challenges that have been discussed in this chapter. For the purposes of simplicity, the different considerations have been set in the context of testing a person search application, though the principles discussed also apply if the component being evaluated is part of a broader application.

This chapter has discussed the design of a test focused on assessing recall, precision, hit ranking and configurability; these being central to the performance of any identity matching system. In practice, many more factors are likely to be covered in the assessment, including the speed of the search and the ease with which results can be reviewed. However, these four key criteria define the performance of an identity matching component and should form the core of any evaluation. In order to be sure that these features are effectively assessed, it is necessary to take a structured approach to the test design and the analysis of results. Significant weaknesses can be overlooked if the test design is not sufficiently robust.

Though the evaluation process is time-consuming when done correctly, it should result in the selection of an effective tool that can be deployed across the organisation and meet the requirements of all relevant business processes. This is an important first step in the organisation-wide alignment of search procedures. The next chapter looks at the implementation of standardised search criteria to support this process.

Chapter 14: A Linguistic Search Standard

14.1 The Need for a Search Standard

The identity matching industry is currently experiencing a shift in the paradigm on which it has been based for decades. Traditional methods still dominate the search technology market, but the improved quality achieved by linguistic search techniques is already evident in a number of software products. Vendors of identity matching tools are starting to build linguistic capabilities into their applications in response to growing expectations from corporate users, regulators, law enforcement and the general public. However, the increased flexibility offered by linguistic techniques has lead to less consistency in the way search technology is applied.

Larger organisations frequently maintain many different identity searches across multiple locations and business processes, often with greatly differing configurations. Significant effort can be saved in the design and testing of these different search processes if their individual configurations are underpinned by the same basic principles governing the definition of true and false positive hits. Consistency across different search processes can also lead to greater operational efficiency and fewer problems with satisfying the requirements of auditors, regulators and other external bodies.

In addition, the very process of defining and approving the principles comprising an organisation's own internal search standard can help to ensure that search requirements receive the management attention they deserve. Often, the tolerated variations in an identity search are considered purely a matter for technical staff, despite the strategic impact they can have on the management of risk and the effectiveness of the systems they support. Agreeing a search standard can assist management in understanding the risks and challenges involved.

For technological reasons, some processes, such as the real-time transaction screening that takes place in the financial system, often use a narrower search than may be appropriate in less time-critical systems. To allow for the different tolerances for false positive and false negative hits inherent in different business processes, it is necessary to define a search standard using progressively broader principles that can be used to specify different levels of search accuracy. This allows organisations to reap the benefits of a standardised search approach while applying the most appropriate tolerances in each process. Section 14.3 describes how an organisation might approach the definition of their own internal search standard.

Beyond the benefits of internal corporate search standards, some commentators have promoted the idea of industry-wide standards to increase the consistency of search processes across particular business areas. The case for such standards is perhaps most convincing in the financial services sector, where search capabilities currently vary widely between different organisations, despite being employed to address similar risks and regulatory requirements. As discussed below, a more standardised approach could benefit all parties involved, from financial institutions to regulators, and on a broader level, provide important protection for society as a whole.

14.1.1 Case in Point: the Financial Services Sector

One of the key drivers of the paradigm shift in identity search theory is demand from within the financial services industry and its associated regulatory bodies. There are a number of reasons why the financial services sector is so keen to harness the benefits that linguistic search techniques can provide. One such reason relates to the many operational areas in which financial services firms can benefit from the improved recall and precision offered by a linguistic search, including customer due diligence processes, transaction screening and data quality management programmes. In addition, financial services firms often maintain very large databases of identity information, so even small improvements in search precision can lead to significant efficiency gains. However, the main reason why financial services organisations are leading the drive for linguistic search techniques stems from the high price that may be attached to overlooking a relevant profile (either due to poor recall or because reviewers missed it in a sea of false positive results). Penalties may take the form of fines, remediation exercises or even the withdrawal of operating licences. With such high costs at stake, no financial services organisation can afford to lag behind as search technology improves.

As part of the global fight against terror, crime and corruption, the ability of the financial services industry to deny less scrupulous parties access to their systems is also of enormous social and economic significance - yet there is currently no standardised approach to identity screening. This can partly be attributed to the lack of guidance provided by regulatory and other international bodies, which provide lists of names to be screened but little direction in terms of which kinds of variations should be tolerated in this process. Financial services firms are left to determine this for themselves, and in the absence of standard guidance may apply very different search configurations. This inevitably leaves some organisations more prone to abuse than others, and the global financial system open to attack through its weaker links.

The lack of certainty over screening requirements puts financial institutions in a difficult situation as they each work to identify and test the most effective configurations. Without guidance on minimum linguistic requirements, the final decision often focuses on acceptable precision. Though it is now generally acknowledged that an "exact-match" search is not a sufficient safeguard in the financial services sector, precisely how "fuzzy" the search should be is far less clear. In practice, the balance is often tipped in favour of greater precision by a lack of linguistic awareness in the design process and / or by legacy IT systems that restrict the use of the more sophisticated matching techniques. This is a situation that parties looking to exploit the financial system can take advantage of. A linguistic search standard could help to encourage minimum standards, thereby improving the security of the financial system.

It is not only financial services firms that could streamline their design and testing processes if an accepted search standard existed for this industry. Software vendors could focus their efforts on helping their clients to meet the standard requirements rather than creating a new approach for each customer. Compliance data vendors would also benefit as they could provide identity data in a standard format rather than having to expend resources on adjusting the content and format of their data to accommodate customers with very weak search technology. Currently, many vendors are adding spelling variations and other variants to their data, which would not be necessary if their customers employed standardised linguistic search criteria. Those data vendors that provide an on-line service for searching their data would additionally profit from the reduced design and testing efforts required to provide a standardised search. Economies in these areas would help improve the entire screening process as intelligence data and software vendors could free up resources to improve the quality of their products.

In addition, the introduction of a search standard would provide regulators and other controlling bodies with a clearer yardstick by which to assess the effectiveness of screening programmes. In many jurisdictions, a financial services firm can expect to comply with regulators' requirements simply by purchasing a popular screening software package. Given the widely varying search performance of some of the market-leading compliance applications and the huge range of functionality included in most compliance products, it makes sense that screening expectations should be set in terms of what the search is able to achieve, rather than in terms of the popularity of the overall compliance application in which it has been included.

A search standard would also allow regulatory bodies to provide financial services organisations with a clearer indication of what is expected of their screening programmes. This is a particularly difficult area for organisations with an international presence, as the expectations of regulators currently vary from country to country and are rarely explicitly defined, leaving financial services firms with the difficult task of assessing requirements in each location before they can attempt to ensure that these, often vague, requirements are met. The potential differences in expectations in each jurisdiction also mean that locations with less stringent screening requirements may attract parties wishing to access the financial system for less legitimate purposes, so the standardisation of global screening expectations would further help to strengthen the defences of the global financial system.

14.2 A Proposed Linguistic Search Standard

A proposal for a linguistic search standard, particularly focused on the financial services industry, was first put forward by Linguistic Search Solutions AG in 2010, after consultation with software architects, data providers and experts in the area of linguistic search. Leaving the specifics of implementation aside, the standard sets out the basic principles that underlie the configuration of an identity search. Though its authors acknowledge that there is still some work to do in refining the principles and defining their interaction, the standard is undoubtedly a solid starting point for any organisation wishing to apply a robust and consistent approach to identity search.

The 2011 version of the proposed Linguistic Search Standard has been adapted here, with the permission of its authors, to demonstrate how an organisation could improve the consistency and effectiveness of its own internal search procedures by adopting a standardised approach.

14.3 Defining a Corporate Linguistic Search Standard

The rest of this chapter considers how an organisation might define a set of guiding principles on which to base its own corporate search standard. It proposes a flexible standard that can be modified for use in any organisation. In a number of places, variations to the principles are suggested to allow each organisation to adapt them based on their own priorities and data conditions. However, once defined, the principles should be applied consistently across the organisation.

Importantly, the proposed search standard is technology-neutral, in that it is not dependent on a particular technology for its implementation. The principles specify the desired outcome of the search without dictating the algorithms or methods that should be used to achieve this outcome. This means that an organisation with any relatively sophisticated search technology in place should be able to implement this standard without investing in new technology, and vendors of any good search software should be able to support the implementation of the standard for their customers.

The principles have been divided between three different search accuracy levels to provide a flexible search definition that can be applied in many different business processes. In this way, a consistent search approach can be maintained throughout the organisation while allowing searches to be more narrowly defined in lower-risk or high-volume processes, and more broadly configured in processes subject to higher risk or poorer data quality.

14.3.1 The Precise Match Level

The Precise Match Level defines the requirements for identifying name parts which are essentially the same. There are seven guiding principles that set the minimum requirements for meeting the Precise Match Level.

Principle 1: Differences in character case or punctuation should not stop a Precise Match from being identified.

Under this principle, upper and lower case characters are treated as matching and punctuation is ignored except as a potential marker of name part boundaries. Thus, *ABC Inc.* matches *ABC Inc*, *McKay* matches *Mckay* and *O'Neil* matches *O`Neil*. This principle further requires that symbols such as *&* match to alternative symbols and words with comparable meaning, so that *A&B* matches to *A+B* as well as to *A and B*.

Principle 2: Different romanisations of the same name should be considered a Precise Match.

The application of this principle ensures that identical names from non-Latin script languages will always be matched, provided that a prominent transcription standard has been followed. For example, *Yeltsin*, *Jelzin* and *Eltsine* should be matched as transcriptions of the Russian name Ельцин, as should the prominent transcriptions of عبد الرحمن, including *Abdulrahman* and *Abderrahmane*. A flexible definition of name parts should be adopted so that transcription variants such as *Abd al-Rahman* and *Abdel Rahman* are not overlooked.

There are over 40 non-Latin script languages that are spoken by communities of over 10 million people, including Arabic, Russian, Japanese and Korean as well as the most prominent languages of China and India. This principle requires that transcriptions of names from each of these major source languages into any of the target languages discussed below are identified as Precise Matches. Additional source languages may be included depending on the organisation's requirements.

There are many different romanisation standards which may be used to transcribe names from each non-Latin script. This principle requires that variants formed using one of the most prominent standards should be matched at the Precise Level. Typically, this will include the standards used in English, Spanish, French, German, Italian and Portuguese text, with each of these target languages potentially using several different transcription standards for each script. Again, the exact target language set to be covered may include additional languages based on the areas of operation of the organisation and the sources of the data to be matched.

This principle also requires that, where a name is presented in Latin characters with diacritics, any loss of these should not prevent a Precise Match from being identified. *Milosevic* should therefore be matched to *Milošević*. Similarly, the transcription of these diacritics should also be tolerated so that, for example, *Müller* matches *Mueller*.

The standard discussed here has been designed to be used with matching systems based on the Latin script. This principle, therefore, does not cover the matching of names across other scripts (e.g. matching a Russian name in Cyrillic with the same name in the Arabic script), though it may be adapted to include this if the scripts in which an organisation's data are presented require this.

Principle 3: Names composed of identical name parts should be matched regardless of whether any of the parts have been merged.

In some languages, distinct name parts can be presented separately, hyphenated or merged. The application of this principle ensures that the optional merging or hyphenation of name parts does not prevent a match from being identified. This is most importantly a consideration when matching names of Eastern origin (for example, *Weimin*, *Wei-Min* or *Wei Min*) or Middle-Eastern origin (such as the Arabic name *Abdal Karim* or *Abd al-Karim* or the Persian name *Alinezhad* or *Ali Nezhad*). In part, this principle overlaps with Principle 2, which requires transcription variants of the same name to be matched. However, the merging of given names is also common in some Western cultures, as can be seen in the German name *Hanspeter* or *Hans-Peter*, and this principle also requires that these Precise Matches should be recognised.

Principle 4: Names composed of identical parts should be matched regardless of conventional changes to the order in which the parts are presented.

The order in which name parts are presented is often altered, for example when names from cultures that place the family name first are stored in Western records. The application of this principle ensures that any change to the order in which name parts are presented does not prevent a Precise match from being identified, provided that the change can be explained by reference to cultural norms.

This can often be seen with Chinese names, where the family name is traditionally placed first, as discussed in Chapter 3, but in the Western world may be placed at the end of the name in order to avoid confusion between the name parts for people unfamiliar with the Chinese system. *Wang Jian-Hua* should therefore match to *Jian-Hua Wang*. In addition, many Chinese take a Western name, which may be placed either at the front or at the end of the Chinese name. In Western records this may be combined with a switch in the order of the Chinese name parts; thus *Donald Jian-Hua Wang* should match to *Donald Wang Jian-Hua* and to *Wang Jian-Hua Donald*.

However, this principle should only be applied where confusion is likely to arise over the order of the name parts. A change in the order of the personal and generation names in a full Chinese name would be more unexpected, so *Wang Jian-Hua* should not match to *Wang Hua-Jian* under this principle. Similarly *John Robert Smith* should not match to *Robert John Smith*, as the likelihood of the order of the first and second given names being reversed in an Anglo-saxon name is low.

However, *John Robert Smith* should match to *Smith, Robert John*, to account for the administrative custom of recording the family name first and separating it from the rest of the name with a comma.

It should be noted that this principle does not apply to the components of compound name parts, where identity is bound to the particular order in which the components appear. This could be, for example, in compound Spanish surnames such as *Gonzalez Lopez* and *Lopez Gonzalez*, where traditionally the first compound name belongs to a person whose father's first family name was *Gonzalez* while the second belongs to a person whose father's first family name was *Lopez*. Similarly, this principle does not apply to compound given names, so that *Hans-Peter* is not required to match *Peter-Hans*.

Principle 5: Identical names from non-Western backgrounds should be matched regardless of the way they have been parsed for storage.

The application of this principle ensures that Precise Matches cannot be overlooked as a result of data storage practices. Many global identity data stores have rigid data structures, frequently based on the Western naming convention of first, middle and last names. In many societies, identity data does not readily fit this pattern and names from such cultures may be entered to the data fields in more than one way. For example, *Saddam Hussein Al-Tikriti* may be stored in the database with *Hussein* as a middle name, but should still be identified if *Hussein* is searched for as part of the surname.

However, the principle described here only applies to names from cultures where ambiguity may occur if the names are stored in a Westernised data format. For example, a profile with the given names *James* and *Martin* is not required to match a profile with the full name *James* (given name) *Martin* (family name) at the Precise Level. Where an organisation maintains name data in a format other than the typical Western model described here, this principle should be adapted accordingly.

Principle 6: Established nick names and abbreviations should match to their corresponding full name parts.

Many given names may be presented in diminutive versions, such as *Bill* for *William* or *Ted* for *Edward*, and the abbreviation of common words in the names of groups and organisations, such as *Ltd.* or *Corp.*, is standard practice. The application of this principle ensures that the use of derivative names or abbreviated versions of common name parts cannot prevent a Precise Match from being identified.

An organisation should decide on the range of languages and cultures in which nick names and abbreviations should be recognised, based on those likely to be present in its own data sets. A good starting point for this assessment would be the range of linguistic origins for which transcription variants and homophones are to be covered in the matching system.

Principle 7: The omission of peripheral name parts should not prevent a match from being identified.

Many data sources may include peripheral name parts such as pre- and post-nominal titles like professional positions or academic qualifications. In the case of legal entities, these peripheral name parts may include the legal form of the entity or the geographical location of a branch. This principle requires that, where a peripheral name part is only present on one side of a match, this should not be treated as an unmatched name part.

14.3.2 The Close Match Level

The Close Match Level defines the requirements for identifying name parts which are very similar. The following four principles complete the minimum requirements for the Close Match Level.

Principle 8: Name parts that are both spelt and pronounced in similar ways should be identified as a Close Match.

There are many examples of similar names which are hard to tell apart phonetically. These include forenames like *Markus* / *Marcus* and *Steven* / *Stephen*, as well as family names such as *Meier* / *Meyer* and *Thomson* / *Thompson*. As discussed in Chapter 6, the level of similarity in the pronunciation of different syllables may vary from language to language, so that *Scholze* and *Scholtze* sound the same in German, despite their apparent dissimilarity to native English speakers.

The range of languages for which the phonetic characteristics should be covered may be determined by each organisation based on an analysis of how phonetically derived misspellings may be introduced into the names being matched within their own data sets. As discussed in section 10.2.2, a good starting point for this coverage would be the roughly 70 languages that are spoken by at least 10 million people worldwide.

Principle 9: Names composed of identical parts should be matched regardless of any changes to the order in which the parts are presented.

The application of this principle ensures that Close Matches are not overlooked as a result of changes to the order in which the parts are presented. This principle expands on Principle 4, used in the identification of Precise Matches, to include changes to the order of name parts that cannot be explained by cultural norms or administrative practices. Thus *Robert John Smith* should be identified as a Close Match to *John Robert Smith,* to account for potential data quality issues.

Principle 10: All names comprising identical parts should be matched regardless of the way they have been parsed for storage.

The application of this principle ensures that fielding errors should not prevent a Close Match from being detected. This principle expands on Principle 5, used in the identification of Precise Matches, to include names from Western cultures and other backgrounds where ambiguity in parsing names into a Westernised database would not normally be expected. Under this principle, the names *James* and *Martin*, stored as given names, would match to identical name parts stored as family names, so that *James* (given name) *Martin* (family name) would match to *Martin* (given name) *James* (family name) at the Close Level.

Principle 11: Common spelling mistakes should not prevent a Close Match from being identified.

In many global name matching processes, data quality issues and the potential for human error can lead to the introduction of minor spelling variations in identity data. The application of this principle ensures that Close Matches are not overlooked as a result of the most common minor spelling mistakes. These include the transposition of two characters, the replacement of a character by one that is positioned close to the original on a keyboard, or the introduction of an erroneous additional character by hitting an adjacent key. By matching only these more common errors, this principle requires that *Jordan* would match with *Jordam* but not with *Jordas*. An organisation should determine which keyboard layouts and OCR errors are relevant for the matching of its own identity data, based on the data input methods and sources of external data used.

Given the potential for creating excessive matches, this principle may be applied only to names consisting of six or more characters. This is appropriate as even minor spelling variations in shorter names can indicate completely different names, particularly in names prevalent in China, where *Chen* and *Cheng* are transcriptions of different names, as are *Li*, *Liu* and *Lu*.

If required, this principle could be adapted to allow for spelling errors in shorter name parts in names where other, longer name parts are correctly spelt. Thus *Wei Chen* would not match *Wei Cheng*, but *Penelope Jones* would match *Penelope Jone*.

Principle 12: The inclusion or omission of less significant name parts should not prevent a Close Match from being identified.

This principle requires that the omission of common or otherwise less significant name parts, such as *Der*, *Von* or *De La* should be ignored rather than considered a mismatch. For example, *de Winters* compared with *Winters* should be considered as one matching name element at the Close Level rather than one exactly matched and one mismatched name element. This principle is important in ensuring that appropriate weight is given to mismatched name elements when assessing the congruence of the full names, as described in section 14.4 below.

14.3.3 The Broad Match Level

The final principles expand the match definition further to identify matches at the Broad Match Level.

Principle 13: Any minor spelling mistakes should not prevent a Broad Match from being identified.

This principle expands on Principle 11 to allow for less common, but still relatively minor, spelling mistakes. Under this principle *Capelli* would match with *Capella* on the Broad Match Level, despite the replacement of an *i* with an *a* being a relatively unusual spelling mistake. Again, to avoid excessive false-positive matches, this principle need not be applied to names consisting of 5 or fewer characters unless compensating restrictions are imposed, such as requiring the presence of longer, matching name parts.

An organisation should decide on the degree of flexibility required based on the quality of the data to be matched. If required, broader tolerances (such as allowing for multiple differences) can be applied to longer name parts or name parts where the rest of the name is a good match.

Principle 14: All phonetically similar name parts should match, regardless of the way in which they are spelt.

This principle expands on principle 8 to include matches between phonetically similar names that are spelt in more substantially different ways, such as *Leicester* and *Lester*. Again, the phonetic characteristics of each language must be taken into account so that, under this principle, the French names *Baudaint* and *Bodins* should be identified as a potential match although they may be pronounced differently by an English speaker.

Principle 15: All translations of relevant name parts should match.

This principle has been defined to match the translated given names used by individuals moving between cultural regions. Under this principle, for example, *Ivan Nikolayev* would match with *John Nikolayev*, as an Eastern European named *Ivan* might use the name *John* in Western regions.

This principal does not apply to family names, so that *Mr Smith* should not match *M. Lefèvre*, *Herr Schmied*, *Sig. Ferrari* or *Gosp. Kuznetsov*. It does, however, apply to terms used in the names of legal entities, so that *ABC (Deutschland) Ltd.* should match *ABC (Germany) Ltd.*

14.3.4 Summary

The following table summarises the handling of each of the key sources of variation to be addressed in any identity matching system.

	Precise Match Level	Close Match Level	Broad Match Level
Punctuation	**PRINCIPLE 1:** Differences in character case or punctuation should not stop a Precise Match from being identified.		
Transcription	**PRINCIPLE 2:** Different romanisations of the same name should be considered a Precise Match.		
Name element borders	**PRINCIPLE 3:** Names composed of identical name parts should be matched regardless of whether any of the parts have been merged.		
Order of unfielded name elements	**PRINCIPLE 4:** Names composed of identical parts should be matched regardless of conventional changes to the order in which the parts are presented.	**PRINCIPLE 9:** Names composed of identical parts should be matched regardless of any changes to the order in which the parts are presented.	
Fielding of name elements	**PRINCIPLE 5:** Identical names from non-Western backgrounds should be matched regardless of the way they have been parsed for storage.	**PRINCIPLE 10:** All names comprising identical parts should be matched regardless of the way they have been parsed for storage.	
Derivative Names	**PRINCIPLE 6:** Established nick names and abbreviations should match to their corresponding full name parts.		**PRINCIPLE 15:** All translations of relevant name parts should match.
Phonetics		**PRINCIPLE 8:** Name parts that are both spelt and pronounced in similar ways should be identified as a Close Match.	**PRINCIPLE 14:** All phonetically similar name parts should match, regardless of the way in which they are spelt.

Continued ...

	Precise Match Level	Close Match Level	Broad Match Level
Typos		**PRINCIPLE 11:** Common spelling mistakes should not prevent a Close Match from being identified.	**PRINCIPLE 13:** Any minor spelling mistakes should not prevent a Broad Match from being identified.
Common name parts	**PRINCIPLE 7:** The omission of peripheral name parts should not prevent a match from being identified.	**PRINCIPLE 12:** The inclusion or omission of less significant name parts should not prevent a Close Match from being identified.	

Table 14.1: Principles for a proposed Linguistic Search Standard

14.4 Calculating the Match Level of a Full Name

The principles described above show how matches between individual name parts should be assessed. A corporate standard may go on to suggest how the strength of the matches between each individual name part could be combined to determine the closeness of the match between the full names. For example, the following limits could be set for distinguishing between Precise, Close and Broad matches of full names.

- Precise Full Name Matches: At least 80% of the component name parts match at the Precise Level.
- Close Full Name Matches: At least 75% of the component name parts match at the Close or Precise Level; or the name has more than two component name parts, all of which match on at least the Broad Level.
- Broad Full Name Matches: At least 66% of the component name parts match on at least the Broad Level.

The allowance for the inclusion of additional unmatched name parts provides for more flexible matching of full names. It is common that official records may not hold an individual's complete name, particularly where the full name consists of many parts. For this reason, it is important to allow for the apparent mismatch of some parts of a multi-part name. For example, *Mohammed Hussain al-Tikriti* should match at the Broad Level with *Mohammed Abd al-Majid Al-Tikriti*, to account for an individual whose full name was *Mohammed Hussain Abd al-Majid al-Tikriti*.

14.5 Applying a Linguistic Search Standard

The Linguistic Search Standard suggested here describes the conditions under which individual name elements could be matched and how a full name match could be identified based on the results. The standard does not specify how each principle should be fulfilled, though several of them could clearly only be satisfied using linguistic search techniques if appropriate precision is to be maintained. The standard also does not comment on the calculation of match scores or other methods of prioritisation as these will be specific to each implementation. In practice, the prioritisation of matches can be realised in many different ways.

Clearly, the proposals made above do not cover all the questions that must be answered when configuring an identity search system. However, they comprise a set of guiding principles for dealing with the most important sources of variation in names. Though this is far from being a detailed prescription for implementation, these principles represent a sensible approach to ensuring that relevant identity matches are not overlooked. It should also be recognised that many of the search systems currently in use fall far short of several of the principles discussed in this chapter. As a result, though not fully comprehensive, the application of these principles could provide significant improvements and efficiencies in many of today's business processes.

Afterword

As identity search professionals, we have spent many years helping organisations to optimise their search technology and screening programs. We have been involved in projects as diverse as client screening in financial institutions, enquiries into large-scale corruption, the investigation of misallocated state aid, and the identification of assets left unclaimed after the Second World War.

A huge number of strategically important projects require an identity search component and we have always been amazed at how little information is available to help management select the most appropriate search strategy. The new generation of linguistic search techniques has revolutionised the way identity data can be searched, but after decades of working with older technology, the belief that recall is an unavoidable casualty of any improvement in precision is still widely-held. In this context, it is not surprising that largely outdated methodologies are still very much in evidence in even large and otherwise forward-thinking organisations - but as search professionals it was frustrating to see just how many opportunities were being missed.

We have written this book to help those charged with leading compliance, investigative and data management projects to understand the tools and techniques available in the identity matching sphere. We hope the linguistic background provided will help management determine the minimum requirements for their search systems. For too long, the scope and functionality of identity search tools have been assessed with reference to purely technical objectives, such as response times, hit rates and ease of integration. We hope that in opening up the debate on linguistic search requirements, this book will encourage closer scrutiny of identity search tools, so that technical objectives can be more appropriately balanced against the crucial linguistic criteria.

Index

A

B

C

R

S

V

W